surf & art

VEERLE
HELSEN

CONTEMPORARY
SURF ARTISTS
AROUND
THE WORLD

Lannoo

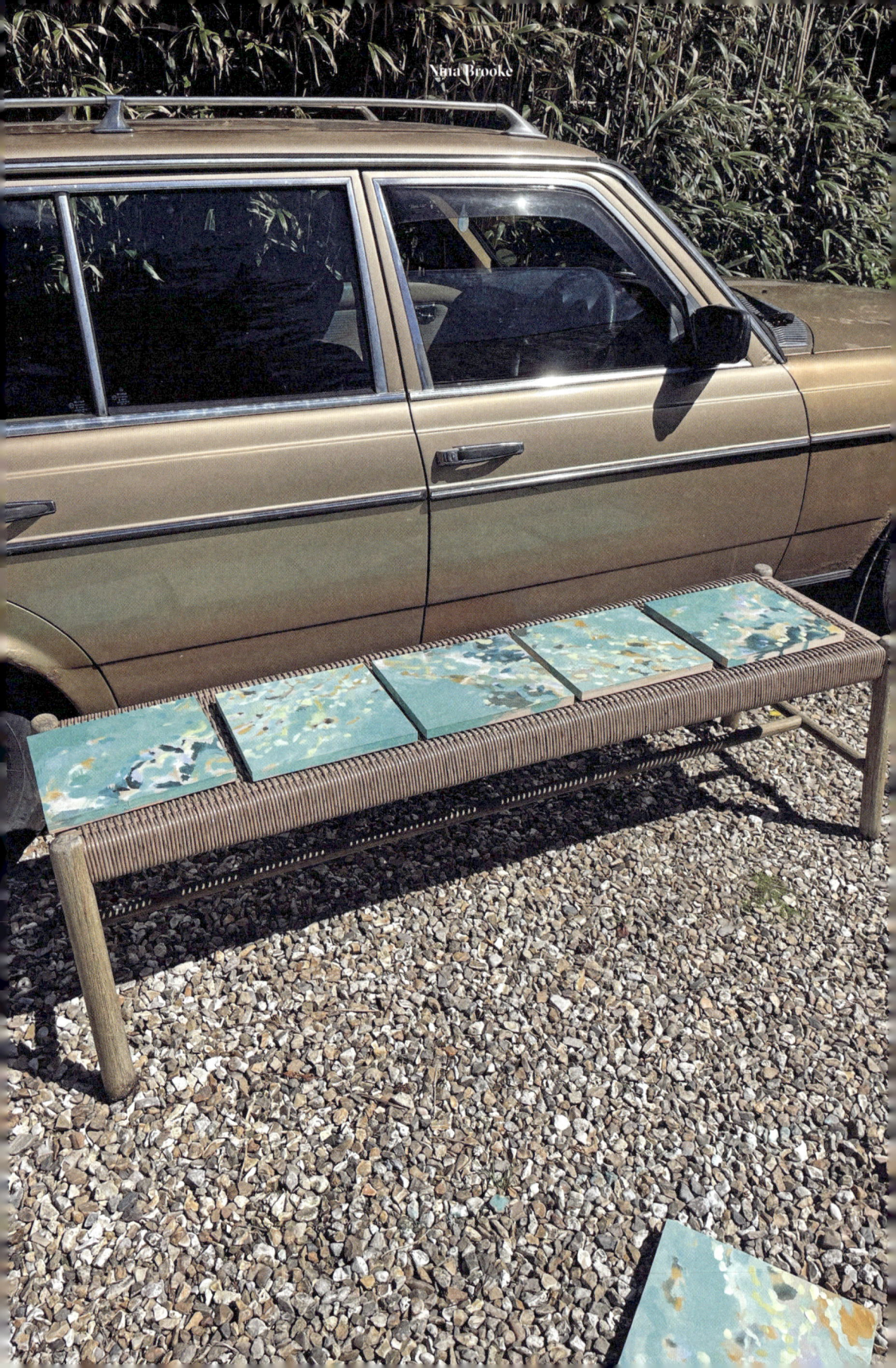
Nina Brooke

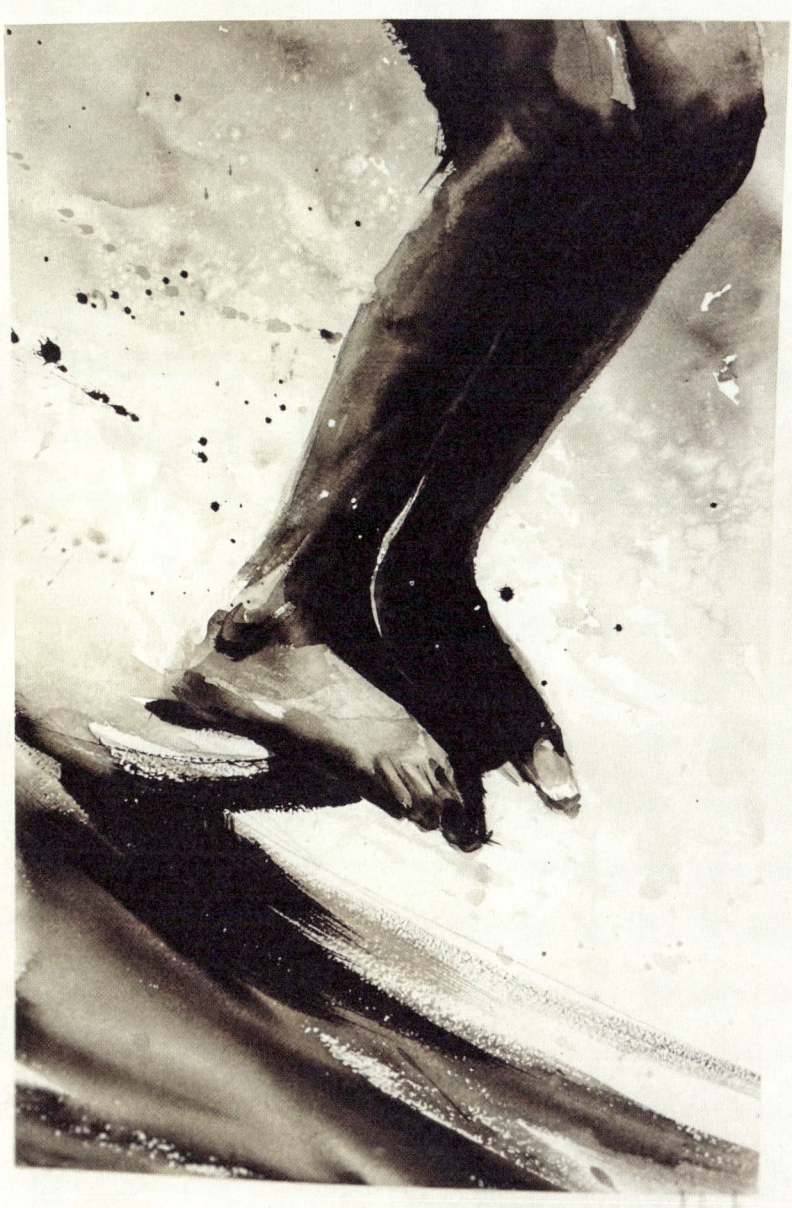

Johny Vieira

It all started with an illustration I bought from Portuguese artist Lizzy back in 2018. I had come across her work during a camper trip when I was on the road for my first book, *Surf & Stay*. It was a woman gracefully dancing on water; she was dressed in blue, and the waves appeared to be pink. Like a shimmering sun had sprinkled them with a magic pencil.

Ever since, I've been collecting illustrations or paintings centred on my absolute favourite thing in the world: surfing. When I'm out in the waves, I lose my sense of reality, finding myself in a fairytale universe. Where worries don't exist, and butterflies fill the air. To me, surf art is all about capturing those moments. Just take a glimpse at the cover and you'll understand what I mean. You see a surfer in the water, waves wrapping around him, clouds drifting dreamily in the sky and a red-soaked sun smiling down on it all.

Having published two editions of *Surf & Stay* – European travel guides with surf photography and recommendations on where to surf, eat and sleep – I felt it was time for a new book adventure. Somewhere along a path where the rhythm of the sea meets strokes of creativity. This book is a tribute to surf artists worldwide. To how they capture the essence of surfing and translate it to canvas, paper or digital spaces.

The cover image was created by Jonty Storey, a talented artist from Wales who turned out to be one of my most exciting discoveries during the compilation of this book. Throughout my interviews with various artists, I asked the same question to everyone: 'Who is an absolute must-have in a book about surf art?' Jonty's name popped up on Fabian Lavater's list, the Swiss painter who can make the sea dance with just a few blue lines. I also stumbled upon the magnificent work of Jim Drouet, whose women drift in the wind and make you think summer is always around the corner.

That's the beauty of this project: it kept growing organically, with every artist suggesting the next name to add to the mix. With limited pages, I couldn't include all the artists I wanted to and I'm secretly hoping this book takes off so a second edition will flow naturally.

Another question I asked each artist: 'What motto do you live by or what quote inspires you?' Enjoy discovering their answers because they'll bring you drops of wisdom in waves. The catchiest one, for me, comes from Ty Williams: 'Salt water can fix that.' If something is broken, the water will glue the pieces back together. I hope this book will simply take you to the ocean.

01

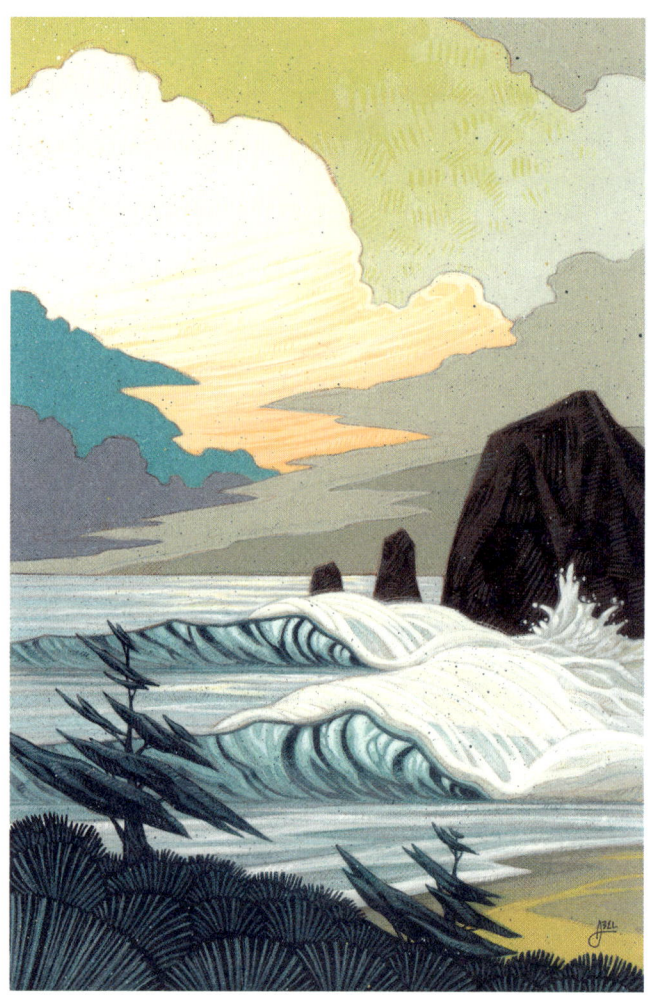

Break in the storm

Pencils on wood

Erik Abel

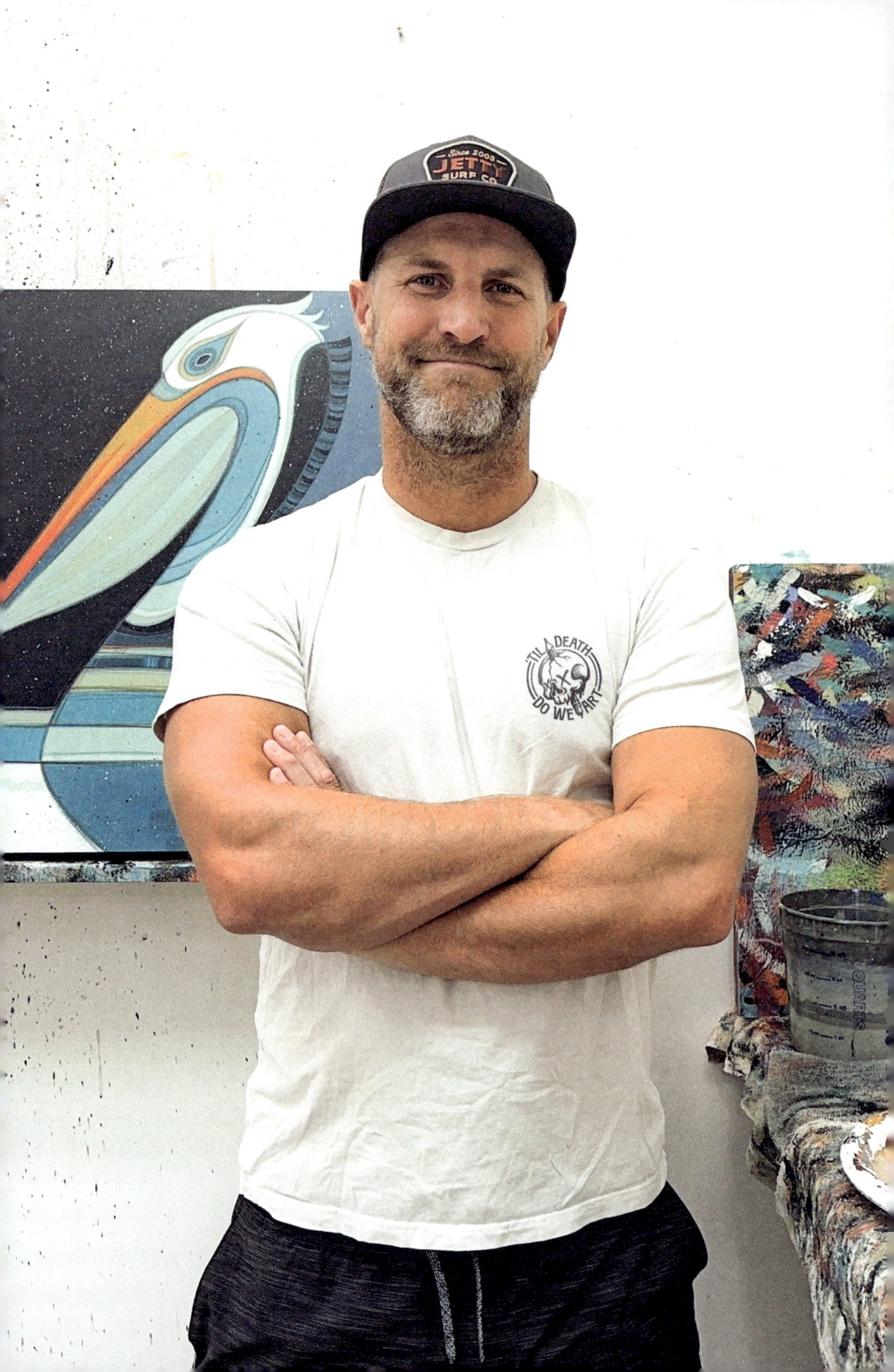

American artist Erik Abel grew up surfing in Southern California and has been influencing surf art for over 20 years. Not interested in painting anything man-made, his art deals mostly with natural elements: the ocean, animals, plants and mountains.

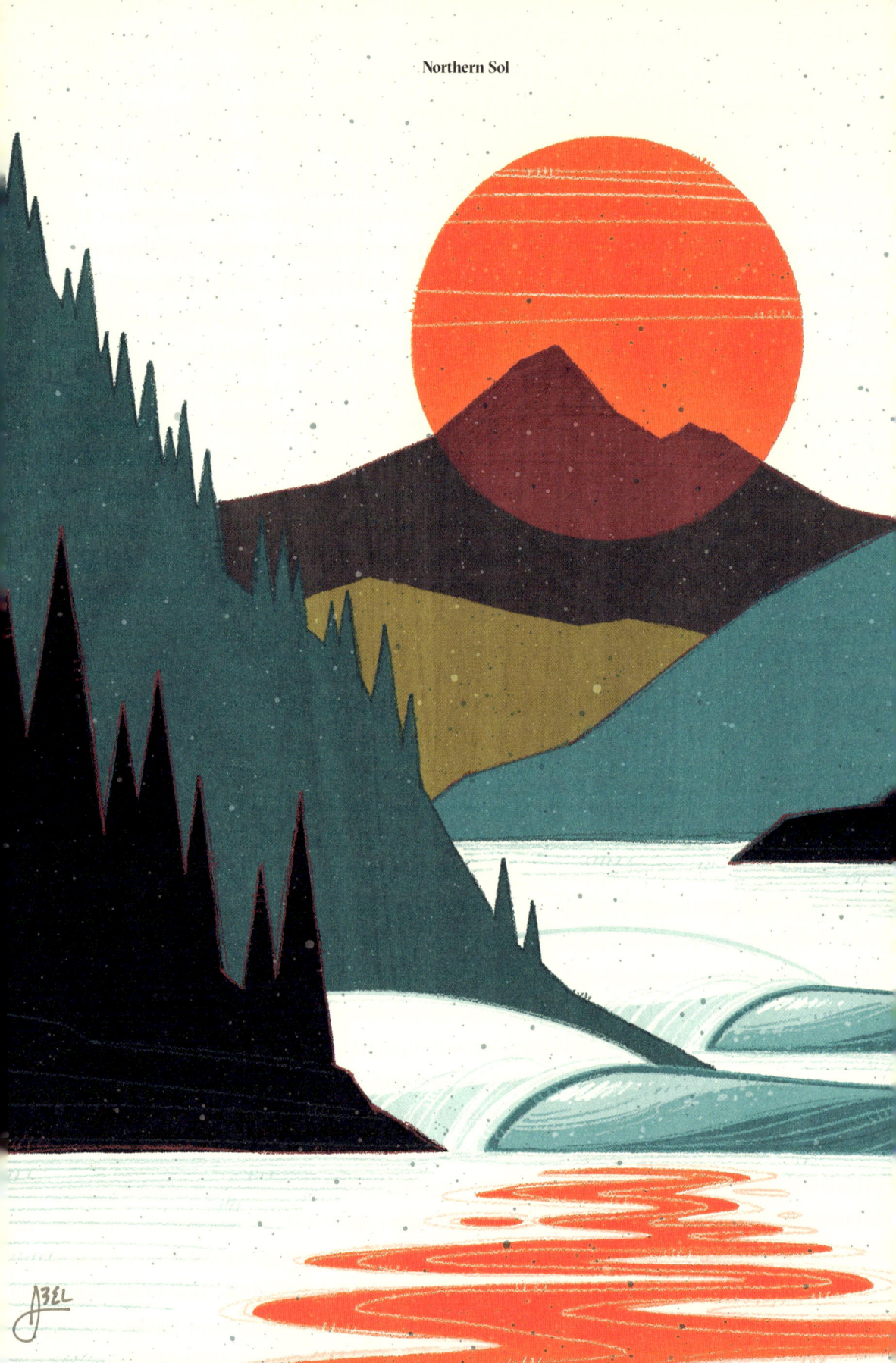

Northern Sol

'Surfing around the Pacific Northwest is a unique experience. It's a lot more raw and wild than where I grew up in Southern California', says Abel. 'These two digitally designed pieces represent some of those elements.'

There's something about the moon in his art. Its circular form often complements his geometric figures.

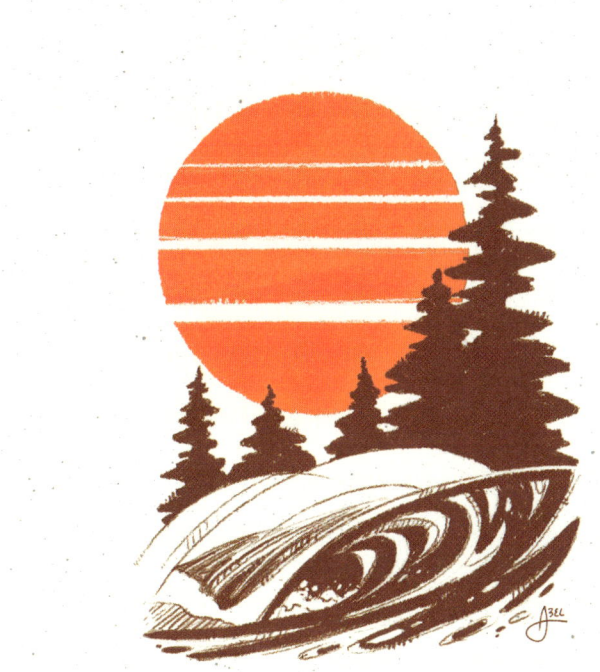

I was born to make art. One day in class when I was about 10, I drew a girl in a bikini that was on my shirt. I made Xerox copies and sold them to the boys in my class for 25 cents a piece

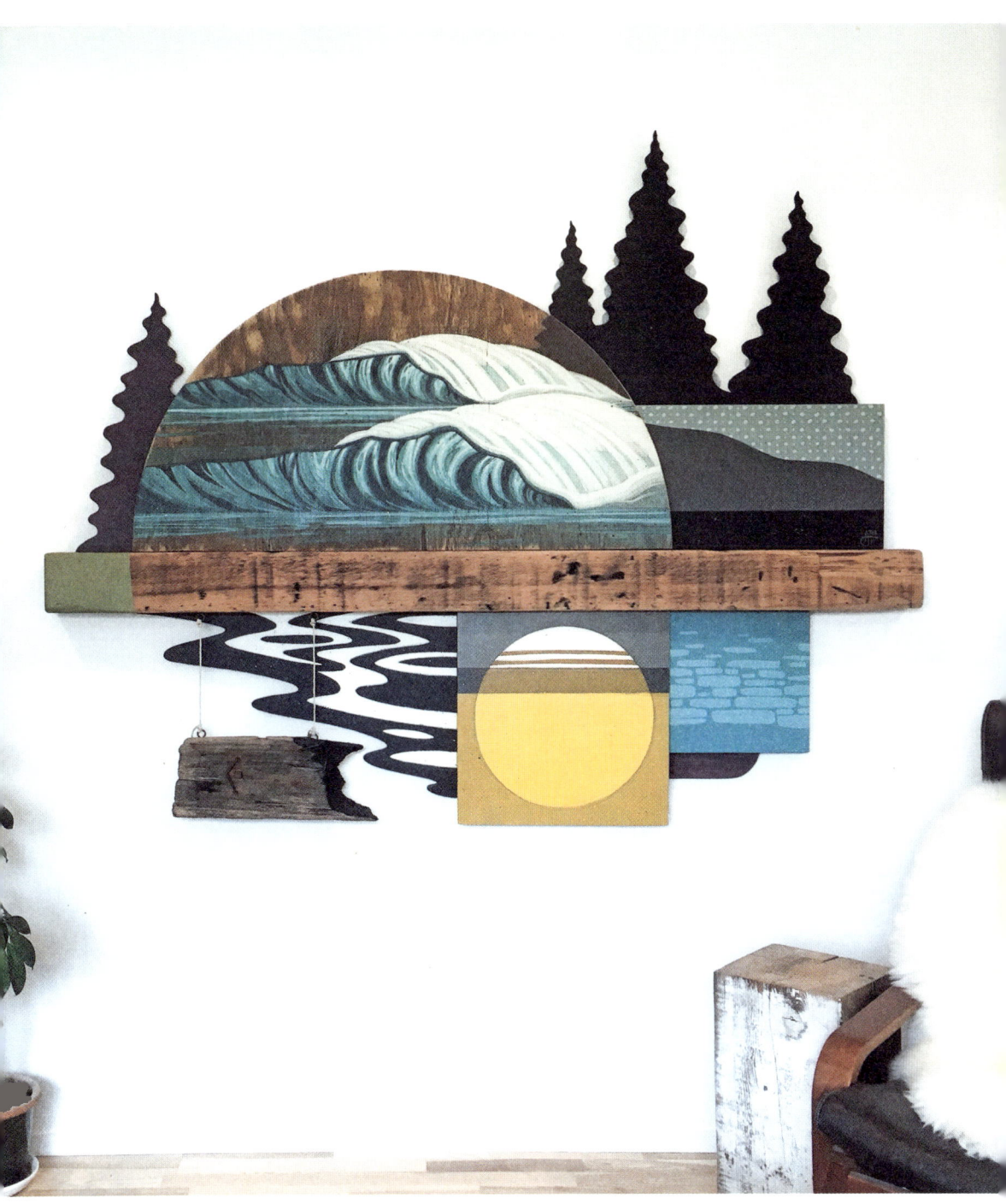

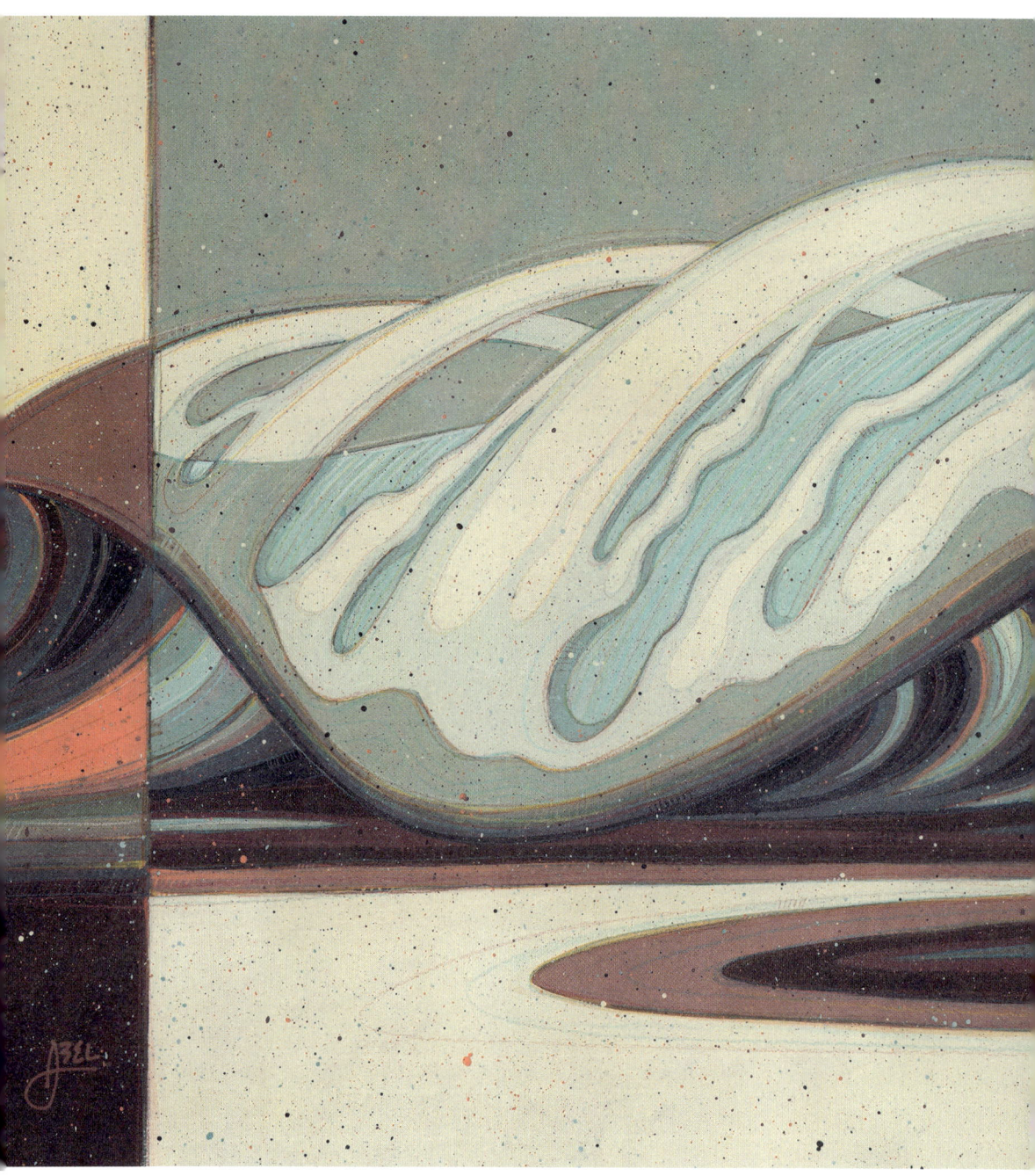

Slabtastic

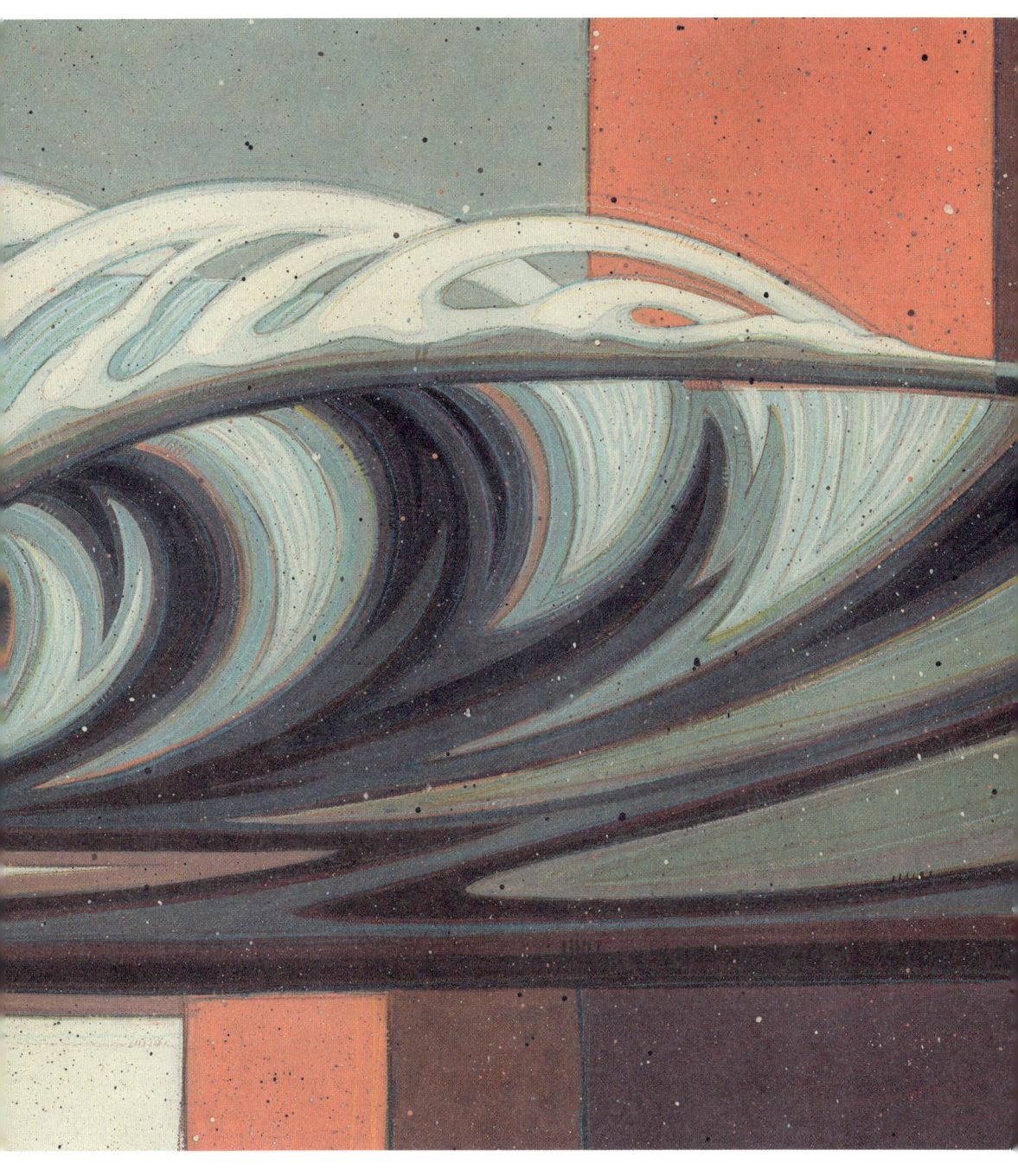

Abel is known for his works
made using acrylic and coloured
pencils on wood, and featuring
geometric shapes.

Q & A

Erik Abel

Who is Erik?
I'm an artist and designer living in Oregon, USA. I grew up surfing in Southern California. I've been lucky enough to make a living as a full-time artist for over 20 years now. It's been an honour to work with some of the biggest brands in surfing. Recently, I was able to check off a life-long goal and build my own art studio. I have a wife and two kids. I'm a hot tub junky and I have a weakness for Bloody Marys.

What came first: surfing or drawing?
I've been drawing since I was in diapers. It was clear from the start that I had artistic talent. I grew up playing on the beach and was always somewhere in or around the ocean as a kid, but it wasn't until I was 11 years old in Junior Lifeguards that I fell in love with surfing.

How important is the ocean in your life/work?
If I hadn't grown up playing in the ocean, I have no idea where I'd be in life or what my art would look like.

If you were to describe your art in a few lines, you'd say…
My art deals mostly with natural elements: the ocean, animals, mountains… I'm not interested in painting anything man-made. I have a background in graphic design and illustration and I think viewers can see that influence in my fine art. It's stylised with geometric shapes and colour separations mixed with organic, sketchy line work. Lately I've been veering off into another direction. I call it Abstract Pursuits and I consider it my artistic alter ego.

Your work is being sold in galleries from the USA to Japan. When did you first think: I can do this for a living?
I always wanted to be an artist, and there was nobody telling me I couldn't. My family and friends have been supportive and I feel there was just no other option. I was born to make art. One day in class when I was about 10, I drew a girl in a bikini that was on my shirt. I made Xerox copies and sold them to the boys in my class for 25 cents apiece. So from a young age, I knew I could make money with my art… even if it just bought me a chocolate milk at lunch.

How does your art come to life?
For the last 10+ years I've gravitated towards acrylic and coloured pencils on wood panels. I enjoy making simple thumbnail sketches in my sketchbook until one of them stands out. I don't go into too much detail or make any colour decisions in these sketches because I like to save those decisions for when I'm actually painting. I mix in some paint markers and coloured pencils throughout the process and finish it off with a lot of coloured pencil work and my little paint splatters.

Can you recommend any other books about surf art?
Artist Robb Havassy has published two giant volumes titled *Surf Story*. They are absolutely humungous books and feature just about every surf artist on the planet, with art but also images and a story from each artist.

Do you have a favourite quote that inspires or motivates you?
'The worst days of those who enjoy what they do are better than the best days of those who don't,' by Jim Rohn (American entrepreneur and motivational speaker, ed.). This quote changed my life. I saw this one day and decided to quit my art director job in Los Angeles, saved up some money and bought a one-way ticket to New Zealand with nothing but a backpack and a surfboard bag. I ended up in many different countries and had the adventure of a lifetime that lasted almost three years.

Where do you currently live or surf?
In 2020, I moved back to Ashland, a small town in Southern Oregon. It's where I went to college and where my wife is from. We have a little mountain to snowboard but it's a little too far from the beach for my liking. I never thought I would live this far from the ocean again, but life happens.

What does your quiver look like?
My entire quiver in my garage right now are Roberts Surfboards out of Ventura, California. I used to airbrush for Robert fresh out of high school. I've been riding them ever since. I've got an 8ft fun shape with a pulled-in nose and tail; a mid-length for weird Oregon waves; a fish; a diamond nose swallow tail wave-eating machine; and about six or seven various shortboards and step ups.

Has surfing given you anything in life?
It's hard to even fathom how much my life has benefitted from surfing. It's given me almost everything. I just feel so fortunate to have grown up in and around the ocean. My dad had a fishing boat and we'd always go out to the Channel Islands off Ventura to fish, snorkel and explore. I grew up getting pummelled in the shore break from before I can even remember. And when I learnt to surf, it was all I wanted to do: that and draw. Surfing has challenged me, given me lifelong friends, kept me healthy, allowed me to get to know the ocean. It's taken me to exotic countries all over the world and has been the biggest source of artistic inspiration in my life. •

02

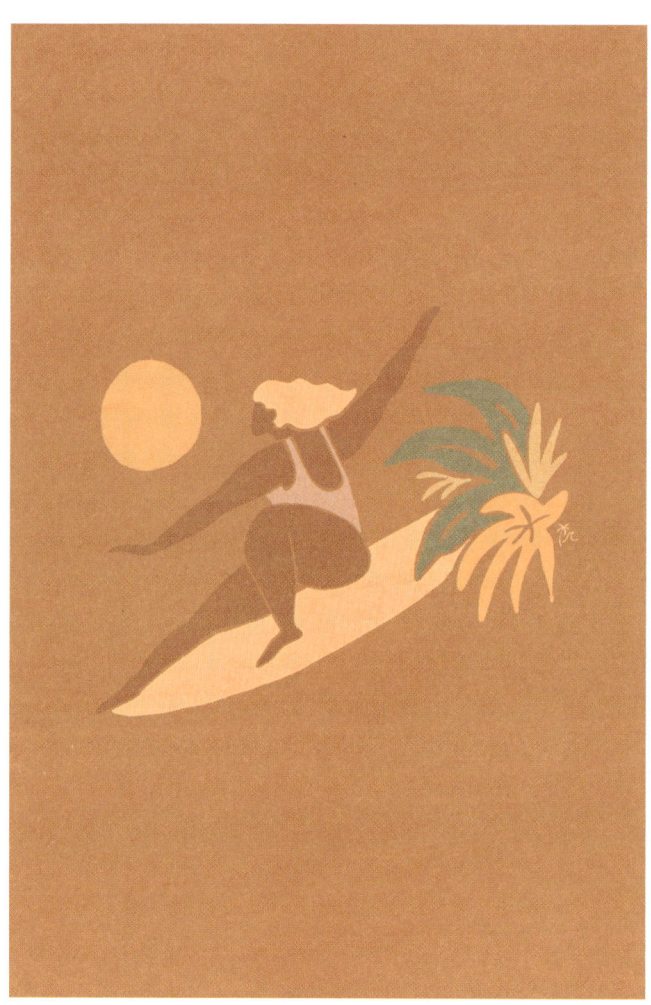

Mama loves surfing

Tropicolours

Ceri Lou Bathgate

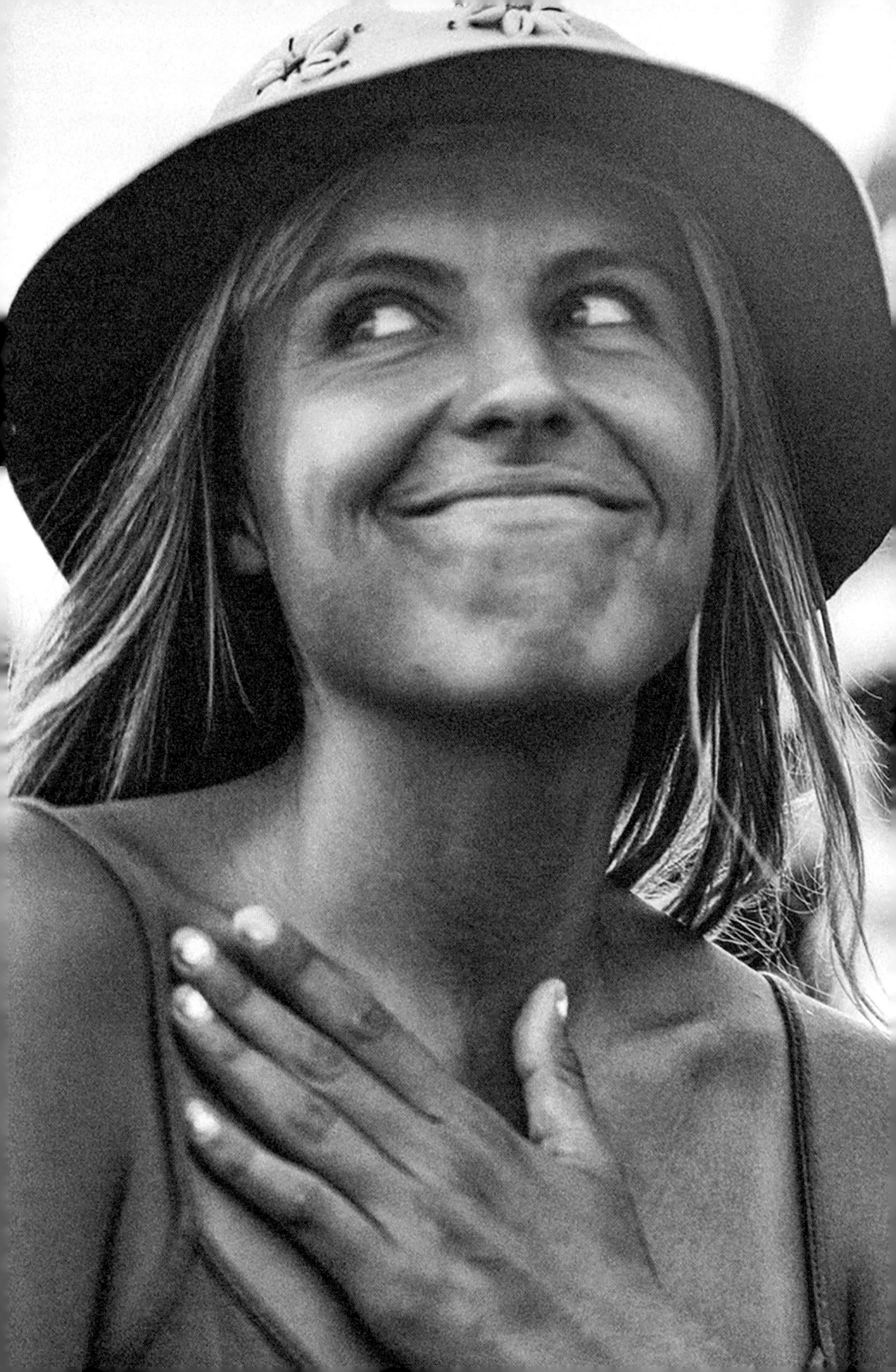

Meet Ceri Lou, aka Tropicool. Originally from Scotland, she grew up in Canada and now travels around the world chasing waves.

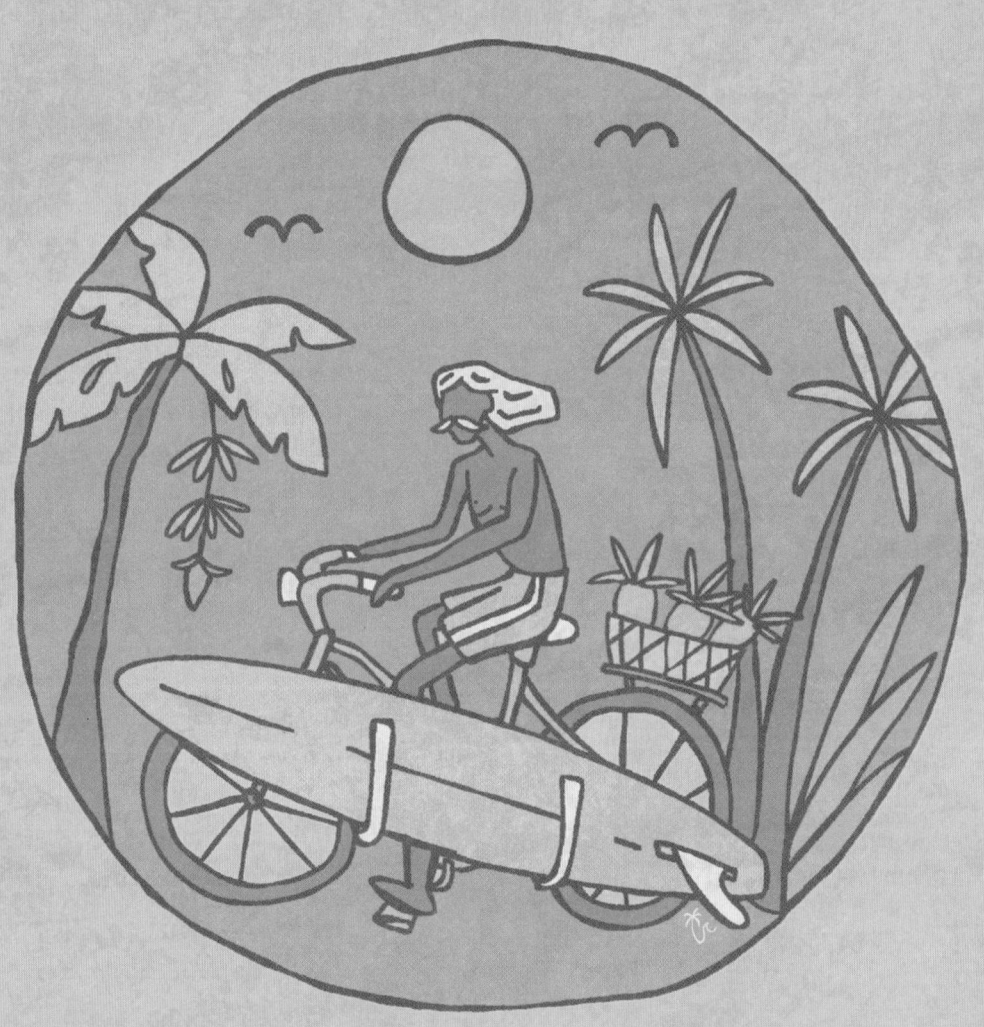

'Ode to LeRoy' (below) is inspired
by the surf photography of LeRoy
Grannis, an iconic American
photographer from the 1960s.

'The 1960s are an era of traditional
surf craft and style', says Bathgate,
'riding longboards in heavy barrel-
ling surf, finding trim in scary places. I feel nostalgic for an era I wasn't
even a part of, and I tend to express
this in my illustrations.'

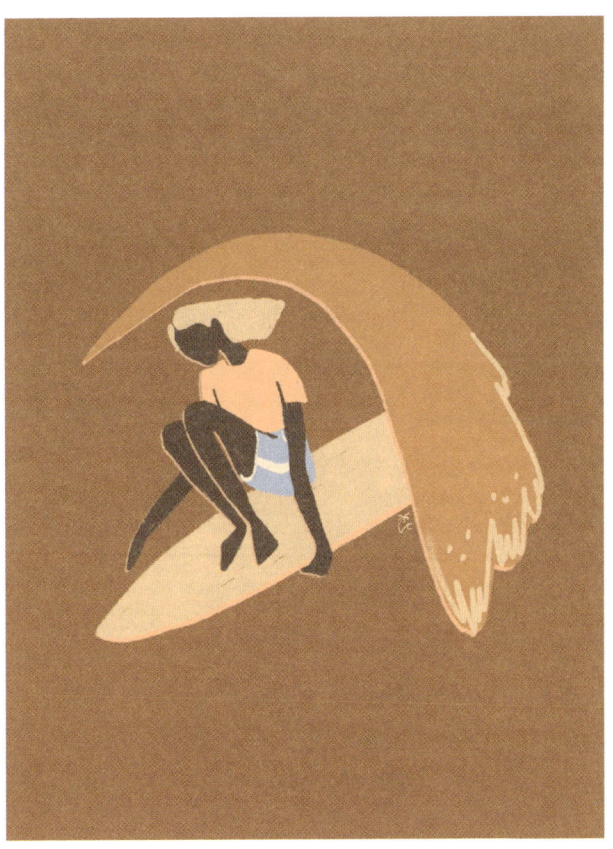

Ode to LeRoy

Q & A

Ceri Lou Bathgate

Who is Ceri Lou?
I'm the artist behind Tropicool Studio. I was born in Scotland, moved to Canada when I was eight and started travelling at the age of 19. I was introduced to surfing when I turned 20 and now that salty blessing dictates all of my movements and funnily enough my current 'career' path.

If you were to describe your art in a few lines, you'd say...
Nostalgic, simple, tropical, retro quirky, joyful and peaceful.

Tropicool is the name of your brand. Does it refer to your style?
I originally chose it because I was living between the West Coast of Canada and the tropics, so I was living a harmonious balance between hot and cold weather. My tagline used to be 'between cold seas and palm trees', but as I've been living primarily in the tropics, I dropped that line, but still love the name Tropicool. I feel it sums up the essence of my work.

It seems like you have a go-to colour palette?
I love orange and earthy colours, at least for graphic art. I find they express the energy of my work and lifestyle well – warm, surfy, tropical. For painting and illustration, I tend to use brighter colours. I experiment more on paper.

When people look at your work, what would you like them to feel?
As if they have been transported to a remote tropical island, lined with bungalow beach shacks, coconut trees, papaya trees, plenty of mantas and dolphins, and warm peeling waves lapping the beach. Oh, and lots of avocados, because guacamole makes everything better.

I think you use a specific kind of paint and sketchbook?
I'm currently exploring gouache paint – Winsor & Newton, Holbein and Turner – as it partners well with mixed media, such as coloured pencils, crayons and markers, so it is a fun way to fill a sketchbook. My current sketchbooks are Royal Talens Art Creations and Strathmore Art Journals. I also love watercolour as it's spontaneous and full of surprises.

When did you first think: I can do this for a living?
While I was in Nicaragua in 2016, I spent my afternoons drawing in the sun, which led to my first client when a local business in San Juan del Sur asked to buy a sketch to print on their shirts. This then led to more work, and over the years I balanced this with a return home to Tofino (British Columbia) every summer to work in a surf shop. Eventually, I got so busy that I sold everything, moved to Mexico, committed to it full-time, and now I've been living off my artwork for over three years.

Do you have an opinion on price setting in the world of surf art?

Surfers tend to be cheap, or on a budget, so it's pretty tricky to earn a good living off just clients within the surf industry. However, the 'laid-back and beach-infused' aesthetic of surfing has bled into many other industries, so I try to attract those types of customers. I think people sometimes assume that, because I'm a fellow surfer, my work might be cheaper, but just because surf art isn't corporate doesn't mean it should be sold cheaply. So I suppose my opinion is: don't undervalue this style of art.

How does surfing influence your work?

There is so much art, style and expression within the culture of surfing, both in and out of the water. It can influence the type of car you drive, the weird haircut you have, the second-hand clothing you buy, the type of camera you use. It's a retro time warp infused with creativity, so the entire culture influences my work, much more than just the act of surfing.

What does your quiver look like?

I currently have a Mitchell Surman 6'10" twin fin – 'The Void', and it has become my absolute favourite board. I was riding a Grant Noble longboard for the last couple of years, which was my favourite board I have ever had, but I decided to explore new avenues of surf and lighten the load as travelling with a log can be so hectic, so I'm currently rocking a one-board quiver, and I love it.

Do you have a favourite quote that inspires or motivates you?

I don't have one particular quote, but I know I had MANY moments with the book *Swell* by Liz Clark that made me stop and think. This is my all-time favourite book.

What's happening in your life right now?

I love the recent projects that I've been hired for. In 2023, I had more big projects than small ones. They ranged from merch for an African safari to an underwater-themed kids book to designing a retro Hawaiian fashion label and branding a surf resort in Indonesia. I kicked off 2024 in New Zealand and am now working remotely on road trips, camping and sailing, so I'm super excited for how my year is already shaping up.

Where do you currently live?

I don't technically live anywhere – for the last few years I have moved every two or so months. In 2023, I was in Sri Lanka, New Zealand, Mexico, Canada, California and Indonesia. I believe I'll be making New Zealand my home base, though, and starting to slow the travel down as it's definitely pretty exhausting and expensive.

Are there other places in the world where you feel at home?

I'm obsessed with Mexico. That's where I feel the happiest. The culture, food, art and of course waves are such a perfect combo for me. I'm not sure I could permanently live there but I could certainly clock up six months a year. Tofino, Canada is another top contender because nothing beats the community and nature there. However, the cold water, rain and cost of living make it a pretty difficult place to call home.

Has surfing given you anything in life?

Everything. Community, fitness, lifestyle, connection, inspiration, a sinus clean, the whole shebang. •

03

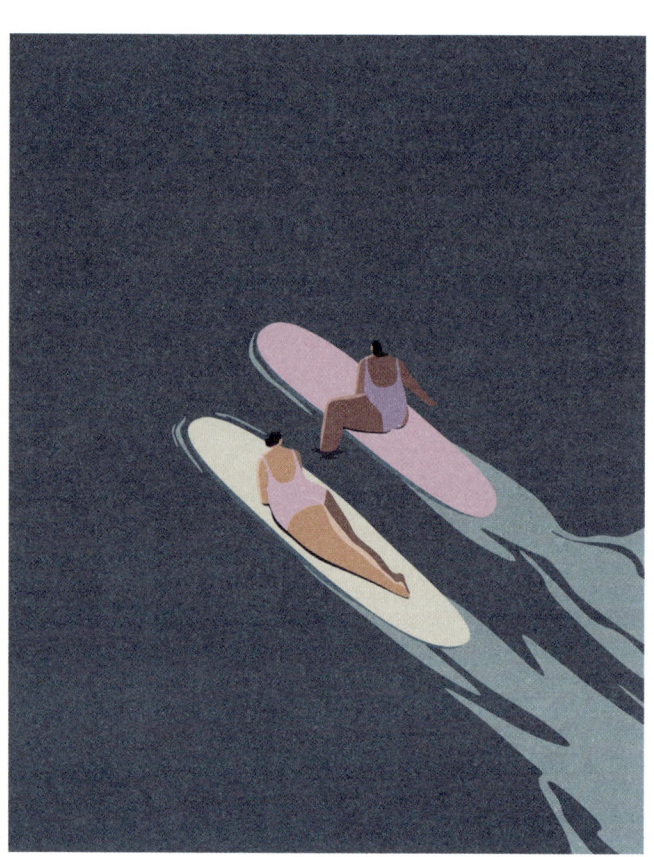

Waiting for waves

Nouvelle vague

Jeanne Beuvin

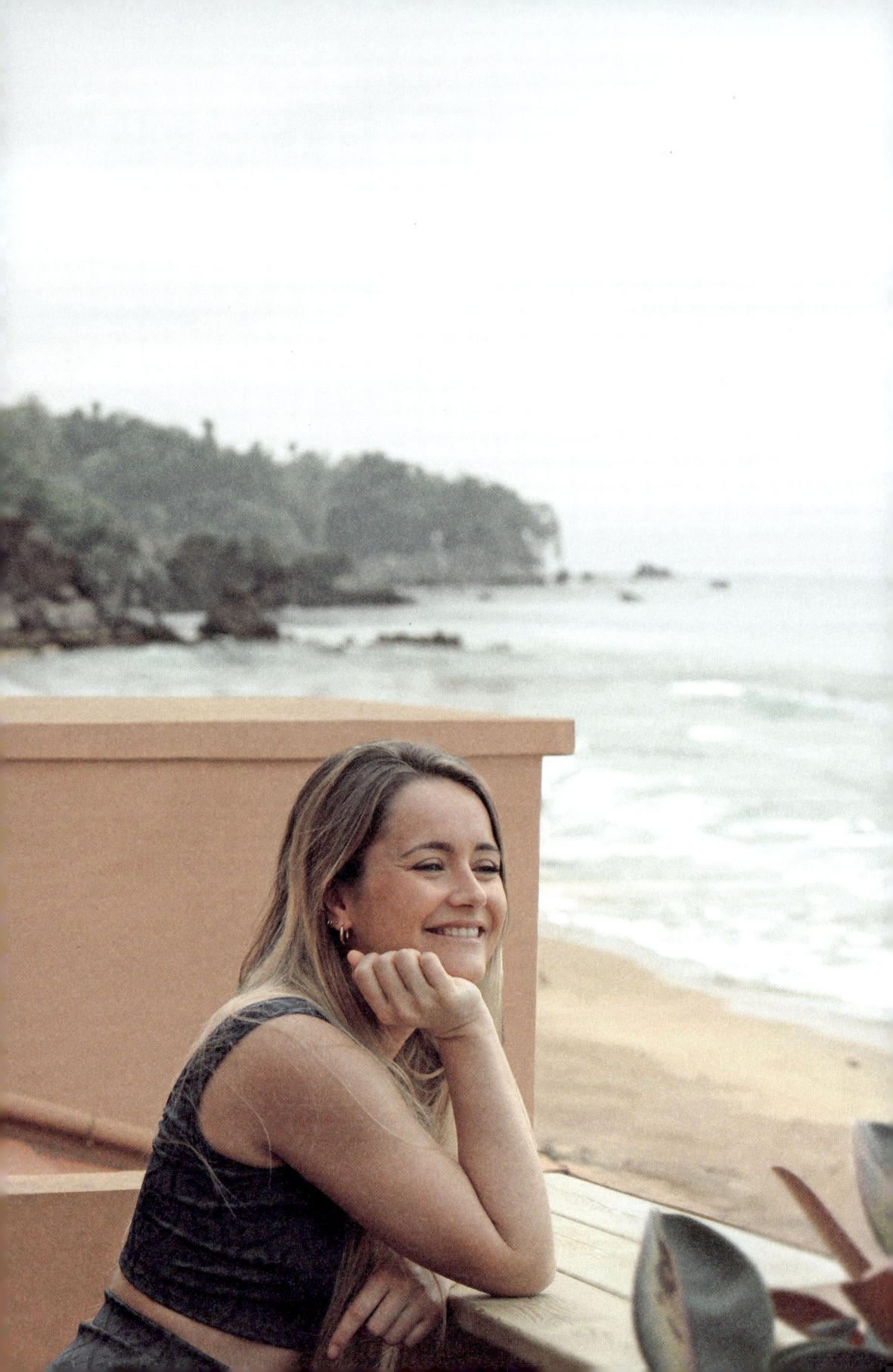

As the founder of Les Filles du Surf, French illustrator Jeanne Beuvin shatters the cliché of the female surfer without any imperfections. There's a softness present in her work, yet it harbours a subtle, empowering message beneath the surface.

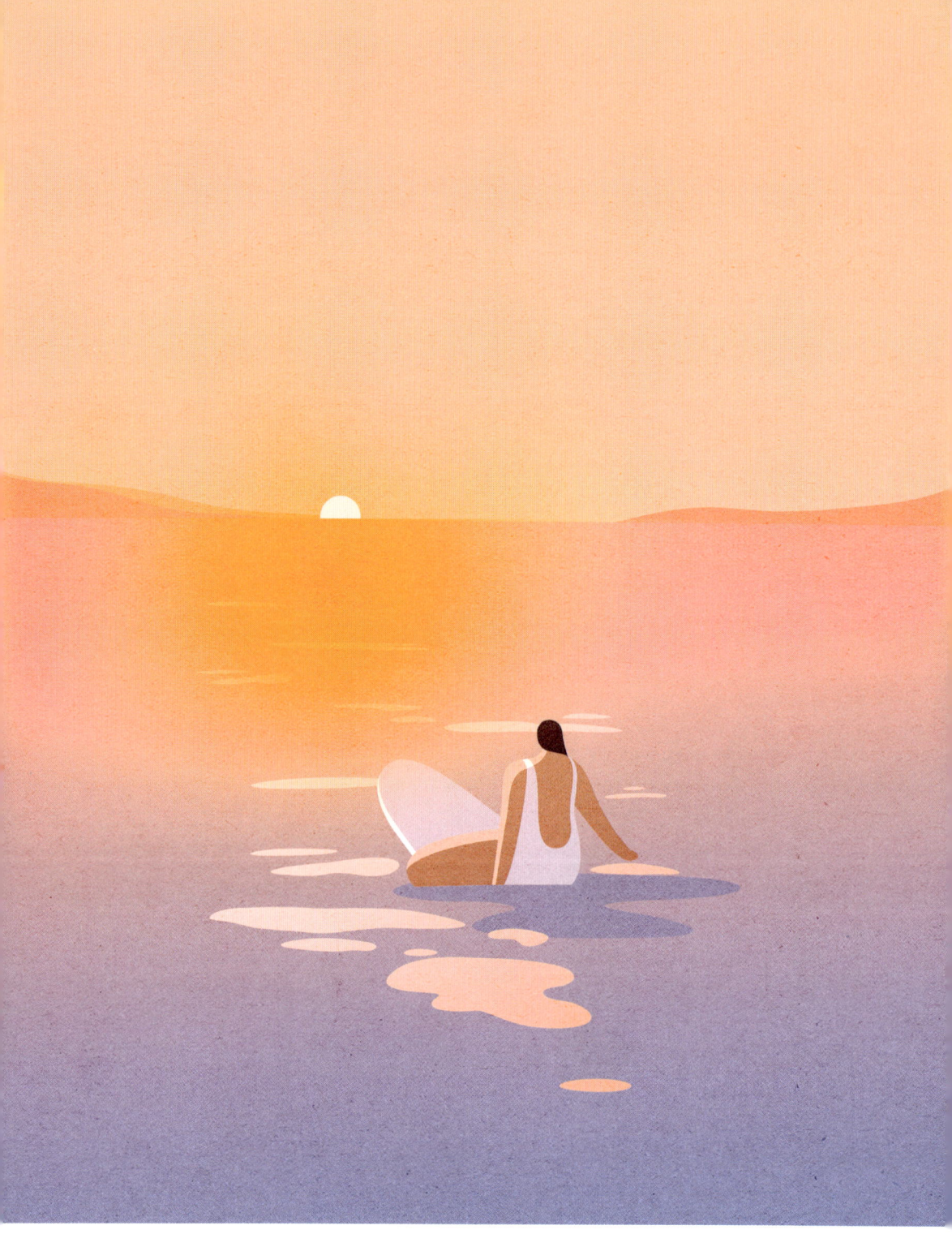

Sunset in paradise

Beuvin created the website and instagram account Les Filles du Surf. Her work features female surfers far away from the stereotype slender bikini girls we know from mainstream surf culture.

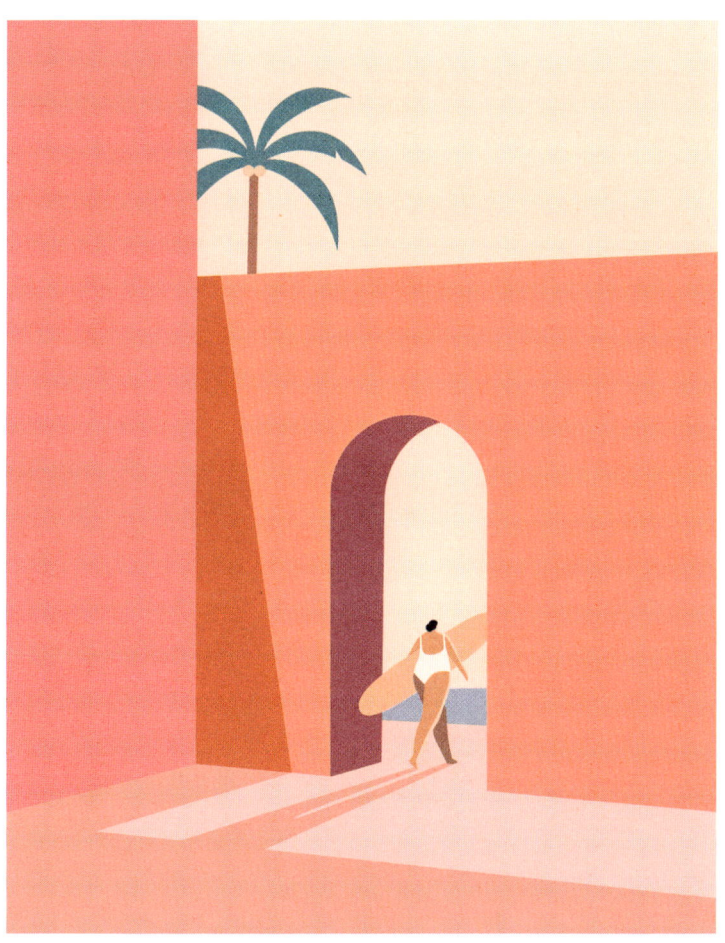

Surf terracotta

I noticed
that the girls
featured in
women's surf
magazines
mostly
confirmed the
cliché of the
slender and
graceful surfer,
without any
imperfections

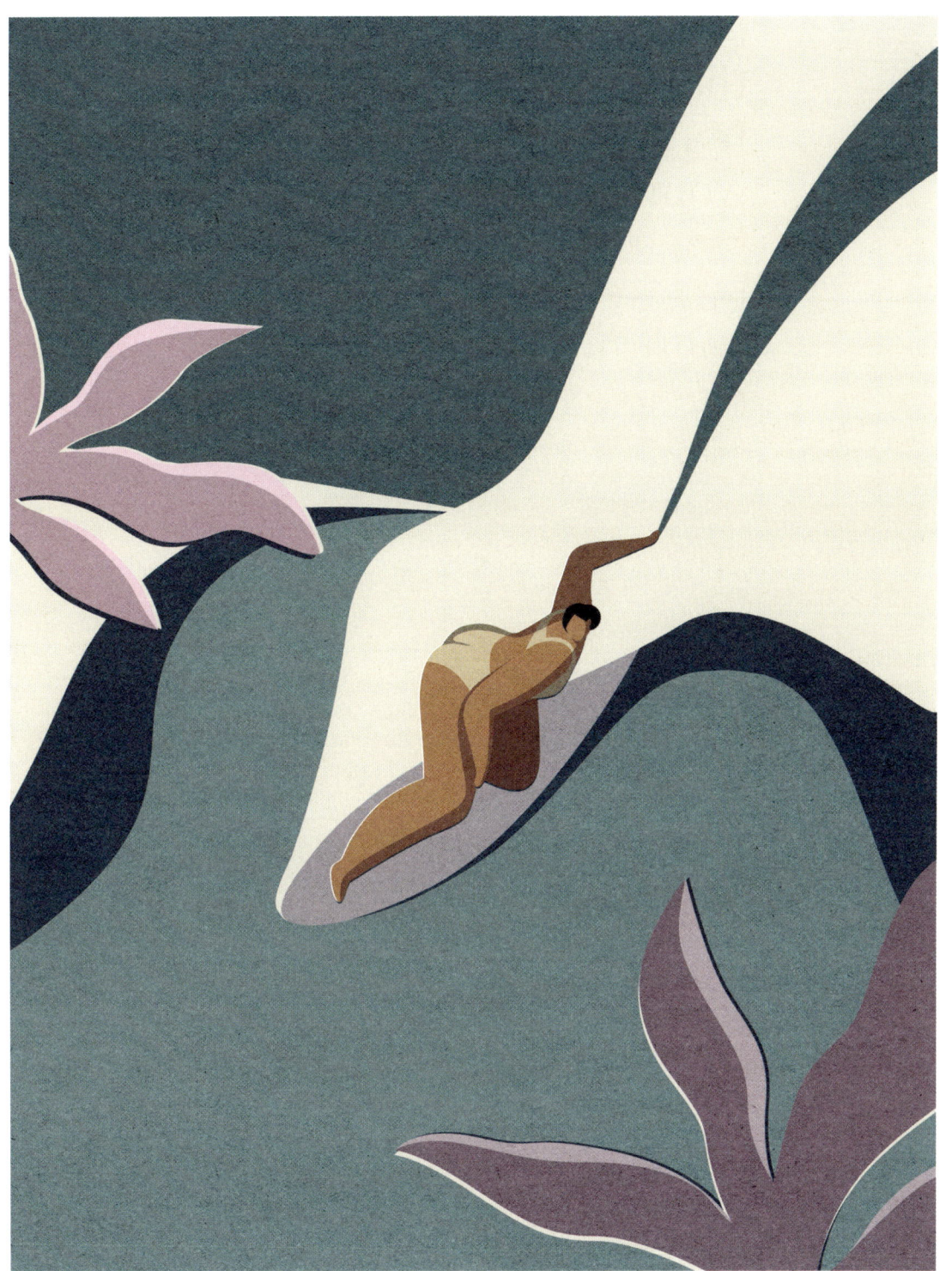

Woman on waves

Q & A

Jeanne Beuvin

Who is Jeanne?
I'm 28 years old and originally from La Rochelle in France. Seven years ago, after my design studies in Bordeaux, I moved to Biarritz. I worked for four years as a graphic designer for a surf magazine and eventually started my own business to fulfil my dream of becoming an illustrator.

If you had to describe your art in a few lines, you'd say…
I illustrate curvy and liberated women in a surf lifestyle universe. I'm a big fan of the minimalist movement, so my lines are simplified to the maximum. I use pastel and muted colour palettes that add a touch of softness and femininity to the drawings.

You are the founder of Les Filles du Surf, a website and Instagram account that is an inspiration for many female surfers. What's the story behind it?
I started Les Filles du Surf in 2019 when I was 23. I noticed that the girls featured in women's press, as well as in surf magazines, mostly confirmed the cliché of the slender and graceful surfer, without any imperfections. So, I thought, 'Why not create a new image of the natural and unburdened woman who surfs freely, without caring about all these stereotypes?' And *voilà*, I started sketching and created the Instagram account Les Filles du Surf.

When people look at your art, what would you like them to feel?
I love this question. No one has ever asked me this, and it's a very important topic for me, maybe even the most important. The initial idea behind Les Filles du Surf was to empower women who want to take up surfing. When they look at my drawings, I would like them to feel calm, softness, and a certain power to do this sport.

Is your relationship with the ocean something important in your life/work?
Without a doubt. I grew up in a house on the dunes. The beach was our garden, the ocean our playground. Today I realise that proximity to the ocean is essential to my happiness. I even believe it is the foundation of all my illustrations.

How does your art come to life?
I don't have a specific creative process. Sometimes I lack inspiration for several days, then suddenly it comes back. At that moment, I stop what I'm doing, put on my headphones and sketch in an old notebook. Then, when I like the sketch, I transfer it to a digital tablet and let it flow. Often, the final illustration looks nothing like the original sketch.

Do you have a favourite quote that inspires or motivates you?
'Le véritable voyage de découverte ne consiste pas à chercher de nouveaux paysages, mais à avoir de nouveaux yeux,' by Marcel Proust. The real voyage of discovery consists not in seeking new landscapes, but in having new eyes.

Where do you currently live or surf?
For the past two years I've been living and surfing in Anglet. It's a neighbouring city to Biarritz on the west coast of France. I loved Biarritz, but Anglet is a more authentic city, less focused on appearance. The waves are rougher, but I'm getting better at surfing every day. It's not as beautiful as Biarritz in terms of architecture, but it is bordered by immense beaches and the ocean as far as the eye can see. Everything I love.

Are there other places in the world where you feel at home?
Actually, no. I feel at home in my apartment. The rest of the world is a playground to discover.

Do you remember how and when you fell in love with surfing?
I fell in love during my very first session on Île de Ré in France. A friend was introducing me to his sport on a huge foam board. I caught my first wave, and it instantly became clear: this sport would become the rhythm in my life.

Has surfing given you anything in life?
Oh, definitely. This sport has brought me serenity, self-confidence, health, energy, and actually the euphoria I need in life to be happy. •

04

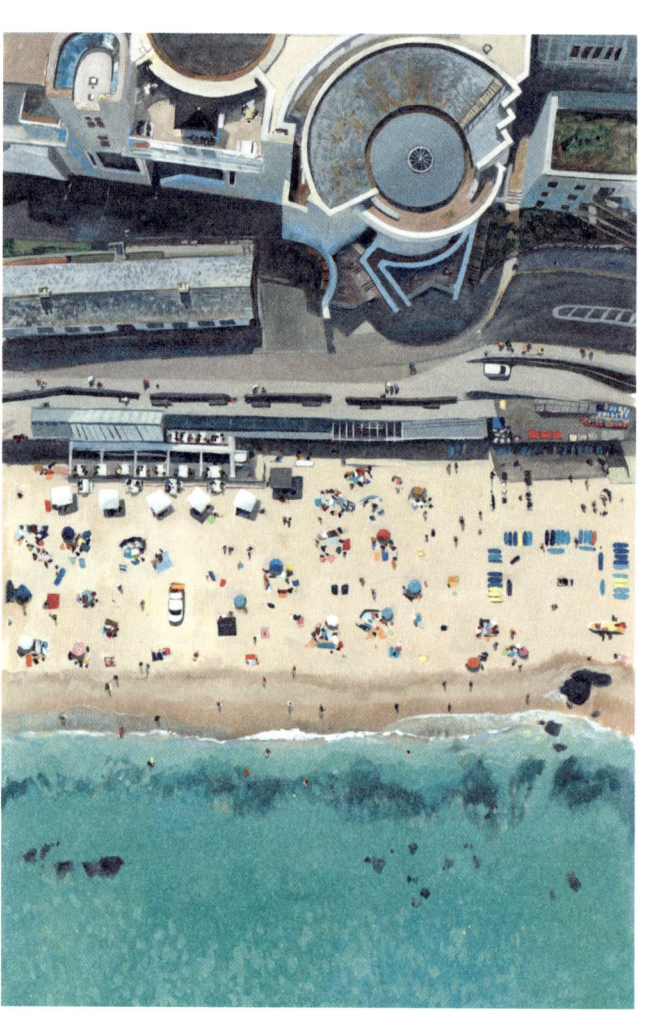

Tate St. Ives

Aerial landscapes

Nina Brooke

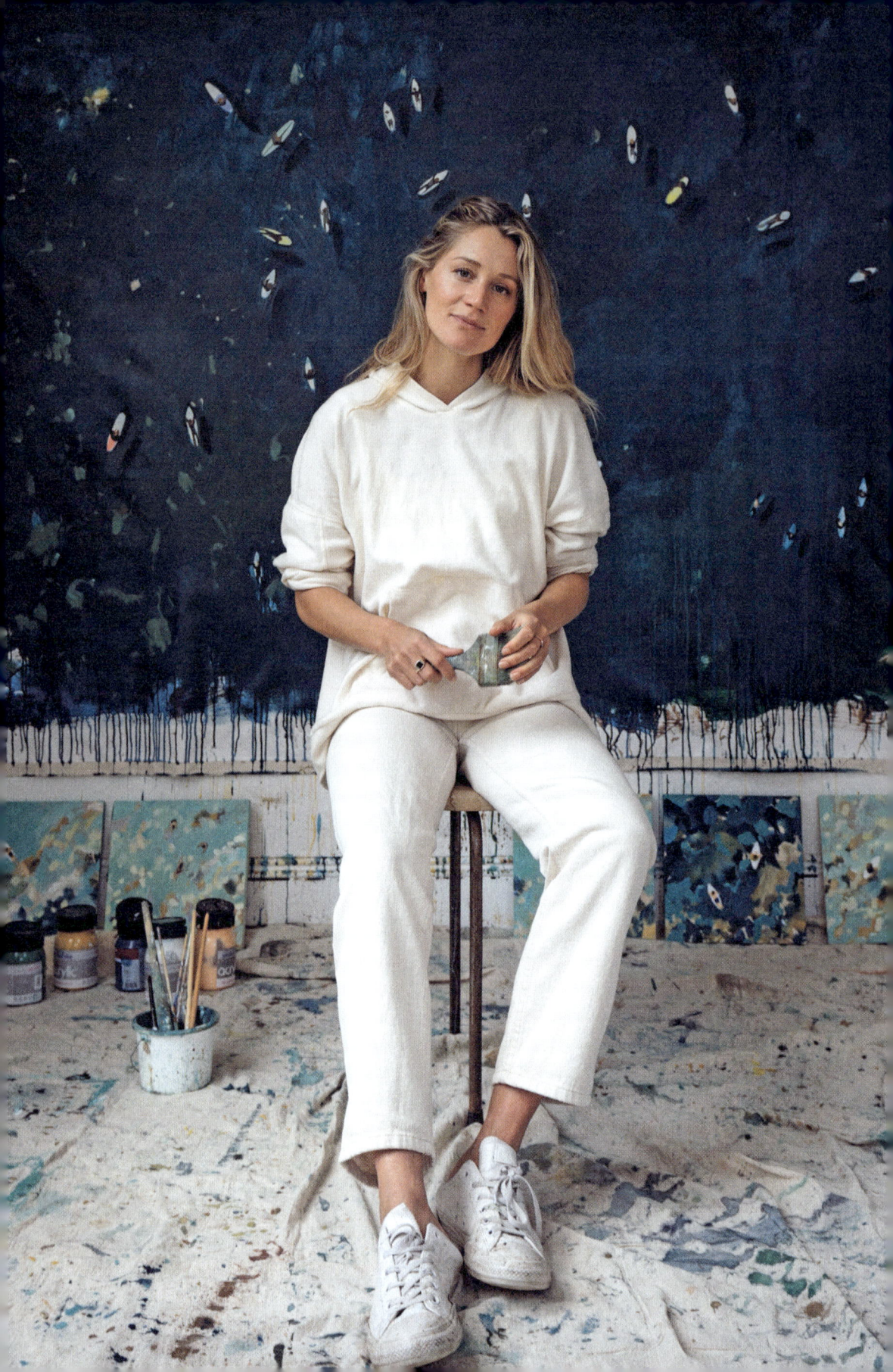

An aerial landscape painter hailing from Cornwall, Nina Brooke has created her own art language. The ocean is her main source of inspiration and shades of turquoise the running theme.

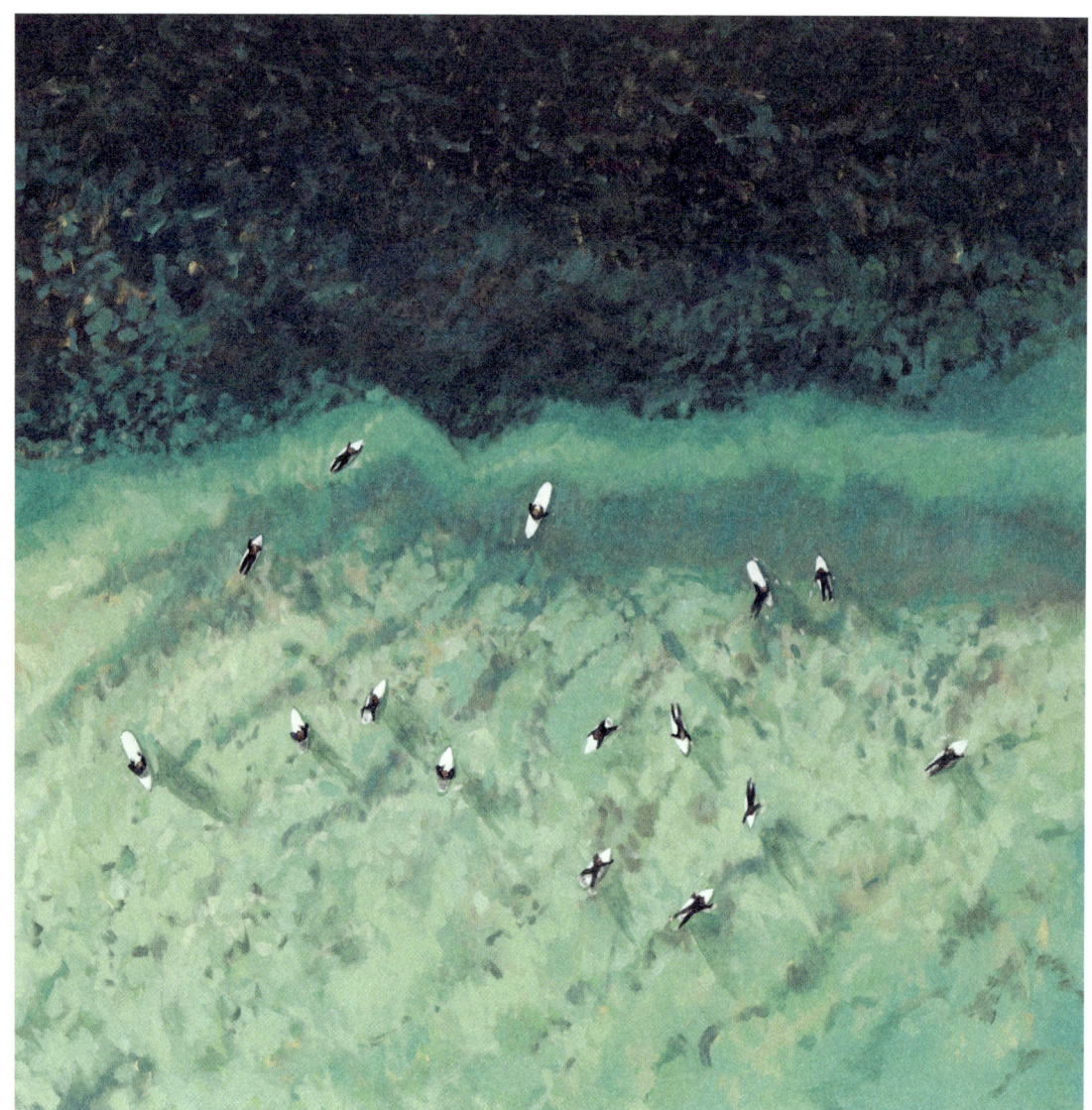

Depth over distance

Brooke's artwork is based on aerial imagery which she captures using a drone.

'I think I have inspired a movement in the artworld, as an aerial landscape painter. It's nice to know that my artwork is unique and no one has done it before.'

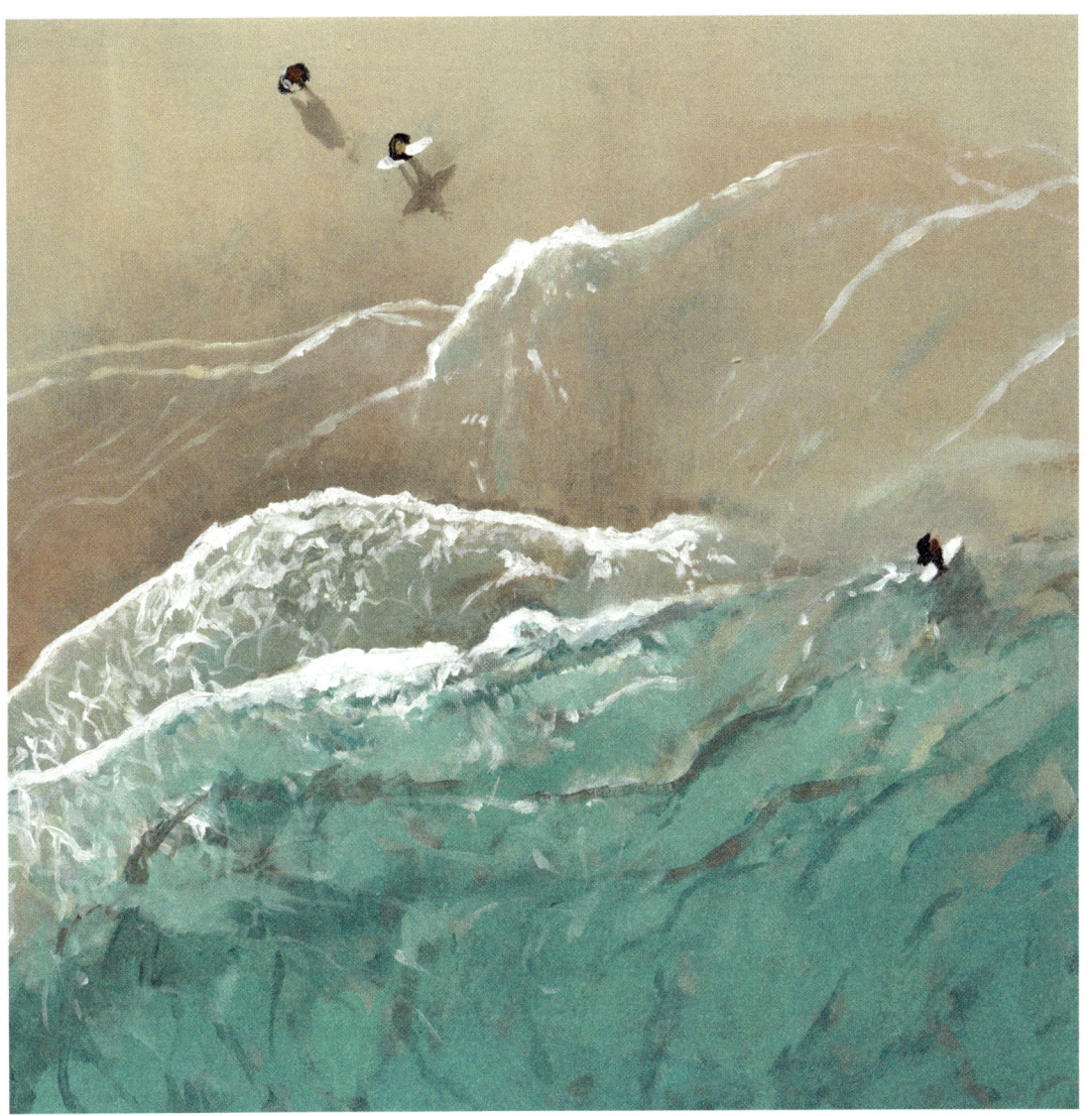

Shoreline, high tide

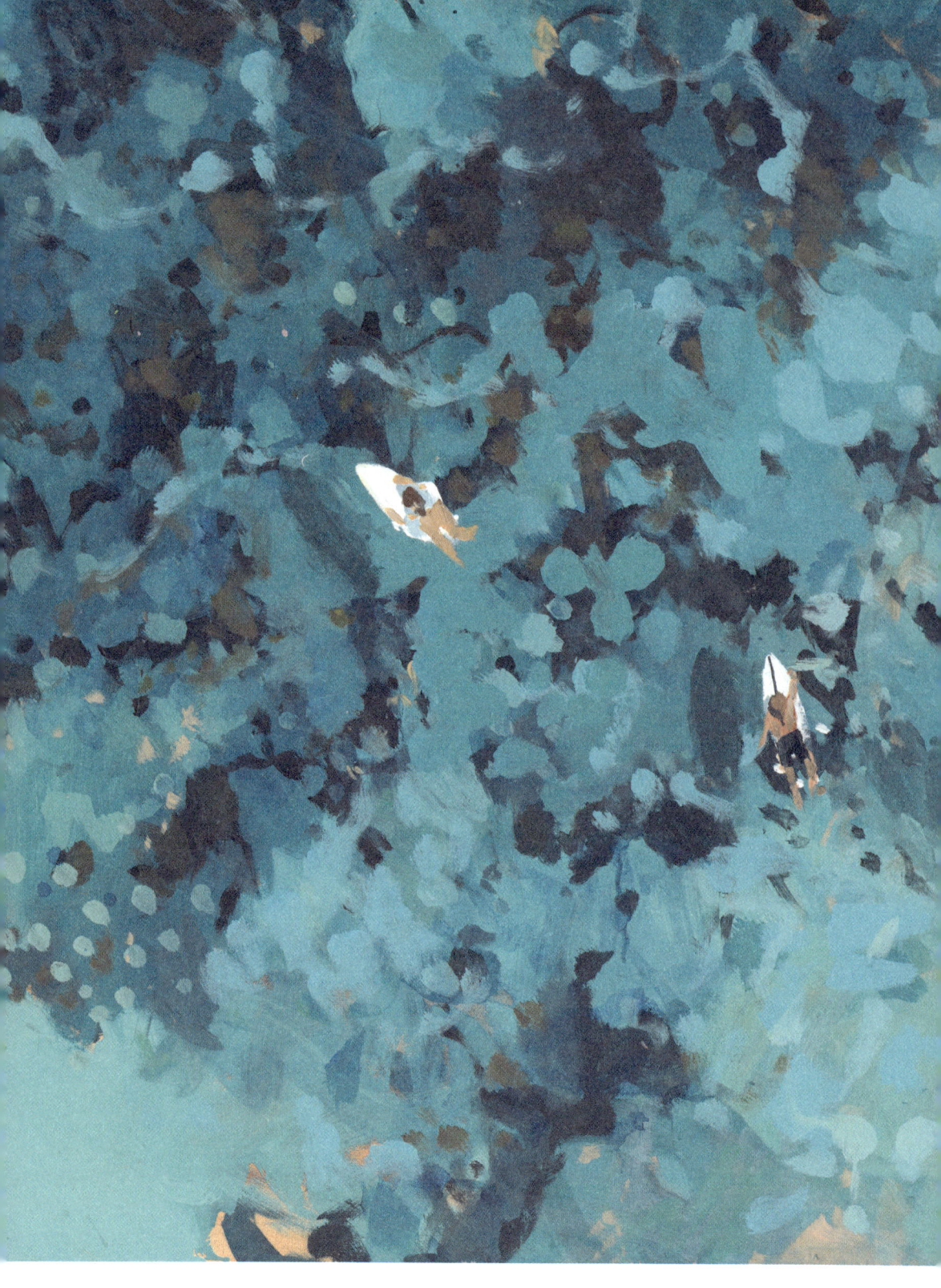

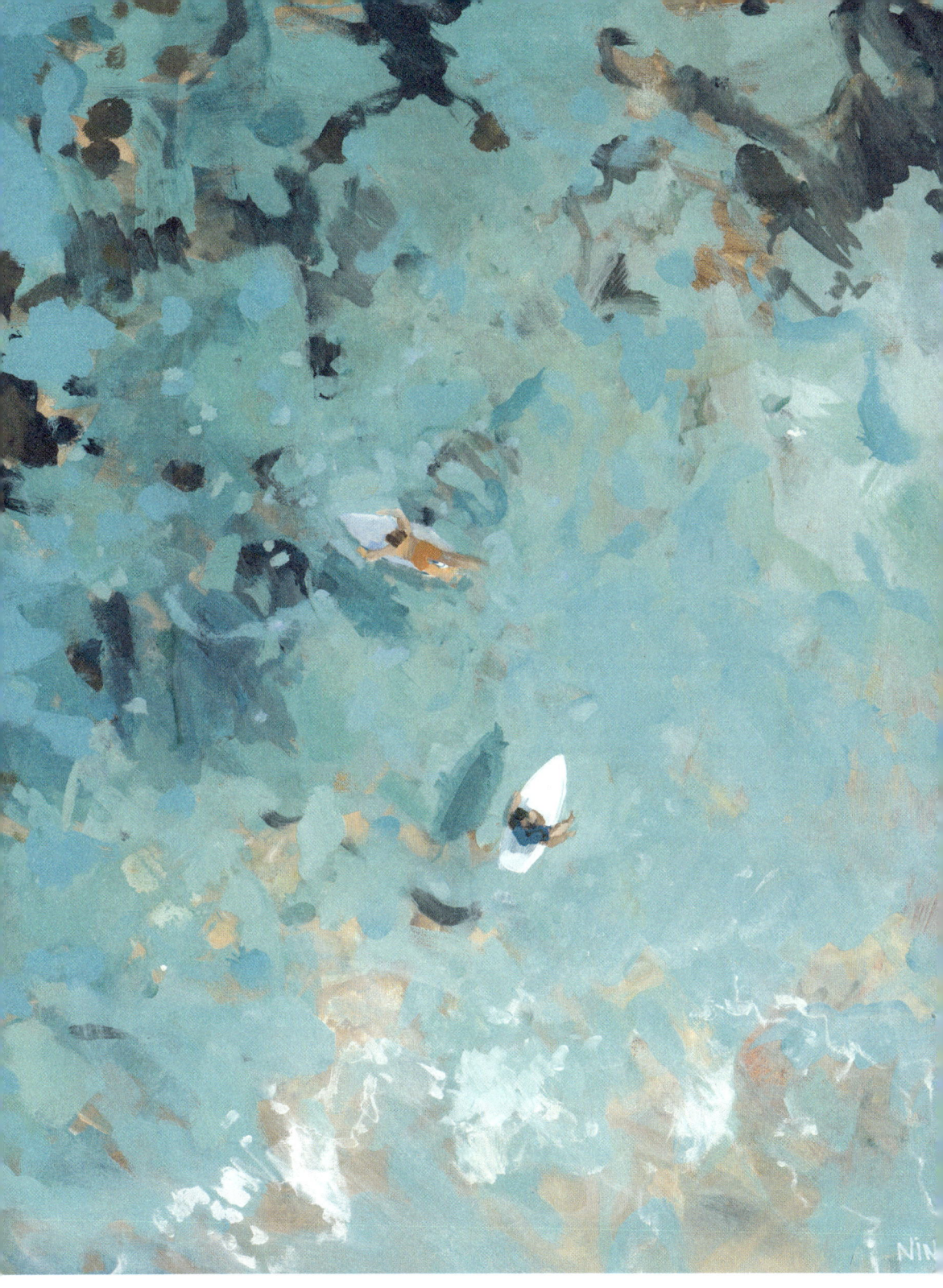

Hermosa surfers

Q & A

Nina Brooke

Who is Nina?
I am an artist living and working in Cornwall in the west of the UK. I've lived here all my life and, despite all the countries I've travelled to and surfed in, Cornwall always inspires me the most.

If you were to describe your art in a few lines, you'd say…
I make contemporary paintings depicting the world as seen from an aerial perspective, emphasising the way human activity creates patterns upon land and sea. My work focuses on human impact (in terms of climate change and migration, for example) but also on a more existential concept of how insignificant we all are. When seen from above, it has a humbling effect. I see my artwork as a symbol of gratitude, a reminder of just how lucky we are to live and wonder upon the natural landscapes of this incredible blue planet.

What came first: surfing or drawing?
Drawing came first — my grandfather taught me from a young age. He was a draughtsman and told me never to use a rubber but to work over your mistakes. Surfing came in my early teens, followed by instructing on Polzeath beach during school holidays, forming a great friendship group who I'm still close with today.

When did you first think: I can do this for a living?
There was a tipping point a few years after I graduated. I had been showing my artwork every year since I left school, and there was this one show that sold out on a weekend at a pop-up shop — I was 26. People just walked off the street and purchased painting after painting. That was when I decided to give up my day job. I was so concerned about taking this big leap of faith, but of course nothing is forever. To be honest it has been really hard work and, although it might look effortless, it's not for the faint-hearted.

How does your art come to life? Do you fly a drone yourself?
The first step is to get to know a place from a bird's-eye view, yes. So I have my drone to shoot aerial images for reference. I fly the drone and capture most of the images myself. In some cases, people will send me reference images, which I can work from too, but wherever possible I like to capture my own images. I take these back to the studio (or beach if I'm working in situ) where I intuitively capture the essence of the place — picking out particularly interesting architectural or natural forms in the landscape alongside human interactions. I use many layers of colour to build an image and it can take weeks to 'finish' a painting.

It seems like you have a go-to colour palette?
The ocean will always be my colour inspiration, and I love how different it can be. So yes — many shades of turquoise is the running theme, usually clear and bold.

Do you remember when you first thought of the idea to paint from a bird's-eye view?
Embedded into my memories are happy moments flying to the Caribbean to visit my grandparents from a very young age. My grandfather was an airplane pilot so we used to fly a lot. This gave me an early introduction to seeing the world from a bird's-eye view. I remember soaring over the islands as a child and being awestruck by the colours. That is what gave me the idea to paint the world from above. My first aerial painting was in 2015, abstract and painted by memory.

Your home base is Cornwall, a magical peninsula in southern England. For people who don't know it: what makes Cornwall so special?
It's just wild and beautiful. The coastline changes dramatically from the north coast to the south coast, and there are so many hidden coves and beaches that need exploring. I live on the north coast of Cornwall, near the popular fishing village of Port Isaac, and my go-to spot is Polzeath.

What is your favourite surfboard at the moment?
I did a collaboration with longboarder and shaper Ben Skinner (European champion and shaper at Skindog Surfboards, ed.). He shaped a most beautiful bespoke longboard, The Quill, and I inlaid a 9ft painting wrapping the edges to the deck, finished with a high gloss and hand-signed by both of us.

What is a perfect surf session in Nina's world?
I recently really enjoyed 'Chickens' in the Maldives — it was out of season and we had the sunset to ourselves. Catching perfect glassy longboard waves with reef sharks, tropical fish and even a manta ray below. The wildlife is incredible — really one for the bucket list.

Has surfing given you anything in life?
Respect, timing, patience, kindness, tolerance, appreciation, good health and energy.

Is there something you are particularly proud of?
That I have inspired a movement in the artworld, as an aerial landscape painter. I created this space and now others are joining. It's nice to know that my artwork is unique and no one has done it before. I created my own art language.

You've travelled around the world and you are often invited by hotels to the most dreamy surf destinations. Are there other places in the world where you feel at home?
That's a tough question. Surfing in the Maldives, Hawaii and Sri Lanka is really stunning, but I think the surfing in Cornwall for some reason is the best. There really is no place like home. •

05

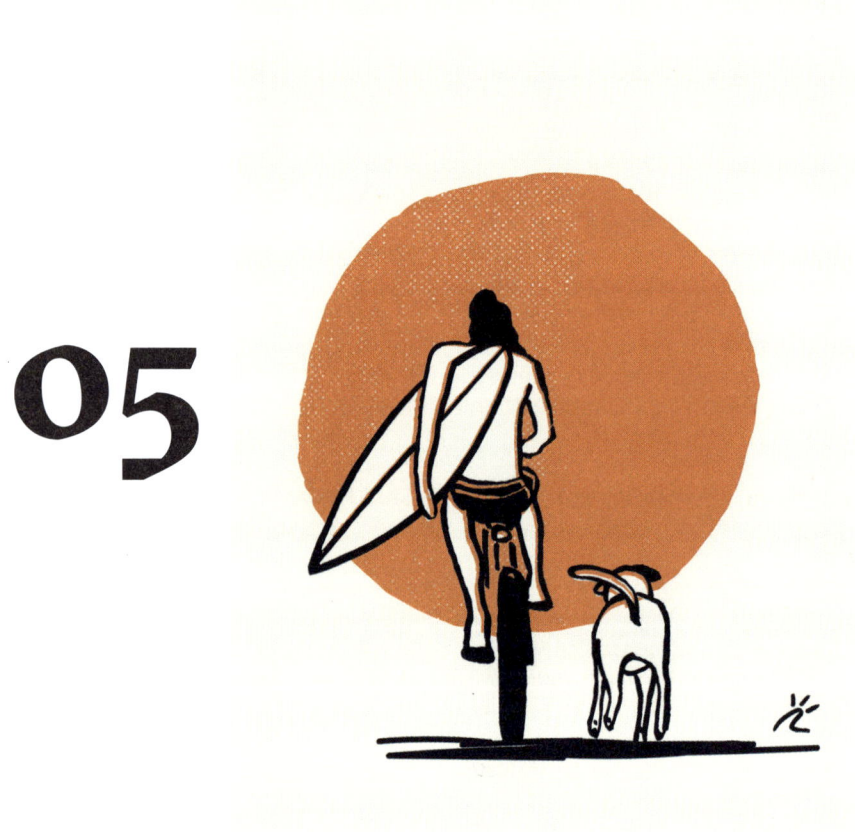

Way home

In between the lines

Raül Casado

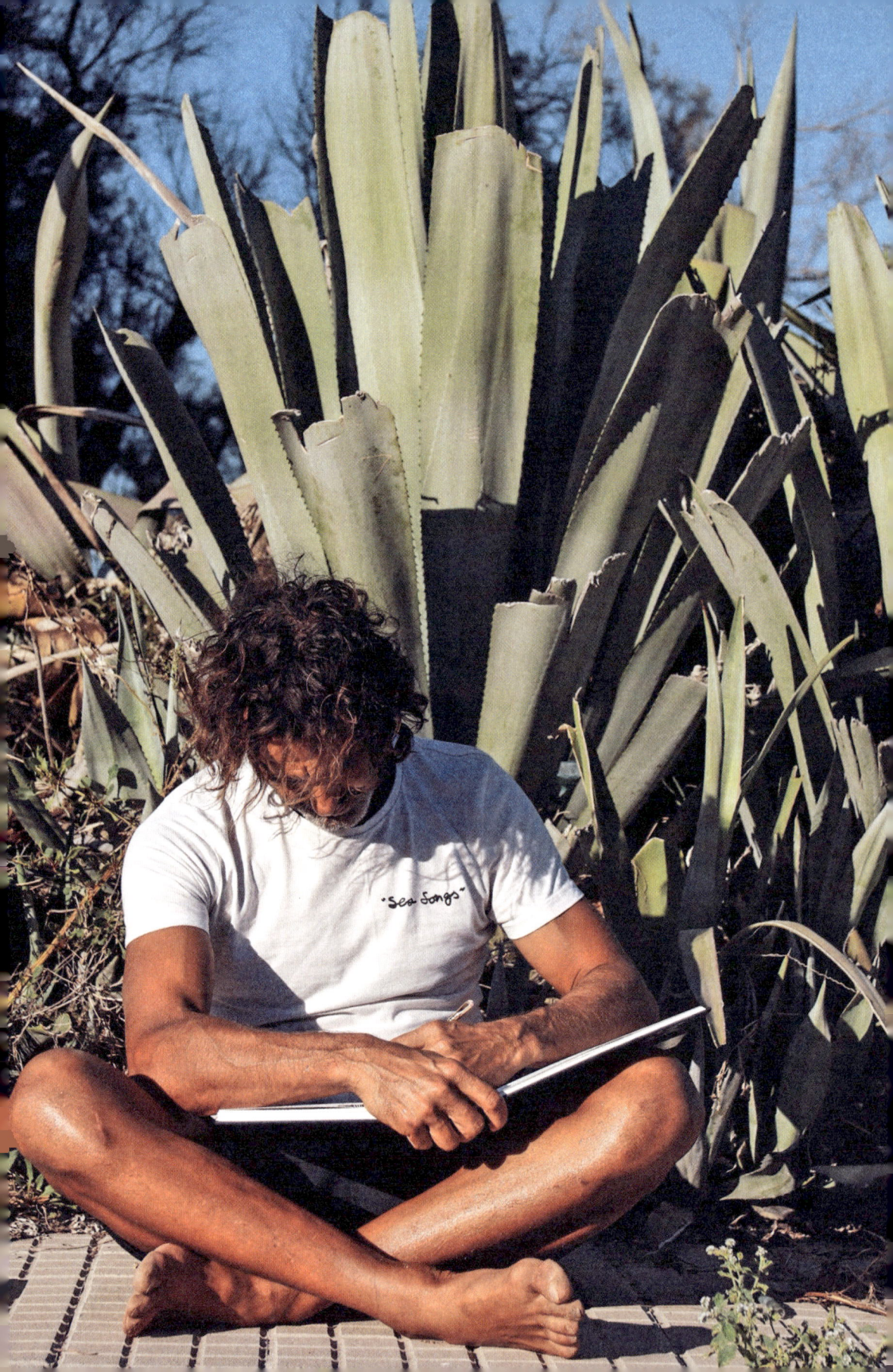

When simple lines tell an unexpected story. Originally from Majorca, Raül Casado is on a quest for the essential. Each stroke is like a word in a visual story, where less is more.

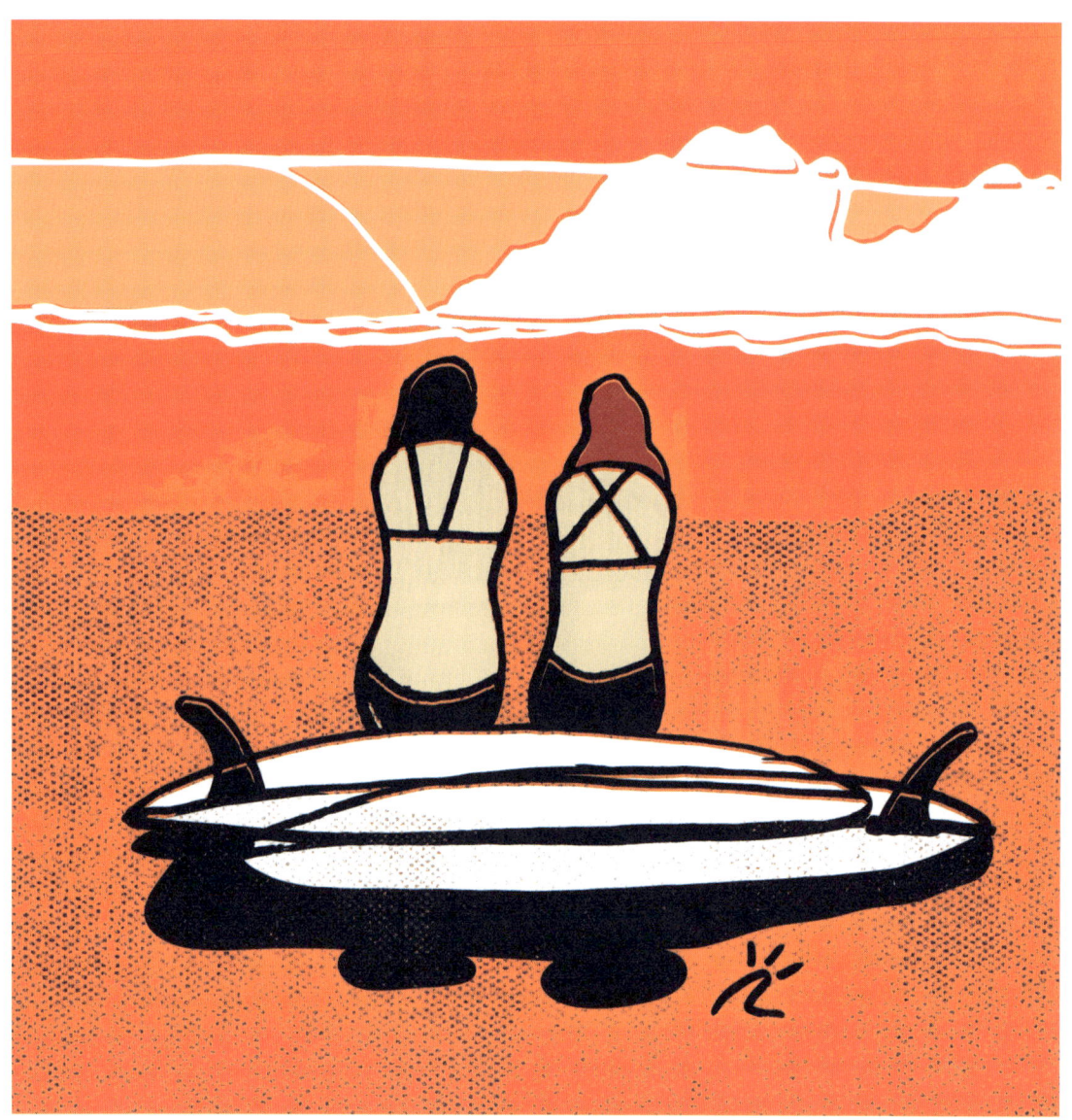

Casado believes in artworks with
an emotive quality. He uses simple
lines to tell a story. 'In the case
of 'Between waves and words'
I envisioned those beachside con-
versations with our friends, gazing
at the waves after a surf session,'
he explains.

He starts by sketching with a pencil
in a sketchbook and then refines the
forms, aiming for simplification and
maximum expression in each stroke.

Between waves and words

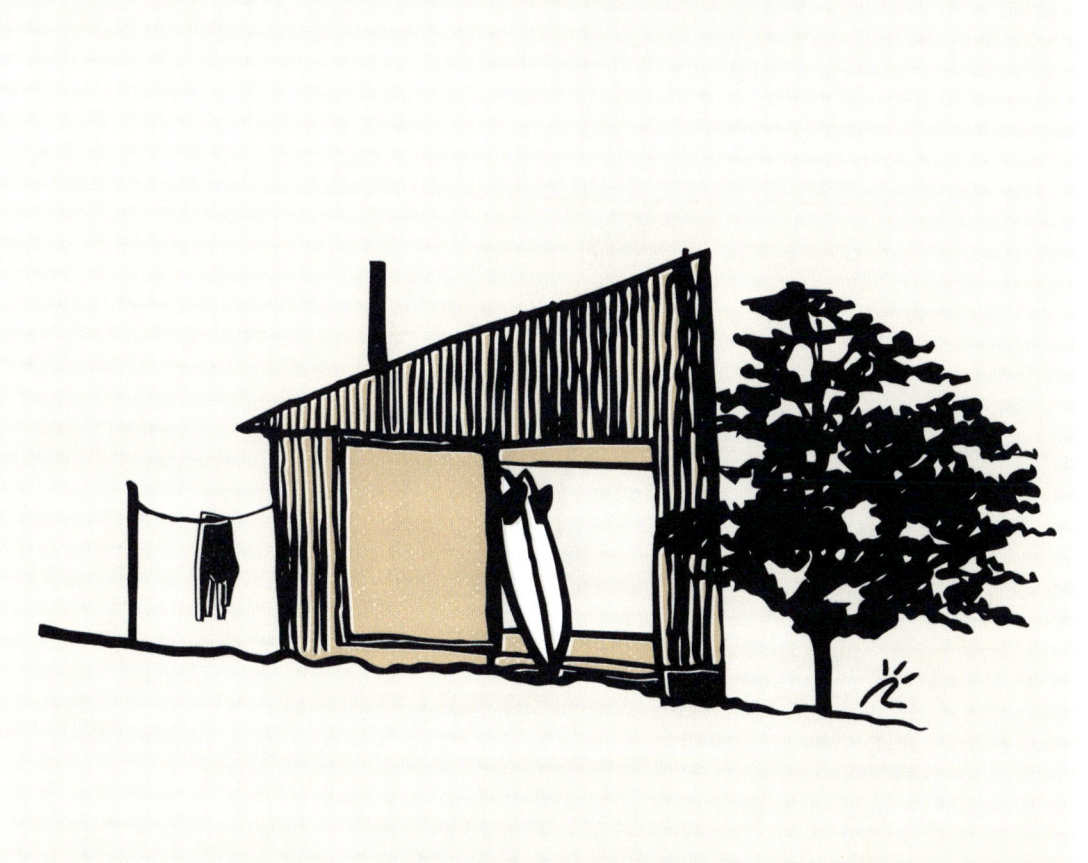

Coastal retreat

My minimalistic
art is not just
a style, but
a quest for
the essential,
removing what
is unnecessary

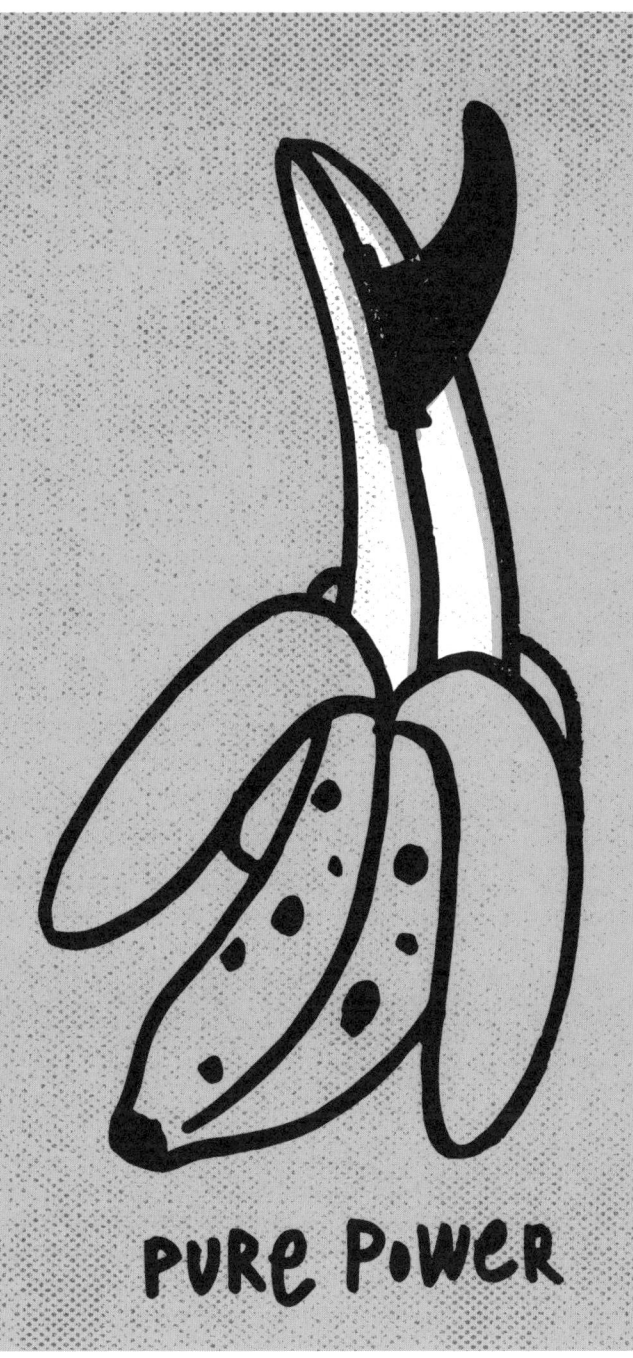

PURE POWER

Eat fruit. Long power

Q & A

Raül Casado

Who is Raül?

I'm an illustrator from Majorca, a small Spanish island in the Mediterranean Sea. Growing up here has profoundly shaped my view on the world, thanks to the surrounding beauty of the beaches, mountains and characteristic Mediterranean light. I've always been passionate about sports and outdoor activities like surfing, swimming and mountain walks. These experiences are mirrored in my illustrations.

How does the ocean influence your life/work?

It's said that those born on an island will always be linked to the sea, feeling the need to have it nearby at all times. Every morning, the first thing I do is go out for coffee and gaze at the sea. It's my zone of disconnection and my main source of inspiration.

What came first: surfing or drawing?

I have early memories of doodling in schoolbooks. From a very young age, I established a close bond with water sports but it wasn't until I was 14 that I was given an old bodyboard, and that's when I felt the thrill of riding a wave. Since then, I've never stopped chasing that surfing sensation.

If you were to describe your art in a few words, you'd say…

In short, my minimalist art simplifies movements and emotions into lines to tell stories. I seek the essence of a subject, using simple lines to convey the main idea. Each stroke is like a crucial word in a visual story, where less is more. It's not just a style, but a quest for the essential, removing what is unnecessary.

When people see your work, what do you want them to feel?

Hopefully they'd complete the story behind them with their own experiences. I want my drawings to transport them to places where they've surfed and felt those emotions – whether it's incredible sunsets, misty sunrises, or a car journey through the jungle in search of the perfect wave.

When did you first think: I can do this for a living?

During the COVID lockdown, many of us were forced to reflect on the direction we were taking. In my case, it was the catalyst to unleash my more artistic side.

What type of paper do you use for your artwork?
I use various materials for drawing, from cardboard and canvases to wood. I like paper with textures that reinforce the illustration, adding something special to my drawings.

Who are your clients? Any collaborations you'd like to mention?
I'm proud to have worked for clients worldwide, including in Japan, Australia and the United States, and with names like Quiksilver, GoPro, Otter Surf-boards, Onewheel, North Shore Surf Shop...

Do you have a favourite quote that inspires or motivates you?
I've always had the phrase in my head, 'They didn't know it was impossible, so they did it.' We set our own limits: dreaming is easy, but turning those dreams into reality is what really takes effort. However, if you set your mind to it, you have a good chance of achieving your goals.

You live in Majorca, a place not very famous for its waves. Or are we mistaken?
The Mediterranean is not known for outstanding waves, not due to lack of quality, but rather regularity. Throughout the year, suitable surfing conditions are scarce and usually coincide with strong winds and storms. The most notable occasions arise when the north wind blows, creating quality waves along the Majorcan coast. On a good wave day, it's common to find around 30 people sharing a small spot.

What does your quiver look like?
My daily board is a 5'6" JS Blak Box 3, and for fun days I have my 5'9" Mark Richards California Twin fin. For trips with more hollow waves, I bring my Lost 6'3", and for smaller days I have a 9ft longboard from a local shaper Leo (Bruskas surfboards, ed.).

Are there other places in the world where you feel at home?
I feel at home anywhere I receive a warm welcome. The north of Spain stands out for the incredible kindness of its people. Surfing, for me, is more than a sport – it's a way to immerse myself in the culture, connect with people and delve into their customs.

What does today's surf culture mean to you?
Surf culture remains fundamentally about those authentic values: connecting with nature, a free spirit and adventure. However, I believe that with the influence of social media, there's a tendency to focus more on the superficial appearance rather than the true essence. It's important to remember and value the essential principles that make surfing so special.

Has surfing given you anything in life?
Surfing has touched everything. From an early age, I adapted my life to the tidal cycles, which inevitably influenced my work, friendships and my way of living in general. This experience has taught me the value of effort, love for nature, living in harmony with my possibilities, and appreciating happiness in the small things. •

06

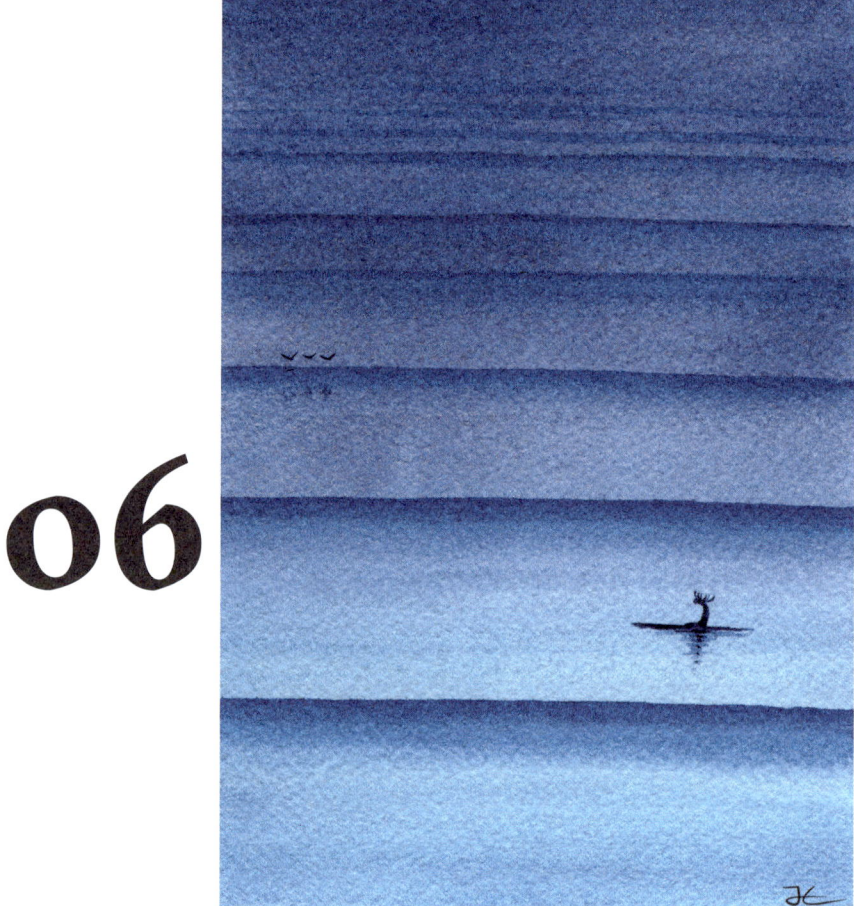

Shades of blue

Dreamy seascapes

Jonas Claesson

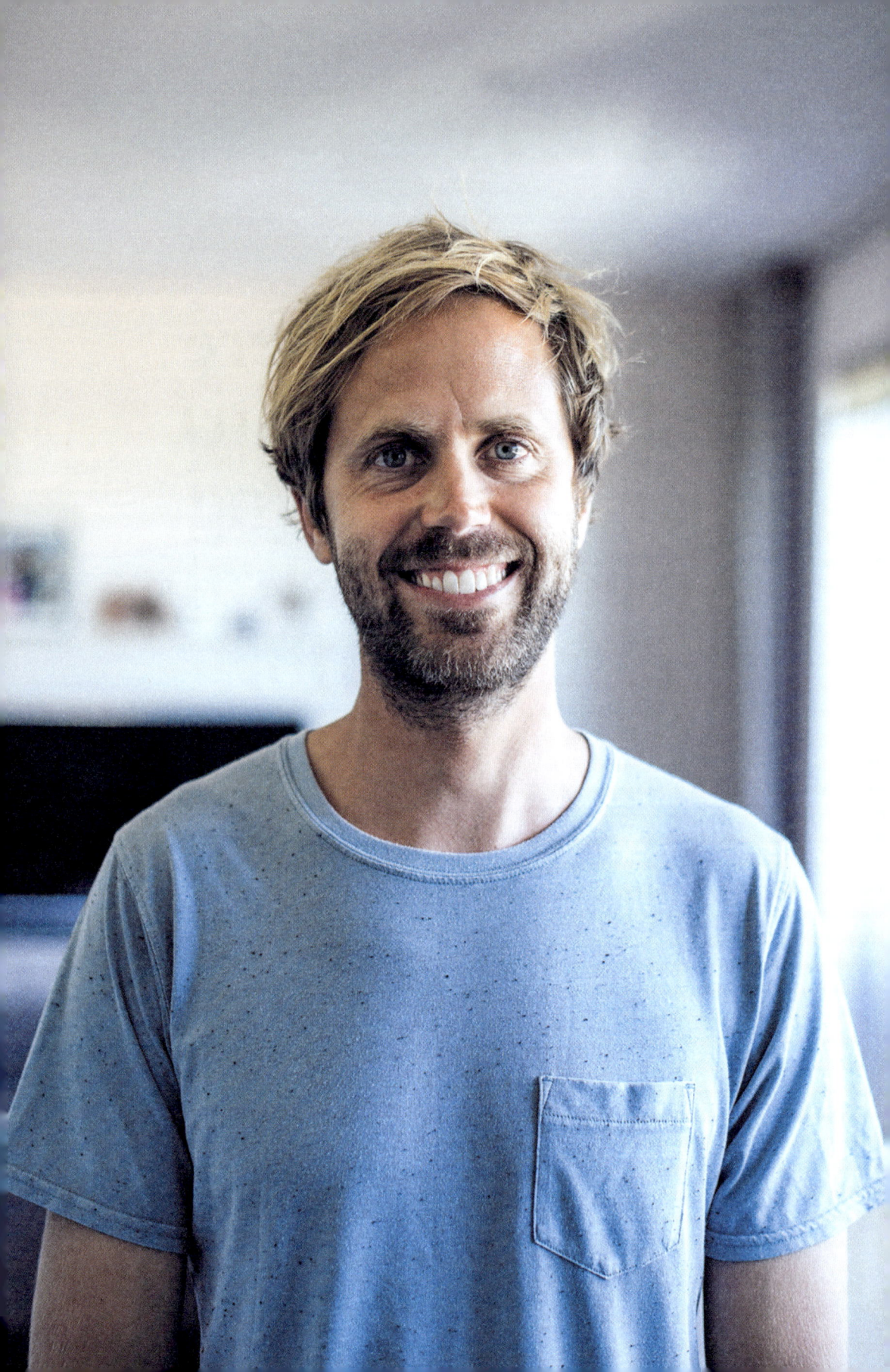

Using ink and watercolour, Jonas Claesson creates fairy tale universes where animals seem to surf in a perfect painting. The Swedish-Australian artist is famous for his otherworldly seascapes.

If you look closely, you'll see that the subjects depicted in Claessons' artworks are actually animals.

'I consider it more fun and playful', Claesson explains. 'Art doesn't always have to be serious. It's a more contemporary way of looking at art.'

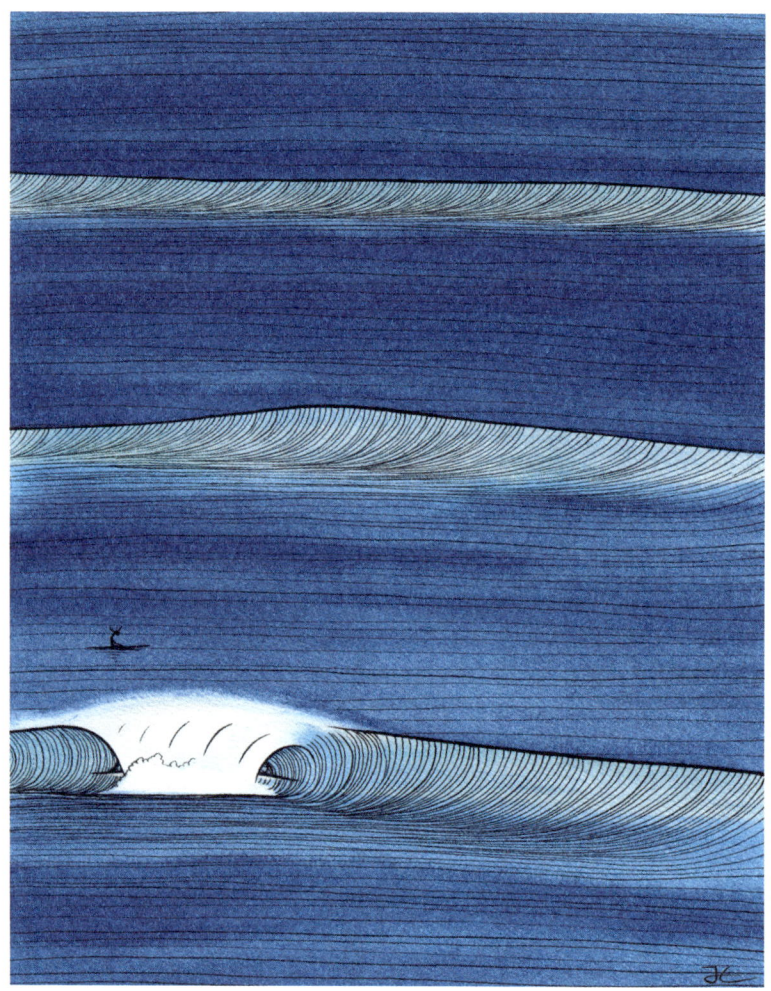

Splitting the peak

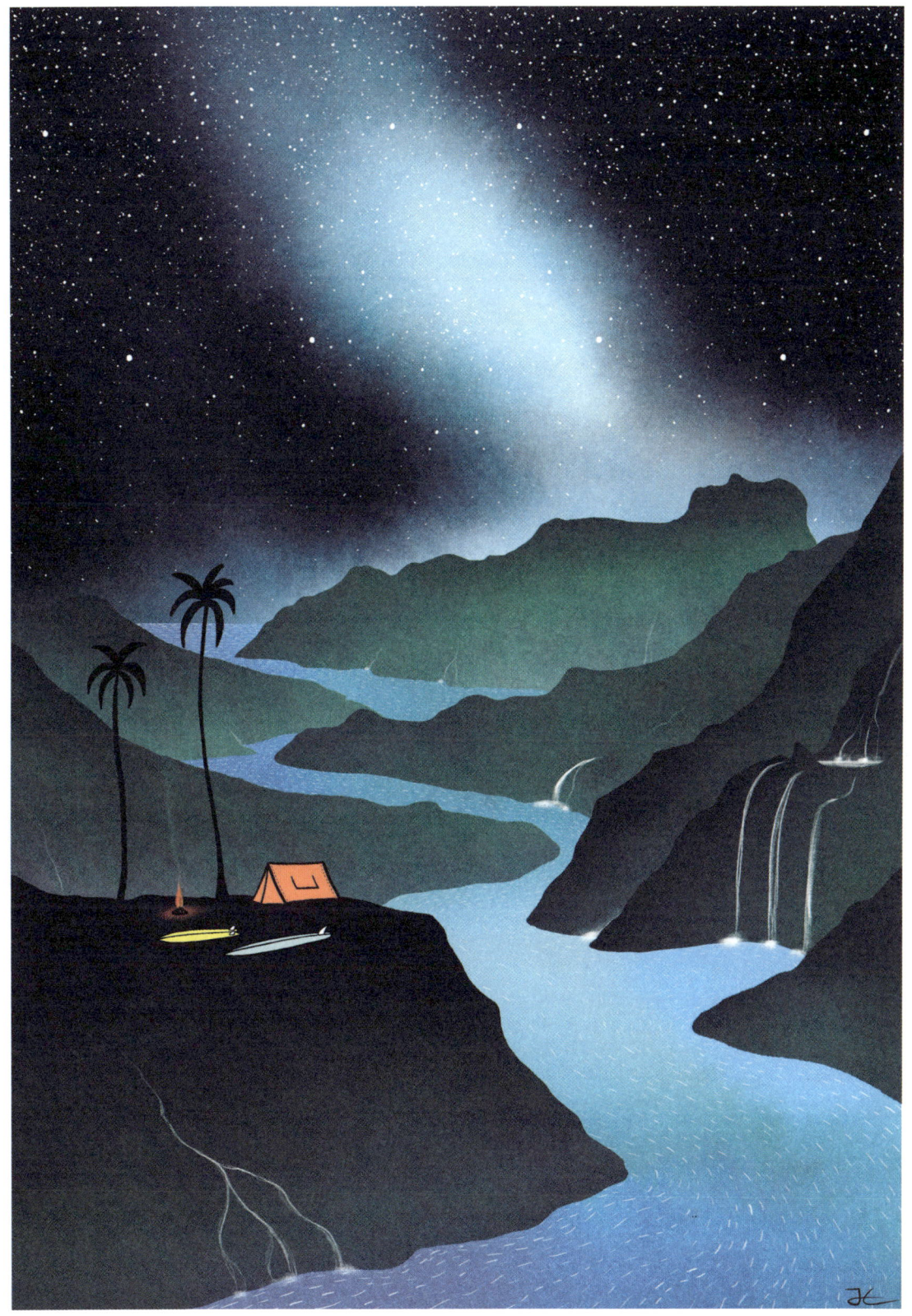

The path

Blue bay

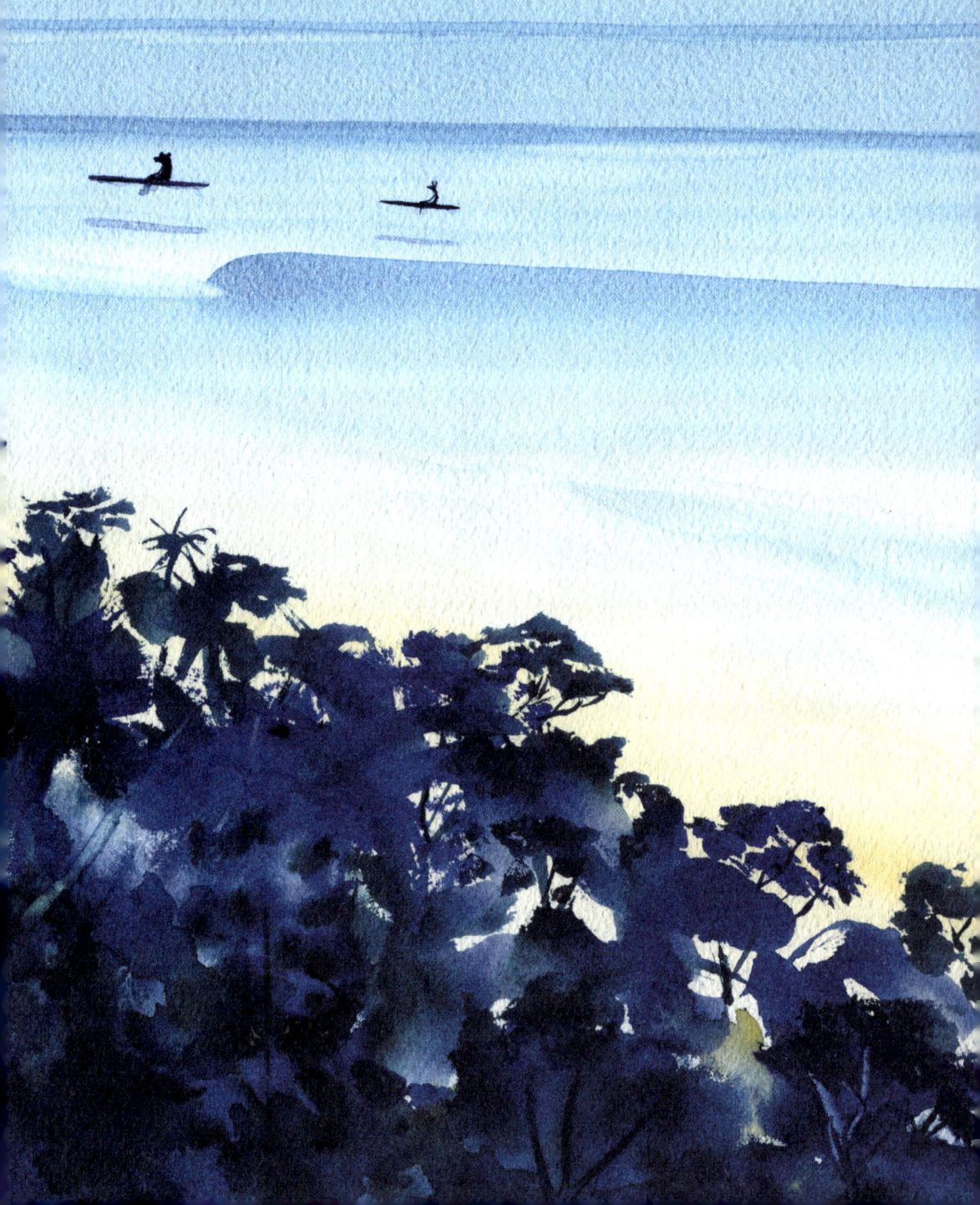

Q & A

Jonas Claesson

Who is Jonas?
A Swede who moved to Australia for the love of surfing and waves.

Did you surf in Sweden?
Yes. We mainly had crappy waves, on a short period and onshore wind, but still surfable. (laughs) I really needed more surf in my life and after high school I spent a few summers in France and Portugal. When I was 20, I moved to Australia.

When people look at your work, what would you like them to feel?
I want to be there/do that!

You draw the moments we all dream about: being out there in the middle of nowhere, few people in the water, dreamy conditions. Do you often experience these sessions yourself?
Not enough but I try to get that experience as often as I can. There is a reef around here that not many people surf where I can quite often get glassy conditions by myself or with just one friend. And if you drive a few hours north or south of here, there are plenty of options.

Do you remember how you came up with the idea to turn your surfers into animals?
I drew some bears skateboarding and surfing for friends who had started a Stockholm based surf brand. And I just kept doing it. I consider it more fun and playful. Art doesn't always have to be serious.

Do you think that is a more contemporary way of looking at art?
I think so. Art can be playful – why not? It's all about what you are personally drawn to. What I like doesn't necessarily have to appeal to someone else.

When did you first think: I can do this for a living?
It happened gradually but probably a tipping point came 10 years ago, when people started to ask me and they paid money for my work. The first 'big' thing that happened in my career was a succesful collaboration with H&M. My friends' Stockholm-based brand launched a sweat-shirt with my artwork and it sold out quickly in H&M stores.

What kind of paper do you use for your artwork?
My favourite paper to print on is Hahnemühle Photo Cotton Rag 308gsm. I love the texture and how it makes the prints look.

For art newbies: what's the difference between prints and originals?
The original is the actual painting, which there is only one of. The print is a reproduction of the original, made by scanning it and then printing.

What kind of clients do you work for? Any collaborations you'd like to mention?
I have been fortunate to work with many awesome brands like Patagonia and Gentemstick. At the moment I am working closely with Columbia in Japan and doing quite a bit of work with KnowledgeCotton Apparel.

Do you have a favourite quote that inspires or motivates you?
'Gravitate towards what fascinates you.' I heard it from Donald Brink (South African/American artist and board shaper, ed.) on his podcast and it really stuck with me.

Is there anything that fascinates you at the moment?
I've recently been doing some larger canvases: acrylics on two-meter paintings. I think I'll be doing more of them this year.

Where do you currently live or surf?
I live in Freshwater on the Northern Beaches of Sydney. It is an awesome spot with a great community and some fun waves.

Do you think Australian surf culture is different from elsewhere in the world?
I think surfing is maybe more immersed in our culture? It's very much a mainstream sport over here. Every beach has a surf club, everyone knows surfing and it's even teached at school. I'm not a surf historian but we also have a lot of surf history originating in Australia, for example Bob McTavish and his boards.

What are perfect waves in Jonas' world?
Small, glassy and uncrowded. (laughs) I can still find them here in Australia, almost on a weekly basis. When I surf in crowds, I don't get the same feeling, always looking for your spot in the water. It doesn't bring me peace. I'd rather choose unpopular spots or moments with fewer people in the water.

What is currently your favourite board?
A Channel Islands 7'10" that I surf in almost every condition. It's big enough for the smaller waves and really fun when the swell is on.

Has surfing given you anything in life?
It's why I moved to Australia and where I met my partner, and now we have a son. I have met a lot of my friends through the common love of surfing. So it means a lot to me. •

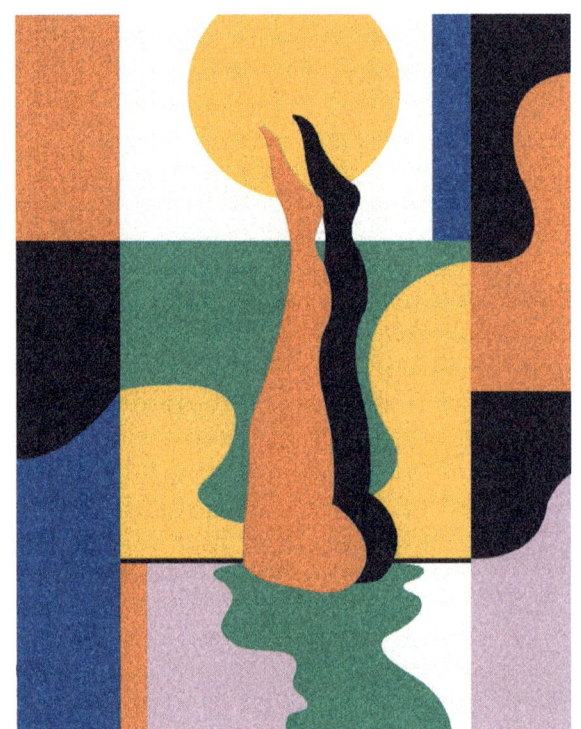

07

Long cool woman

Into graphics

Luís
da Silva

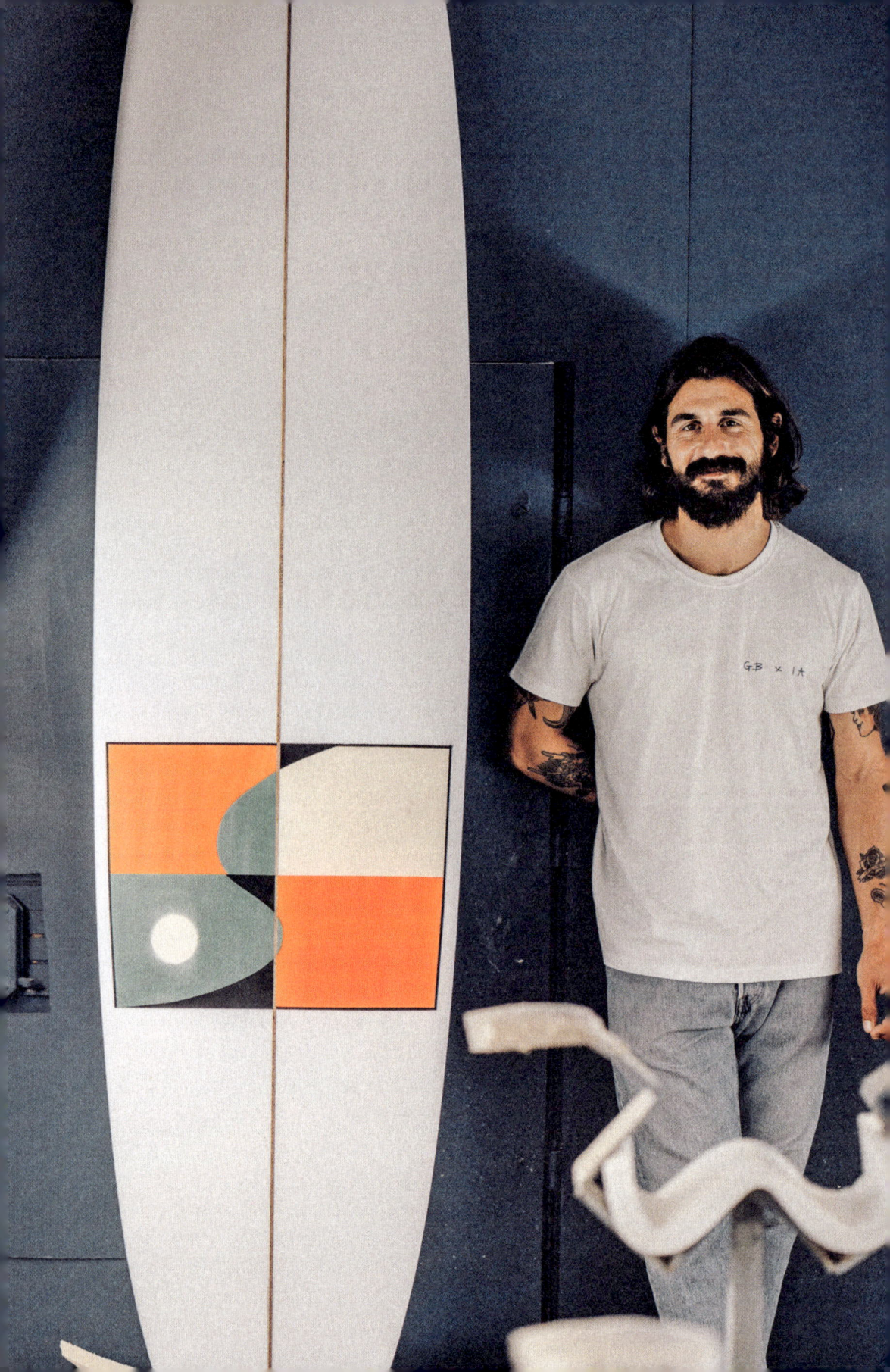

From the north of Portugal, Luís da Silva works with vibrant colours and graphic shapes. His artworks bring a different perspective to surf art.

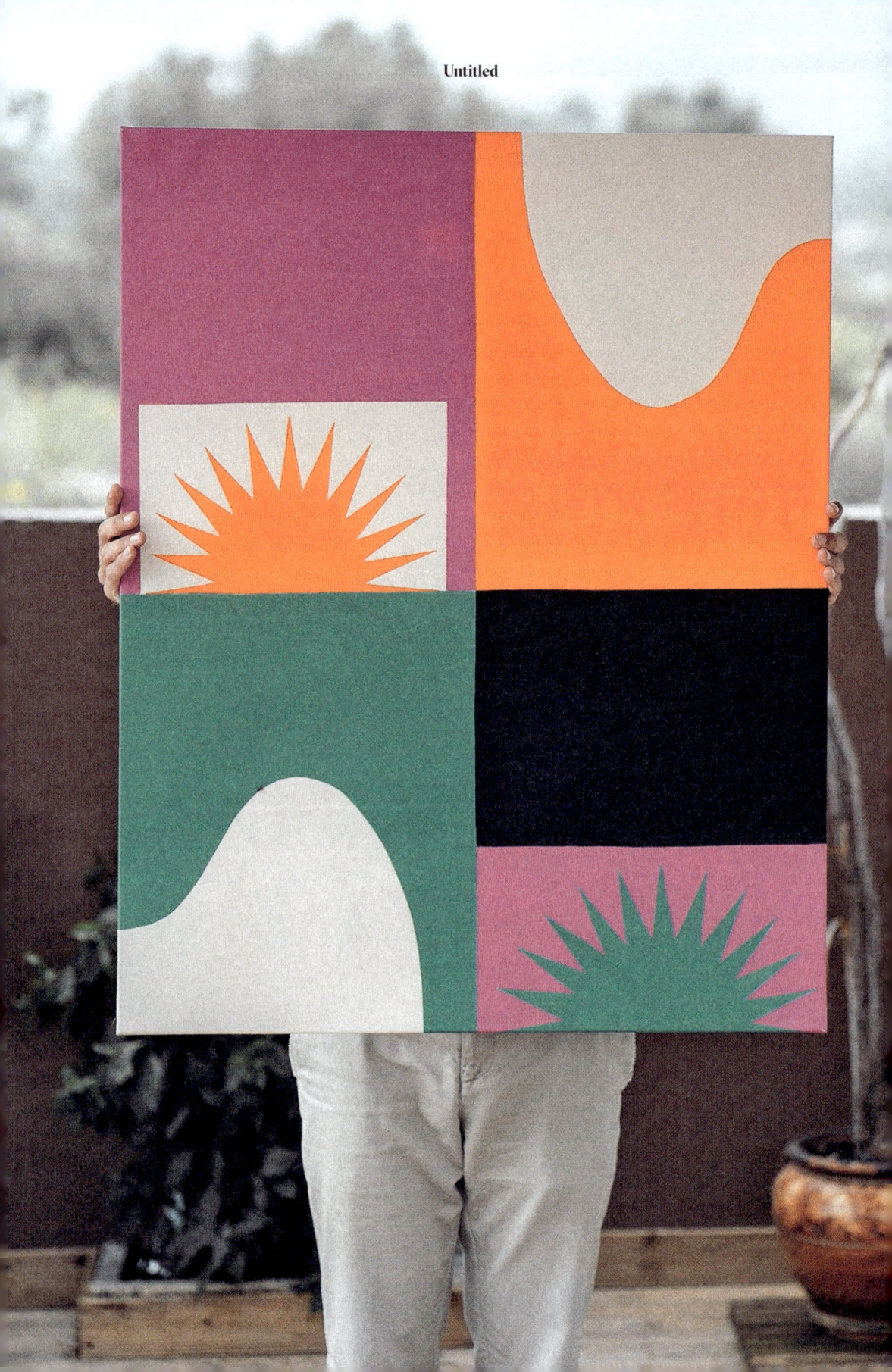

I don't think it's necessary that, when someone looks at a painting, there's something to understand. I believe that if a painting is visually pleasant, it's doing the job

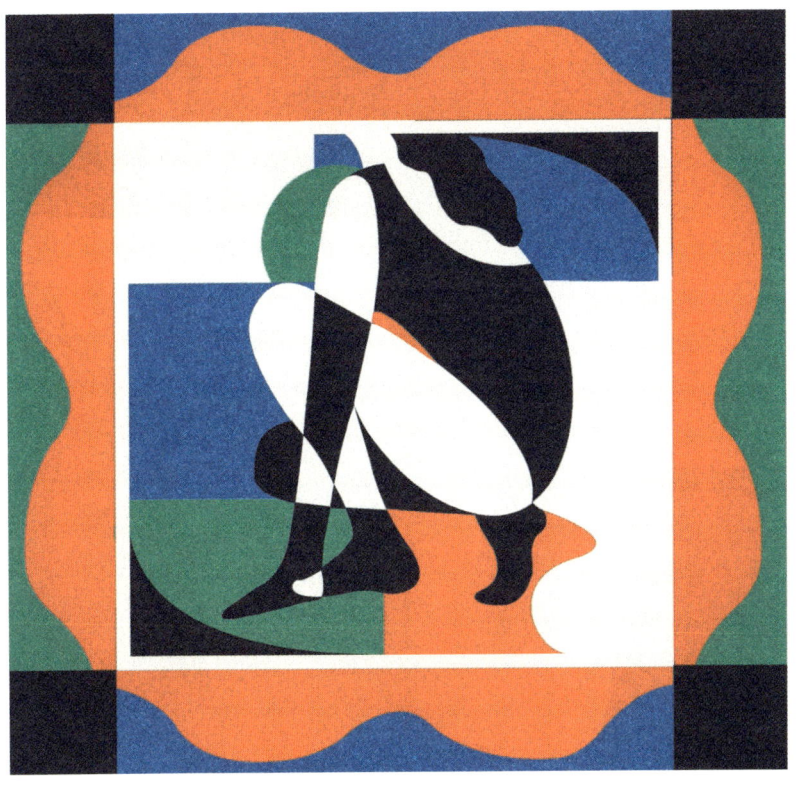

Woman in the sun

Q & A

Luís da Silva

Who is Luís?
I'm an artist from Portugal, currently living in Porto. I wouldn't define my work as 'surf art', but it's certainly related and influenced by it.

What came first:
surfing or drawing?
Drawing came first. I've been in love with drawing and painting since I was nine or 10 years old. I used to love watching the TV show *Art Attack* and I think that was the moment I realised I wanted to do this for a living. Surfing was something that entered my life quite late, especially because I was very much into skating back then. Actually, as far as I can remember I didn't like the surf scene as a teenager.

How does your art come to life?
When I paint, my head keeps thinking about everything and nothing… Good things, bad things, problems and dreams, colours and shapes… And music. Whatever I'm listening to drives me towards the 'destination'. Music is my main influence.

You work under the name SickFaces. What does this refer to?
A lot of people ask me about that. The name originated when I was around 15 years old. I was, and still am, very much into horror movies and 'dark art', if we can call it that. I remember one of my biggest influences at the time was this guy called 'Neck Face'. So you can see the connection. I thought about changing it, but I've been using this name for so long that I don't think it's worth it.

When people look at your work, what would you like them to feel?
I've always looked at paintings purely in an aesthetic way. I was never really into the idea that when someone looks at a painting, there's something to understand (like a hidden message). Personally, I believe if a painting is visually pleasant to the eyes of the viewer, then it's doing the job.

What kind of paper, textiles or paint do you use for your artwork?
I mainly work with canvas and acrylics, even though I'm trying to approach new techniques at the moment. If I'm doing prints, mostly serigraphy (silkscreen printing, ed.), the paper always needs to be of high grammage and the brand Fabriano.

Any painters who inspire you?
There are a few artists that I take as an influence or inspiration on different levels: Quentin Monge [see page 166], Alex Proba, Or Kantor, Nacho Eterno, Alby Guillaume, Hell'o Collective and Lord Mantraste, among others.

Do you have an opinion on price setting in the world of surf art?
I don't have an opinion on what each artist should charge for their work. I do think a lot of people charge way less than they should.

Do you have a favourite quote that inspires or motivates you?
'Sê todo em cada Coisa. Põe quanto és. No mínimo que fazes.' It's from a poem by Fernando Pessoa (considered one of the greatest 20th-century Portuguese poets, ed.) It means: be fully present in each moment. Give as much of yourself as possible, even in the smallest actions.

Where do you currently live or surf?
I used to live in this small town in the north of Portugal, where I was born. It's a quiet area, next to the ocean, with a lot of different spots to surf, waves all year round. I love Praia do Cabedelo in Viana do Castelo. Right now I live in Porto. There's definitely a lot more people surfing here but I still get some fun sessions around Matosinhos.

What is a perfect surf session in Luís's world?
I always think of the autumn sunny days in Praia do Cabedelo. Very cold water but still manageable because of the sun on our faces. Only a handful of people surfing long, right-hand waves. Those were and still are my favourite surf sessions.

Has surfing given you anything in life?
If there's something surf brought to my life, it's friendship. I've met so many nice people along the way and some of them are my best friends now. Apart from that, it also brought me to places I never thought of going. I should also not forget that a lot of the work I've been doing in the last few years is somehow related to surf. •

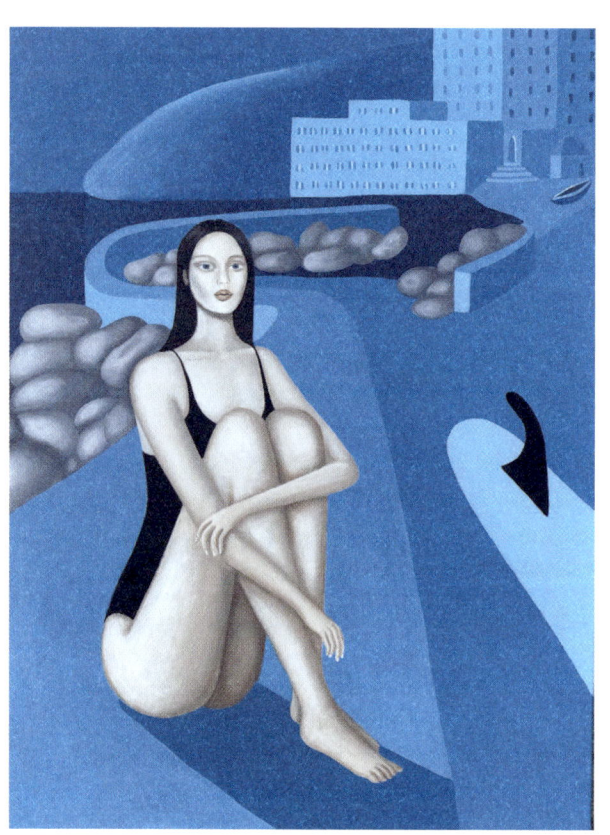

08

Moonlight

Surf &
the city

Pandora
Decoster

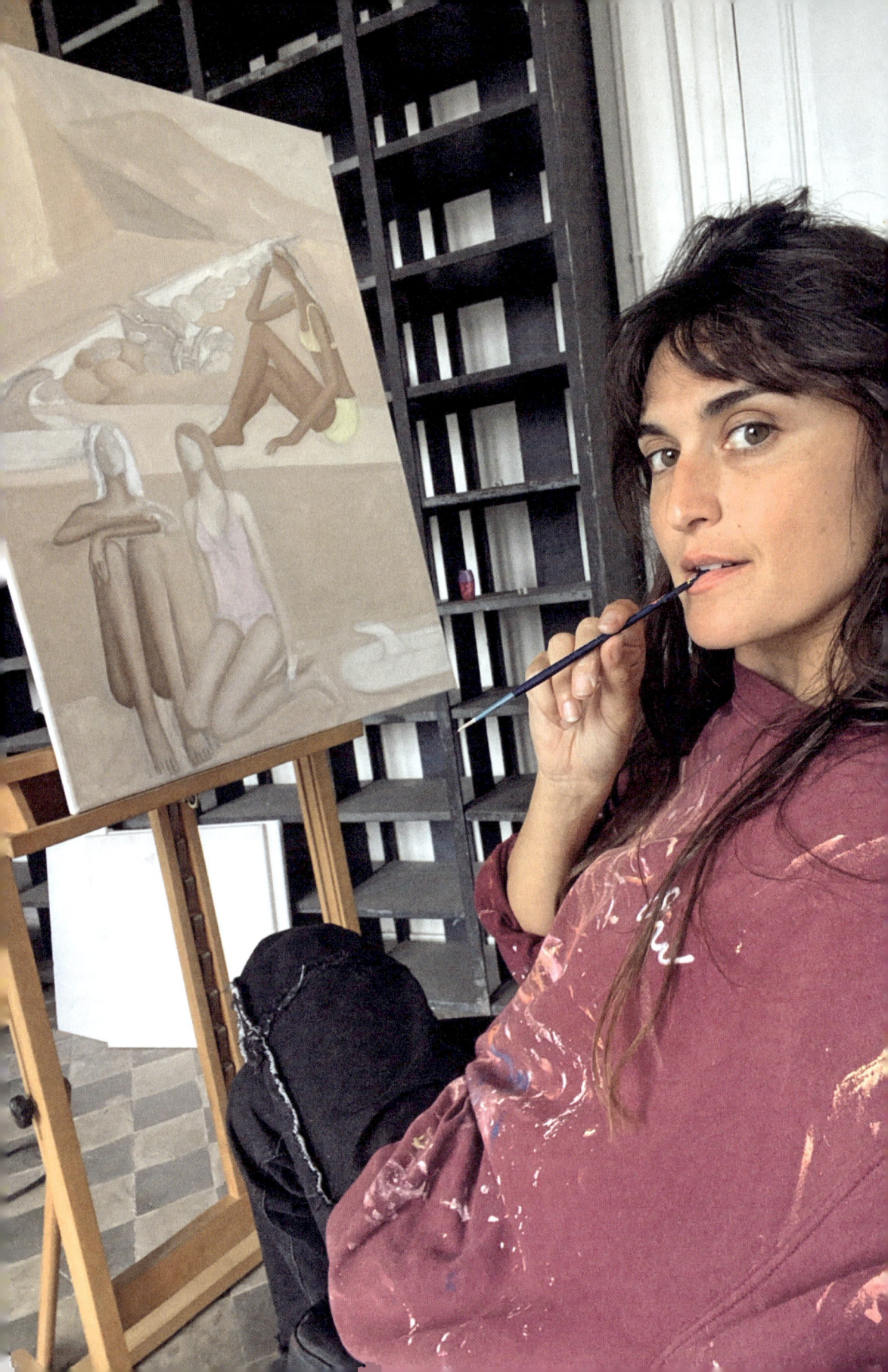

Connoisseurs will recognise the French Basque Country and iconic surf city of Biarritz in Pandora's pastel-coloured universe. Her style is unique and her figurative paintings showcase femininity in a way we hadn't seen before.

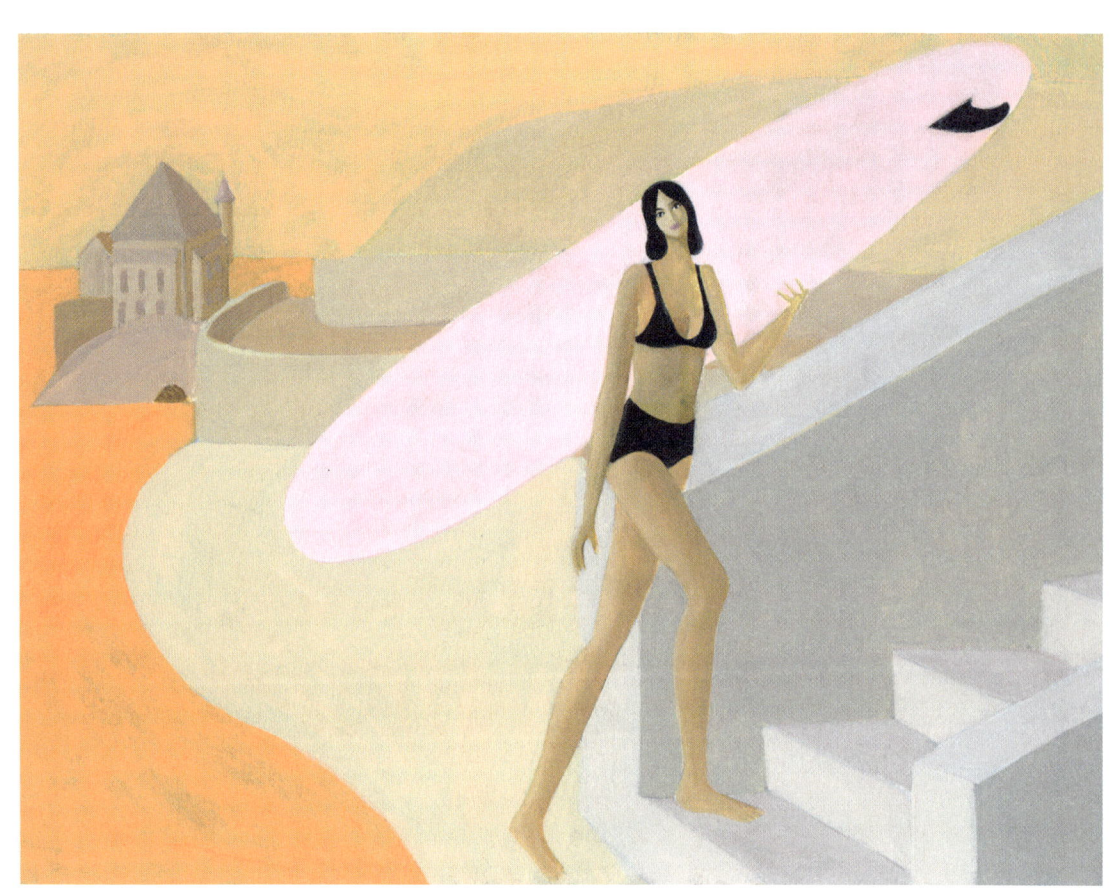

Alaena

Decoster painted 'Alaena' (left) for a collaboration with the eponymous cosmetic brand from Biarritz. They printed the painting on a tote bag.

'Après la pluie' (below) means 'after the rain'. 'I drew this during a little heartbreaking period. There's a cloud in the sky, which you don't see very often in my work.'

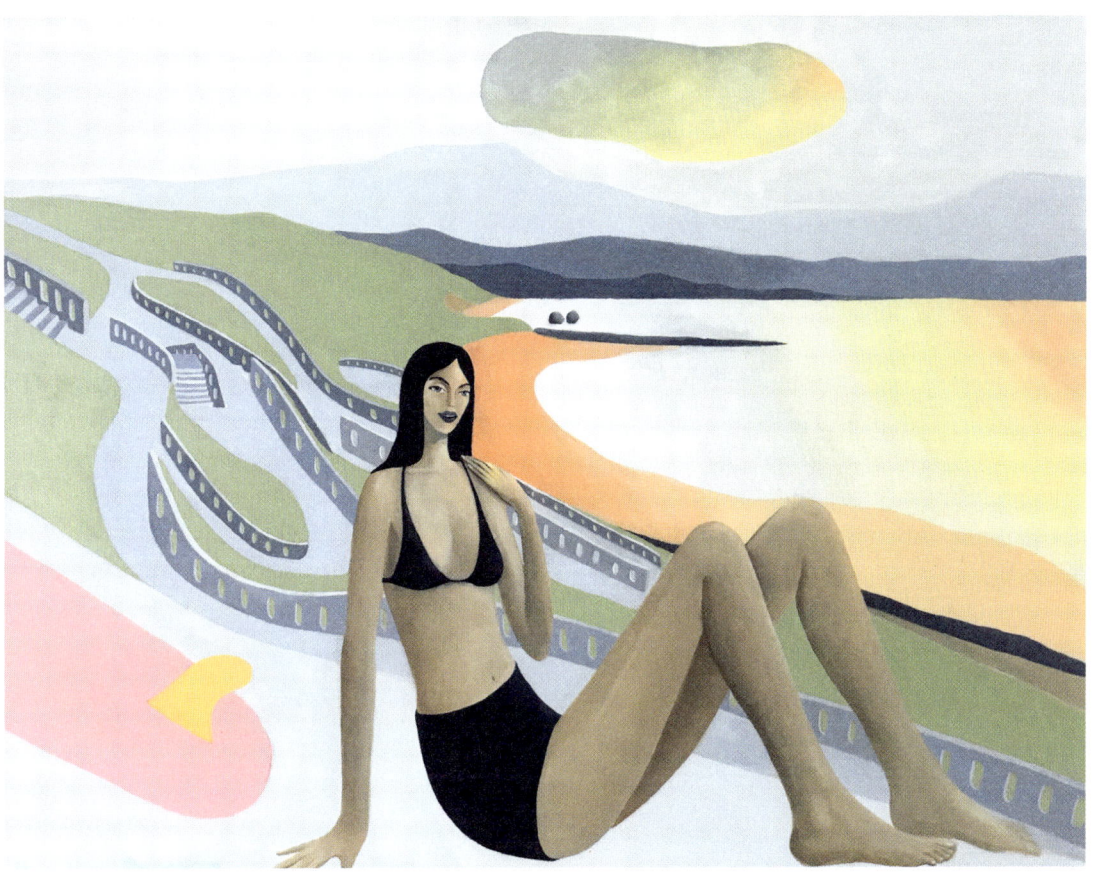

Après la pluie

La Milady, baby

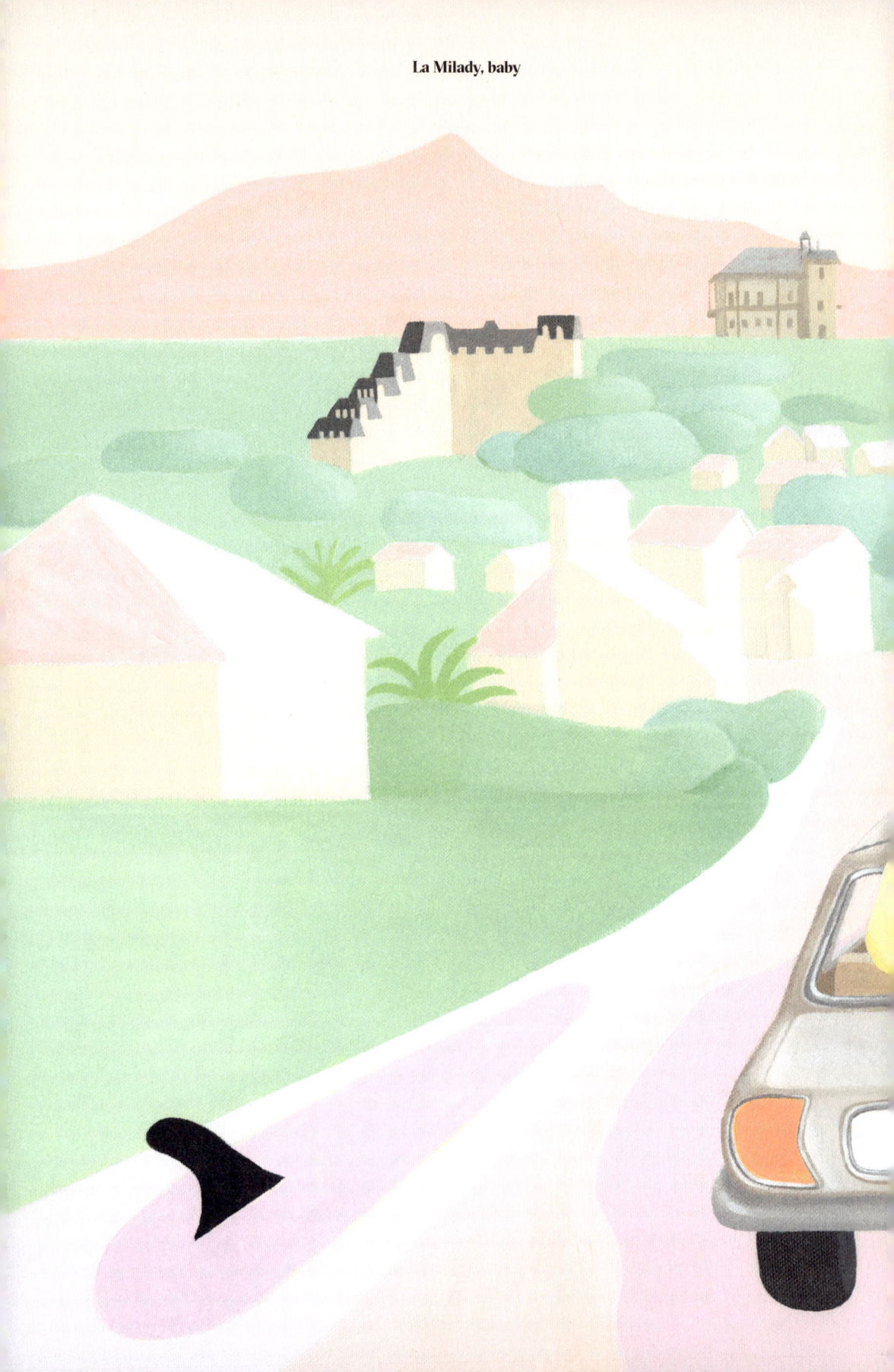

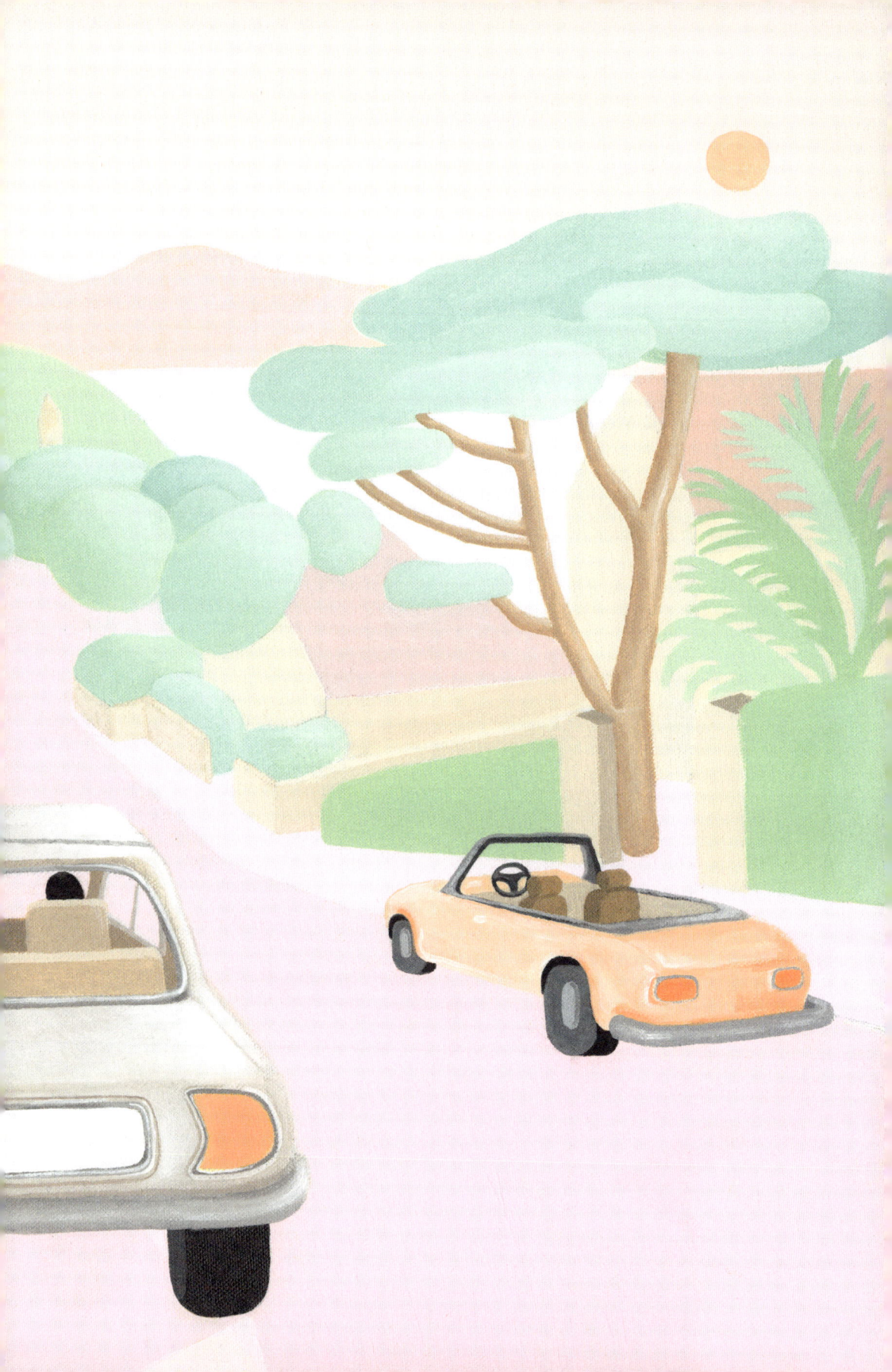

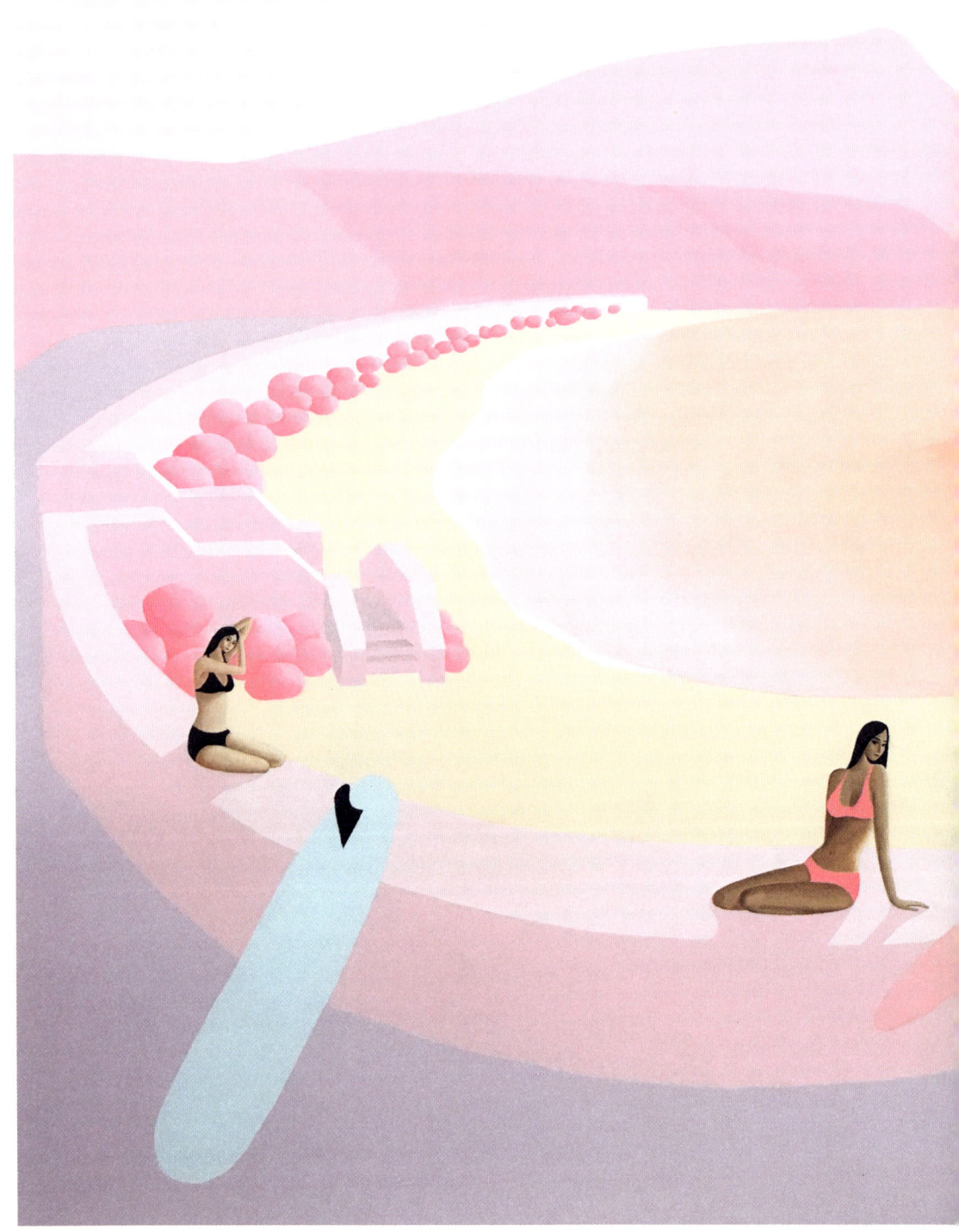

De l'aube à la nuit

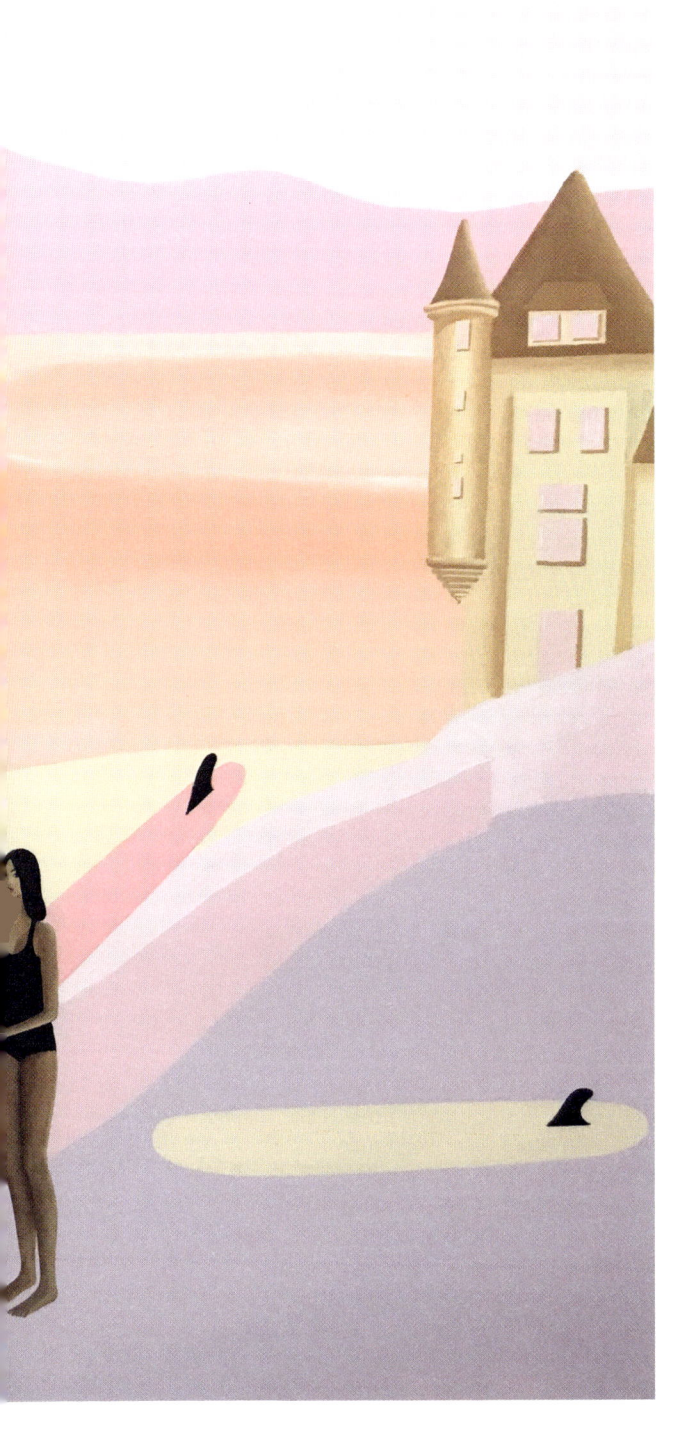

I create figurative artworks with a rather obsessive focus on female surfers in French Biarritz, mainly at the Côte des Basques

Q&A

Pandora Decoster

When did you first think:
I can do this for a living?
I realised this at around the age of
27 after exploring many different
paths. My mother is a painter,
so I always had a desire and
curiosity for this profession.

Who is Pandora?
A painter from Biarritz.

What came first:
surfing or drawing?
Drawing. I have been drawing
since I was a little girl, and
I started surfing at the age of 12.

If you were to describe your art
in a few lines, you'd say…
I create figurative artworks with a
rather obsessive focus on female
surfers in French Biarritz, mainly
at the Côte des Basques. When
I discovered surfing, I developed
a great fascination for this beach,
and I spent a significant part of
my life there.

What do the women in your
paintings represent?
Femininity, grace, strength
and power.

How does your art come to life?
I paint with acrylics in a very
instinctive way — nothing is really
calculated in advance. I make a
small sketch and then transfer it
to canvas. I dive in with colours
without knowing at all what will
happen. Once the balance is
found, I don't touch anything.

When people look at your art,
what would you like them to feel?
A sense of serenity because that's
what I needed to feel after years
of restlessness before that.
But I have a lot more inside me
that I want to express and I'd like
to depict other emotions as well.

Are you thinking of following
a new direction?
At the moment, I still have much
to explore in the direction of
Basque seascapes and bathers
with their surfboards. I wish to
delve more into the exploration
of light, reflections, and skies.
But I also have a strong desire to
paint the countryside, mountains,
trees, and find my own way of
portraying them.

Was it painting that gave you serenity?
Yes. I found serenity thanks to the routine of painting and the meditative state it gives me. As well as through the focus, the soft, calm colours and the serene images I create.

Any painters that inspire you?
I'd say Milton Avery, Georgia O'Keeffe, Frida Kahlo, David Hockney, Edvard Munch, and the painters group Les Nabis. And not to forget surf artists Tyler Warren and Andy Davis.

Where do you currently live or surf?
Right now, I alternate between Guéthary and Paris. I can't choose between a life revolving around nature and calmness, and a life rich in culture. It's a balance that seems perfect to me. I enjoy working in both. In Guéthary, on the Basque coast, I find solace in solitude and immerse myself in a meditative state. In Paris, I go out a lot, meet people, and every day and every night inspires me even more. I paint in a studio surrounded by other painters, and I also like this atmosphere.

How far do you live from the sea?
Five minutes, to be precise.

Has surfing given you anything in life?
I owe everything to surfing! The travels, my job, the opportunities I had when I was younger as a 'pro surfer'.

Do you have a favourite quote or passage from a book that inspires or motivates you?
I really love all of Munch's diaries. I love this small excerpt, translated from Norwegian into English: 'Art is the opposite of nature. A work of art comes from the inner soul of a human being. Art is the form that the image takes once it has passed through the nerves of the human being – his heart – his brain – his eye.' Or this one: 'Explaining a painting is impossible. It's precisely because it cannot be explained that the painting was made.' •

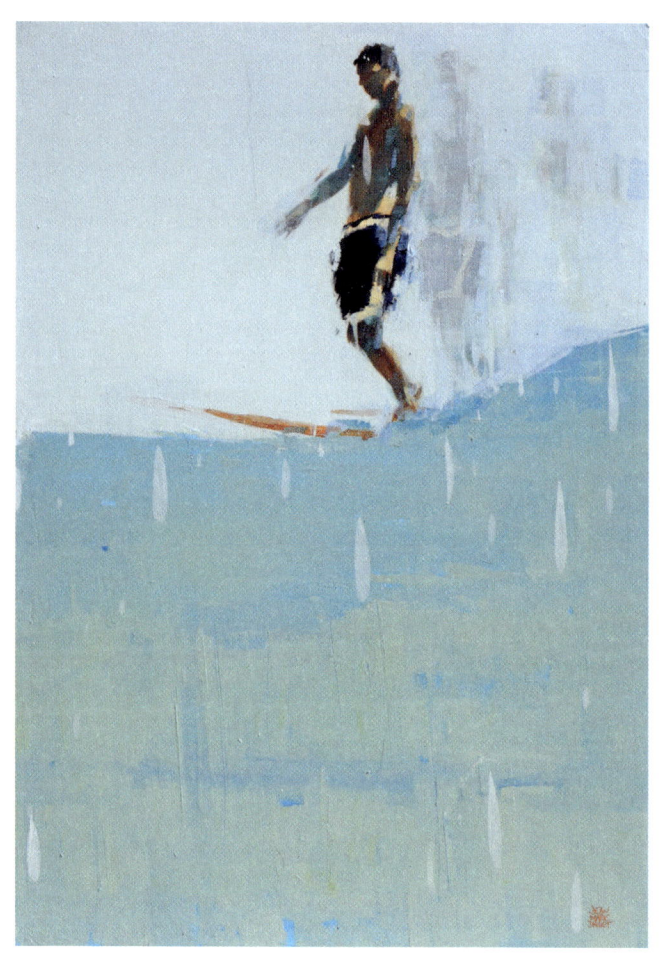

09

Longboard spirit

Beyond cinematic

Jim Drouet

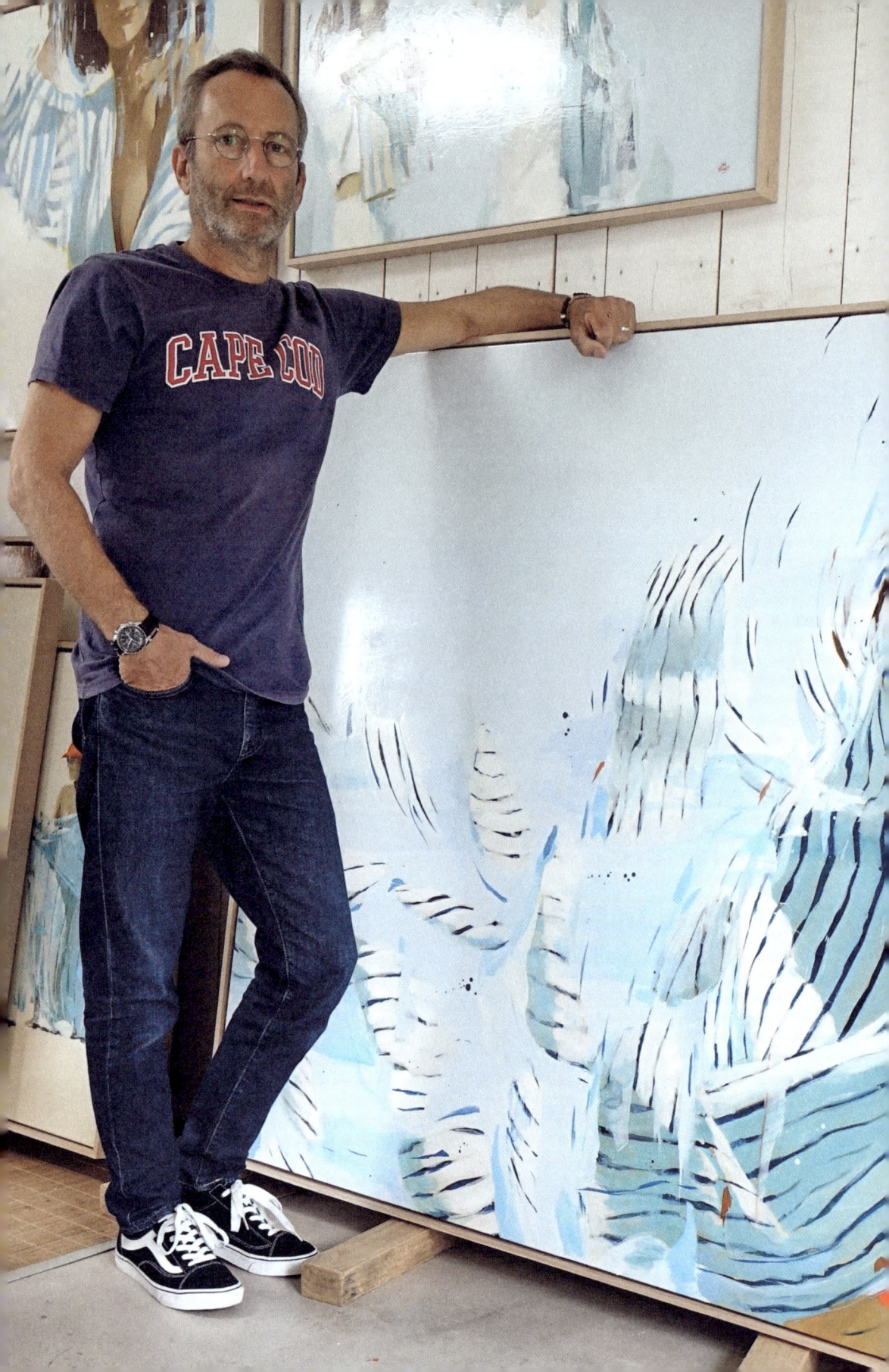

With paintings that almost look like frames from an art film, the work of French painter Jim Drouet is a contemporary kind of impressionism.

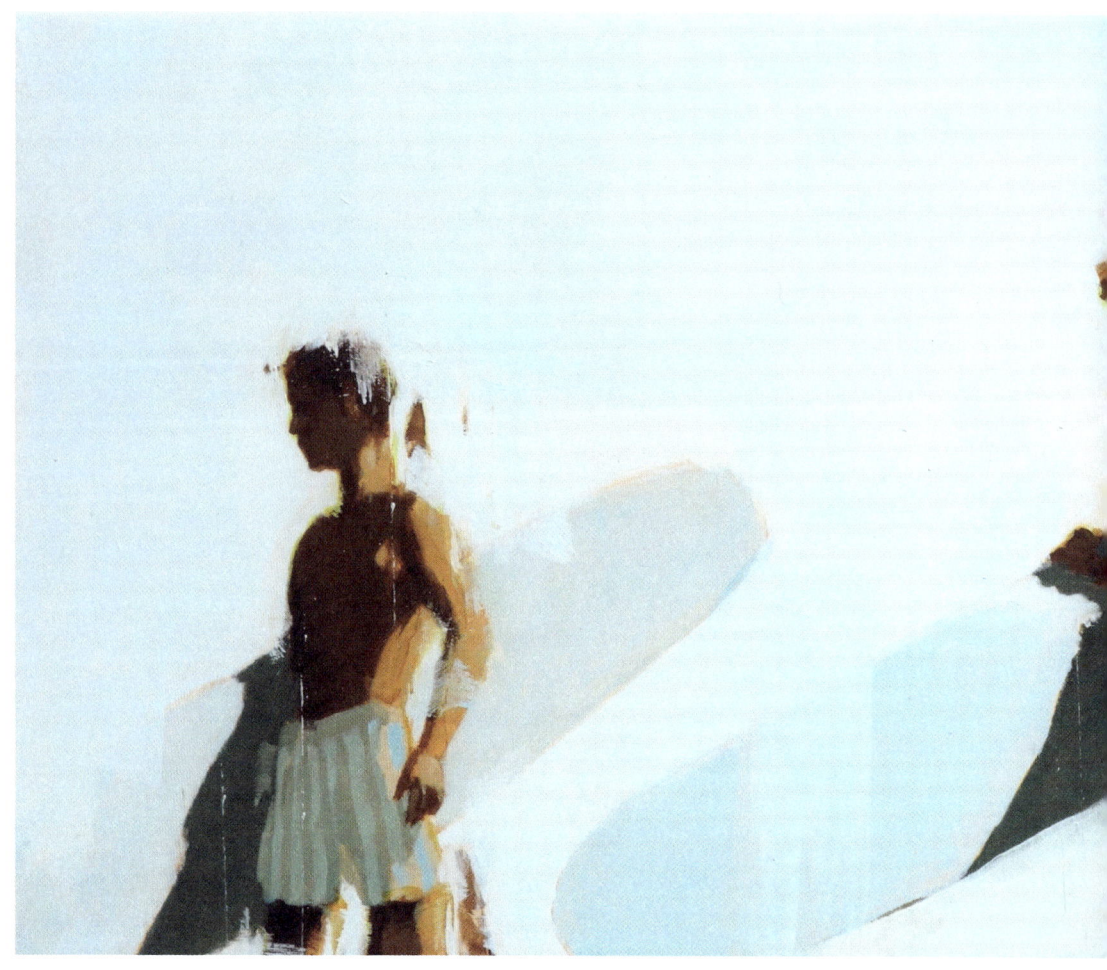

'In this painting, I was aiming for a certain simplicity', says Drouet. 'There's no need to depict the sky or the sea; everything is implied and perfectly understood without showing it.'

The French painter is inspired by cinematic culture mainly from the USA. 'I experienced the beginnings of surfing and windsurfing on the French coasts in the late 1970s and early 1980s with all the imagery coming from California and Hawaii. It was also the era of Spielberg and Lucas.'

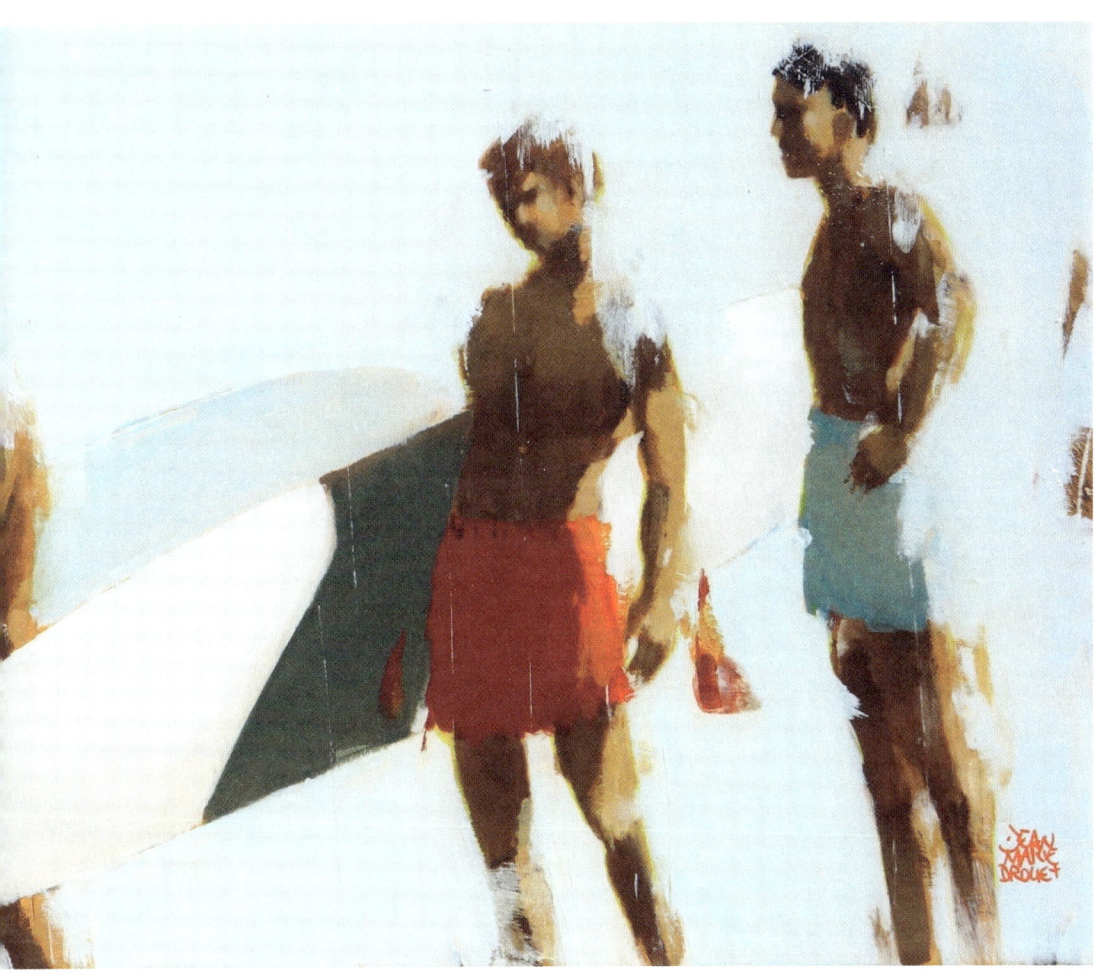

White single

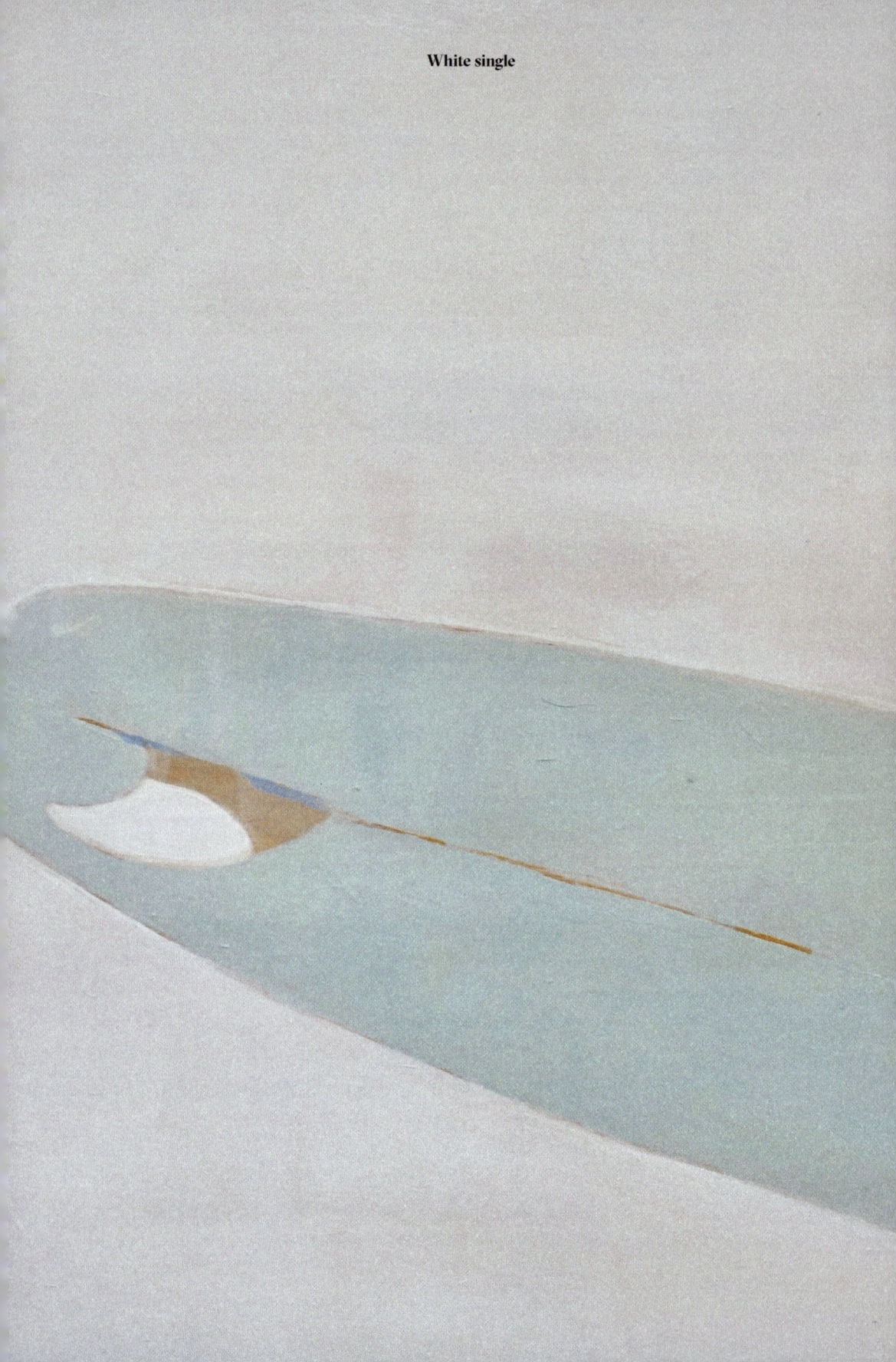

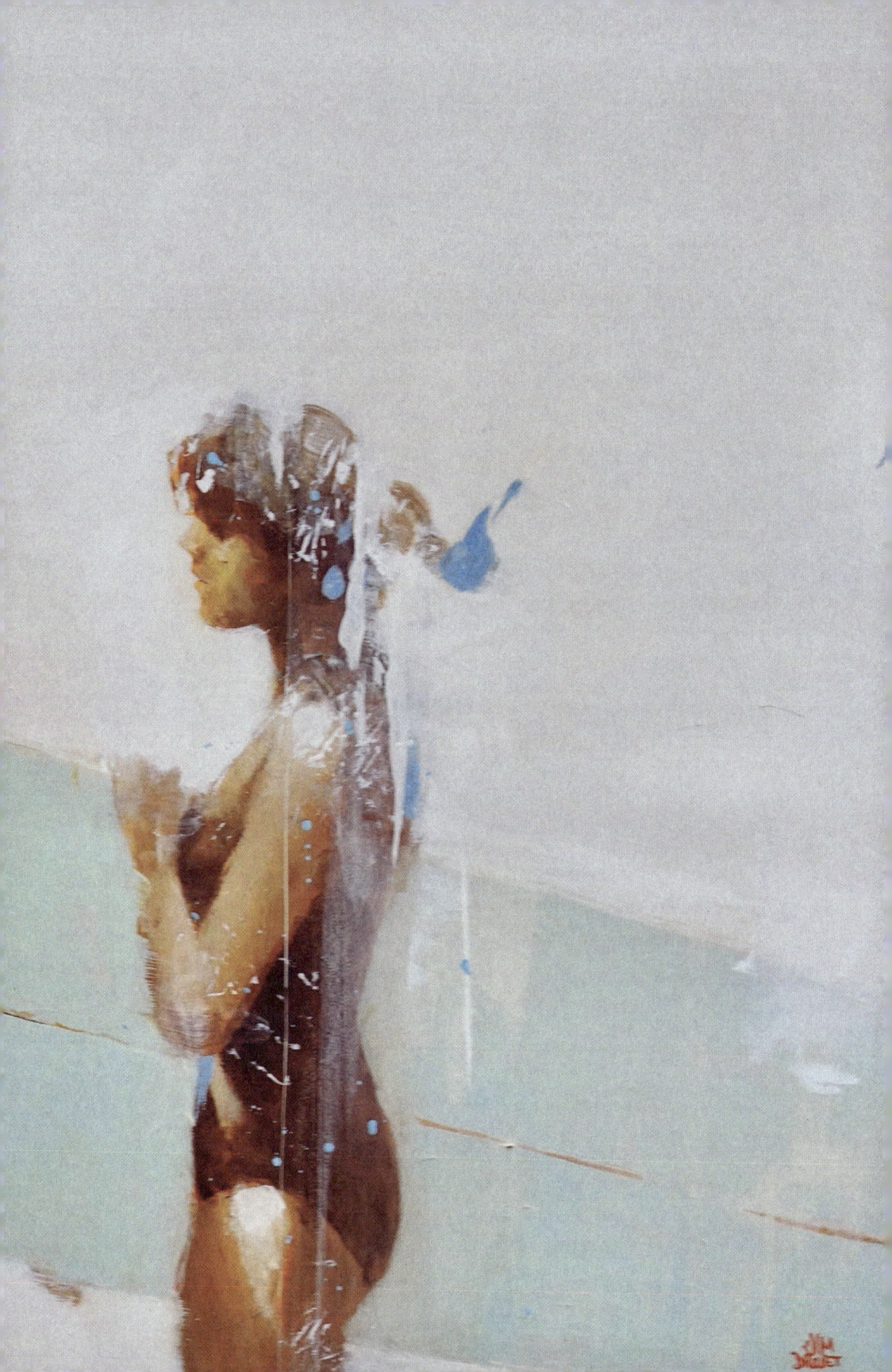

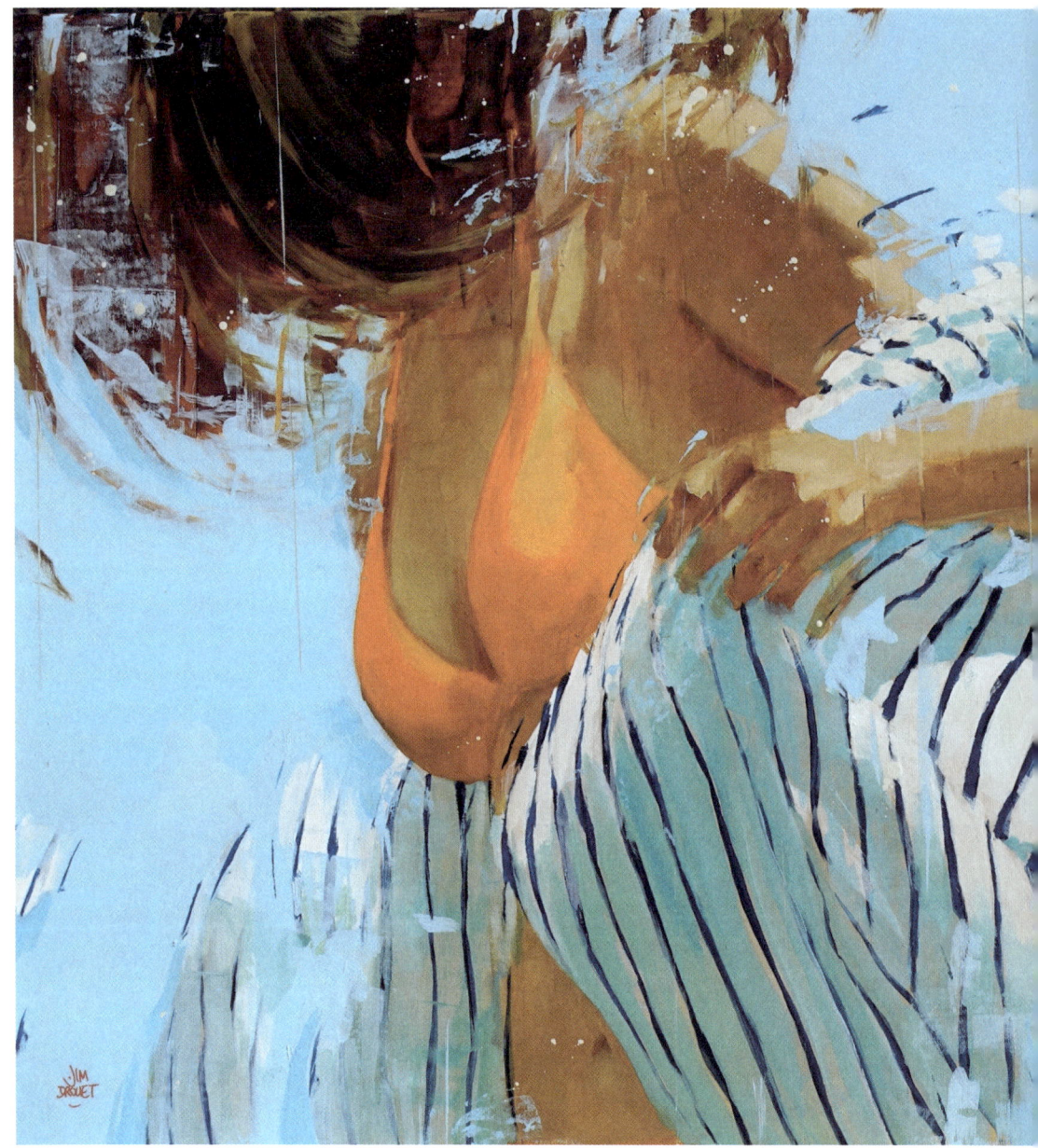

Stripes orange 27

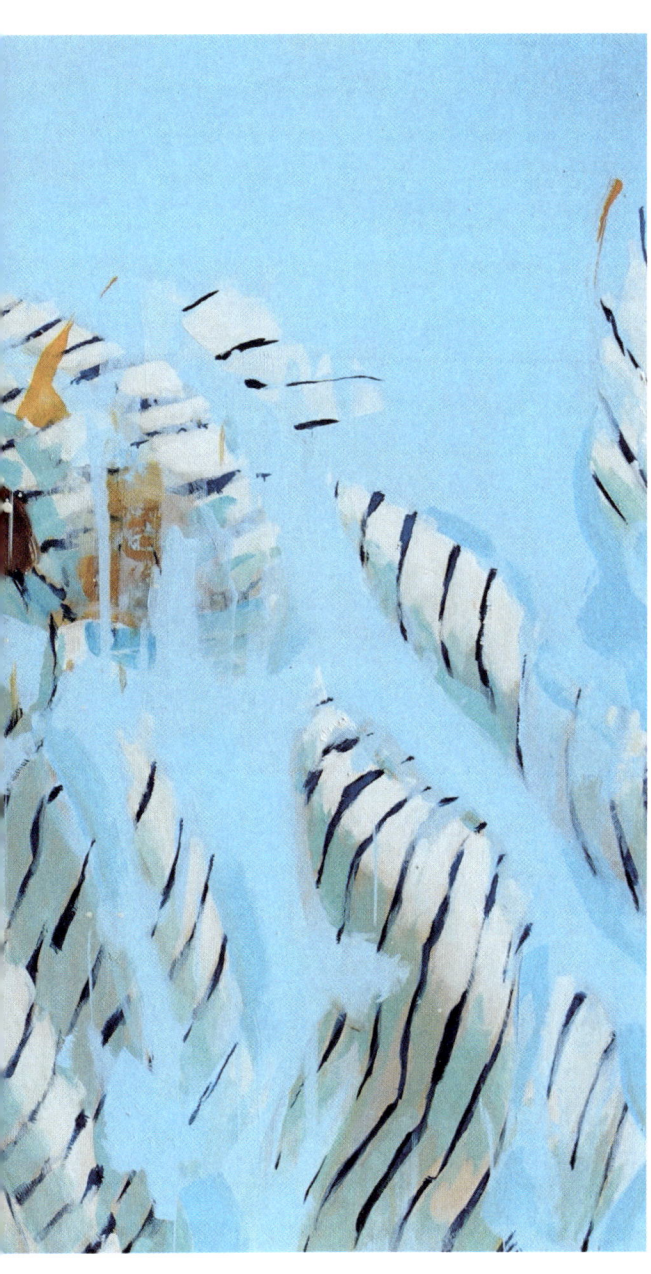

This painting is part of a long series of 'Stripes' by Drouet: 'The stripes have a hypnotic aspect that continues to fascinate me pictorially. '

'The captured movement comes from a person getting dressed on a beach in Minorca. I exaggerated it to create a painting full of movement and light.'

Drouet has a quite distinctive style. Some details are erased but imultaneously everyone can recognise the scene. It gives theimpression of a déjà vu.

Q & A

Jim Drouet

Who is Jim?

After graduating from the School of Fine Arts in Angoulême, I worked for 17 years in advertising before turning resolutely towards painting. Since my first exhibition in 2004, I have displayed my works in several galleries in France and at various international art fairs (London, Amsterdam, New York, Hamburg…). My paintings are part of private collections in France and abroad.

Light and imagination seem to be important?

That's exactly it. My paintings are about life by the ocean so they speak essentially of light. *A la recherche de la lumière.* In search of the light. Sunlight is everywhere and my perspective on the world is intentionally optimistic. I'm influenced by contemporary images and I'm intrigued by cinematic framing.

Would you say there's an 'American' spirit in your work?

I don't know if there's an American atmosphere in my paintings, but what's certain is that they have been nourished by a cinematic culture mainly from the USA. I experienced the beginnings of surfing and windsurfing on the French coasts in the late 1970s and early 1980s with all the imagery coming from California and Hawaii. It was also the era of Spielberg, Wenders and Lucas in the cinema. I believe all of this has shaped my imagination.

We're looking at paintings but we could easily think we're looking at images. There's a sense of mystery beneath the apparent simplicity. You have a quite distinctive style.

Some details are erased but simultaneously everyone can recognise the scene. It gives the impression of déjà vu. You could call it *la touche fragmentée* in French. The fragmented touch. Allowing ample space for light, my painting technique comes close to an impressionistic style, but actually I don't really think about my style or words to describe it. I just paint.

Any painters that inspire you?
I draw inspiration from the approach of American realist painters such as N. C. Wyeth, Edward Hopper or Bernie Fuchs. I consider them storytellers, mood creators and masters in *mise en page*, the visual composition in a painting.

You create a certain mood yourself, using scenes of beach life and characters?
Yes, I tend to paint swimmers, surfers with their boards, women and beach towels or vans parked near the beach. There are always people involved, I don't have any paintings without protagonists. The ocean touches my daily life and seeps into my work. I have always lived beside the ocean, so it's part of my DNA.

Do you have a go-to colour palette?
It's quite limited. From pale yellow to dark brown, through ochres and earth tones. Maybe a touch of turquoise. Essentially a range of warm colours.

When people look at your work, what would you like them to feel?
I just want them to feel happy. There's no hidden message. Above all, it's just a painting. I do understand if people feel a certain kind of nostalgia. If it awakens memories in them, even better.

Where do you currently live or surf?
I live on the Atlantic coast in the French region of Vendée. I've been surfing here for a long time. I still surf, even though I'm not the youngest any more, but maybe a bit less in the winter, admittedly. We have good waves on many beaches and there's always a spot to surf depending on the wind directions. And even though I feel nostalgic about an era with fewer people in the water, it's still just as good. I love the atmosphere on our beaches. I don't know if they are dream beaches, but the light is definitely something memorable.

Is there something you are particularly proud of?
Something very simple: I am happy I've been able to live off my paintings for many years now – a life of freedom and creation. •

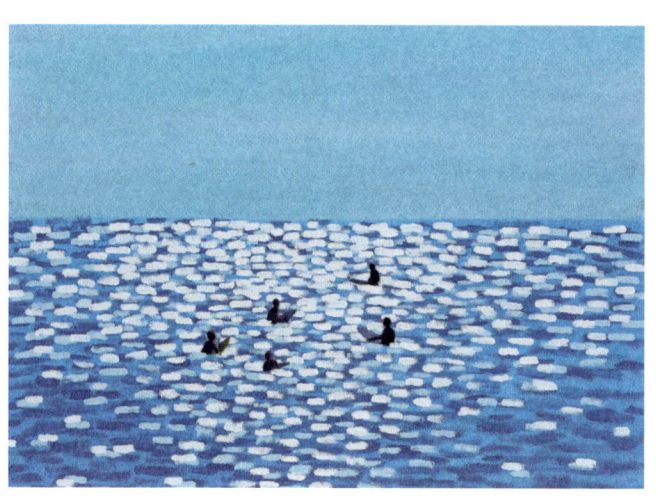

10

Bud Bud

Right on the dot

Jean Jullien

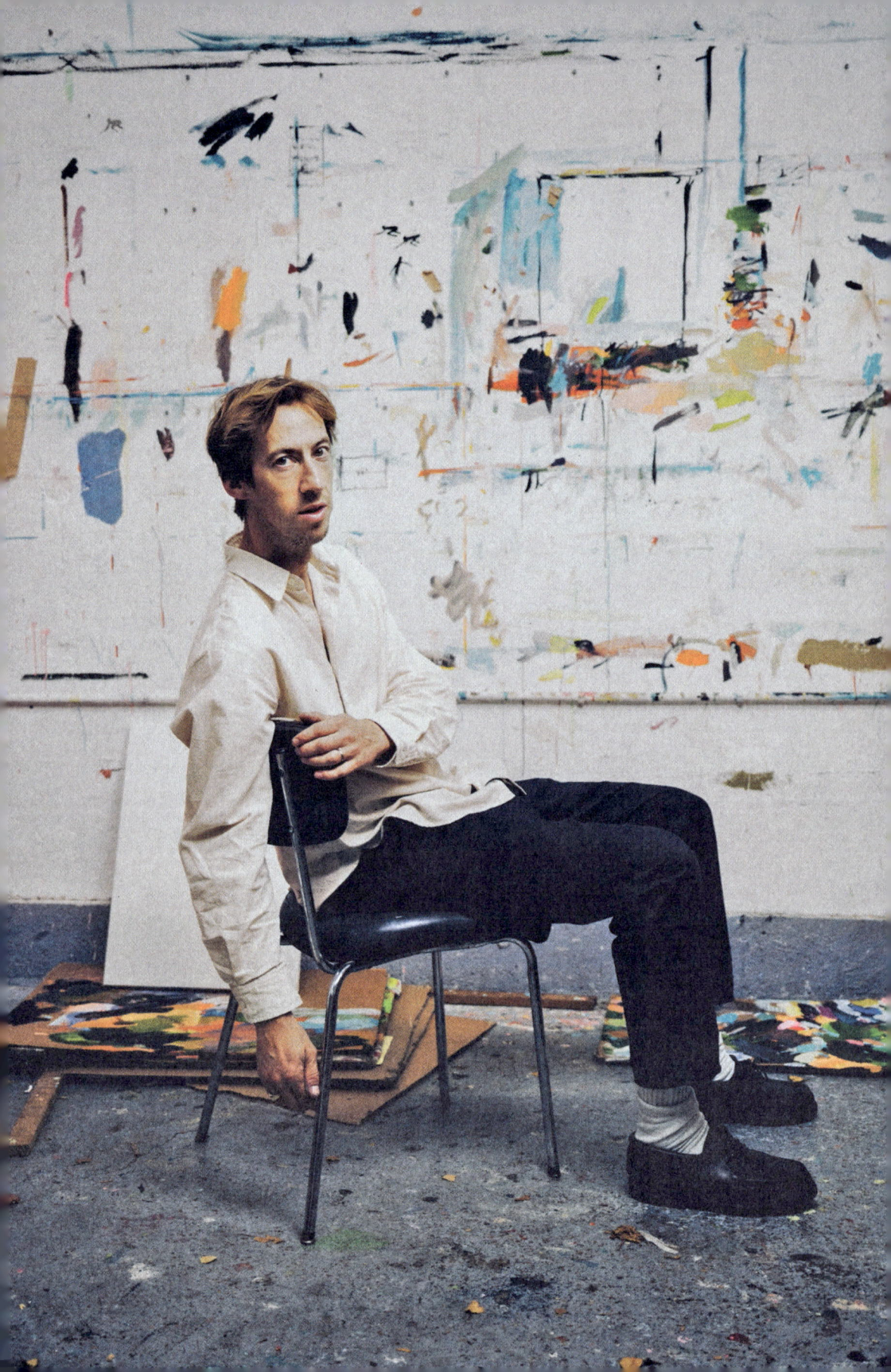

The impressive paintings of French artist Jean Jullien show a little slice of his life, somewhere between Paris and Brittany. With his work touching our imagination, he wins the award for most popular surf artist of the moment.

Charlie

'Surfing has changed my perspective on painting', says Jullien. 'It made me crave a slower way of life, and this in turn is noticeable in my work. I used to be obsessed with surfer's movements but I let that fixation go.'

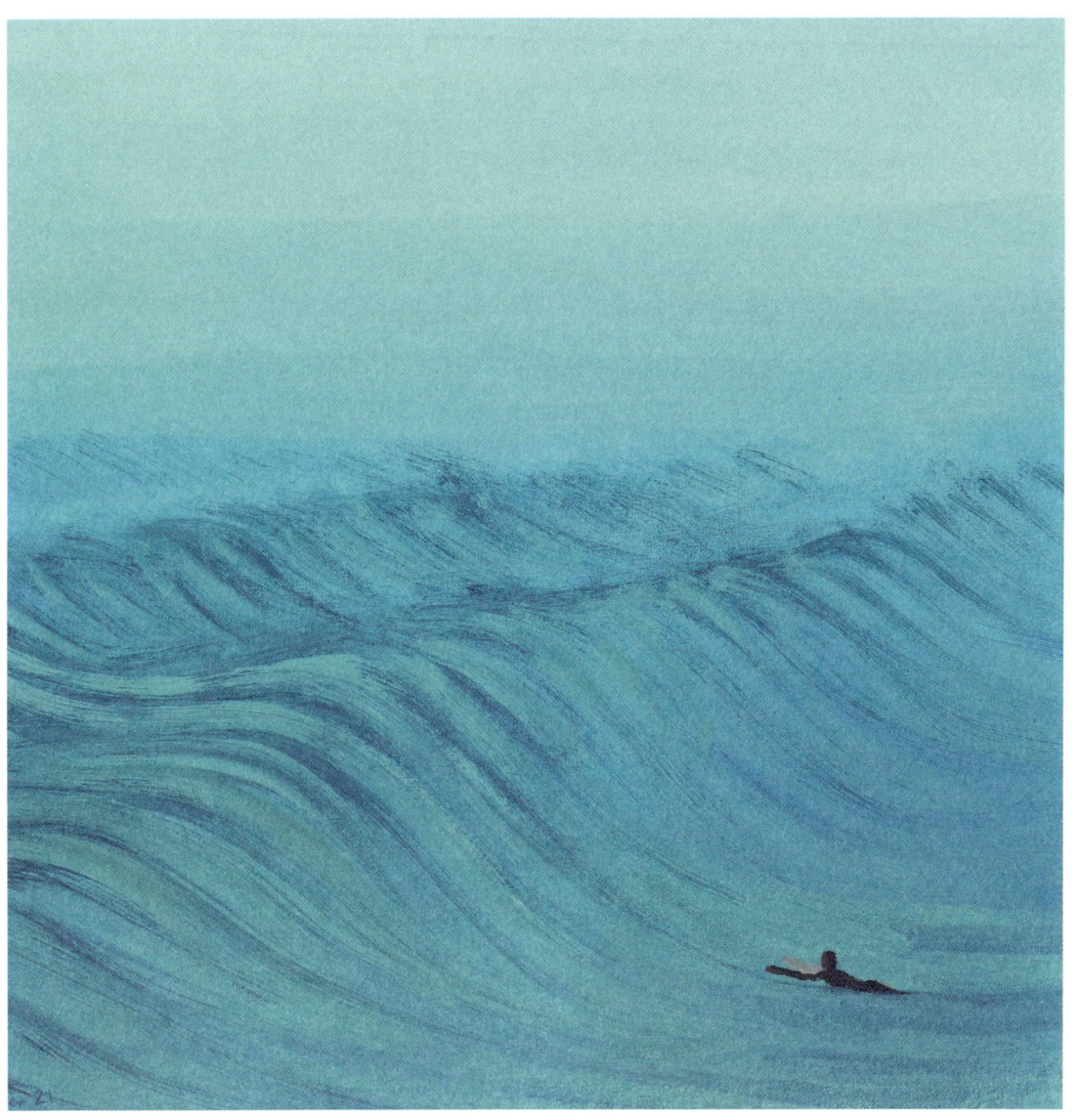

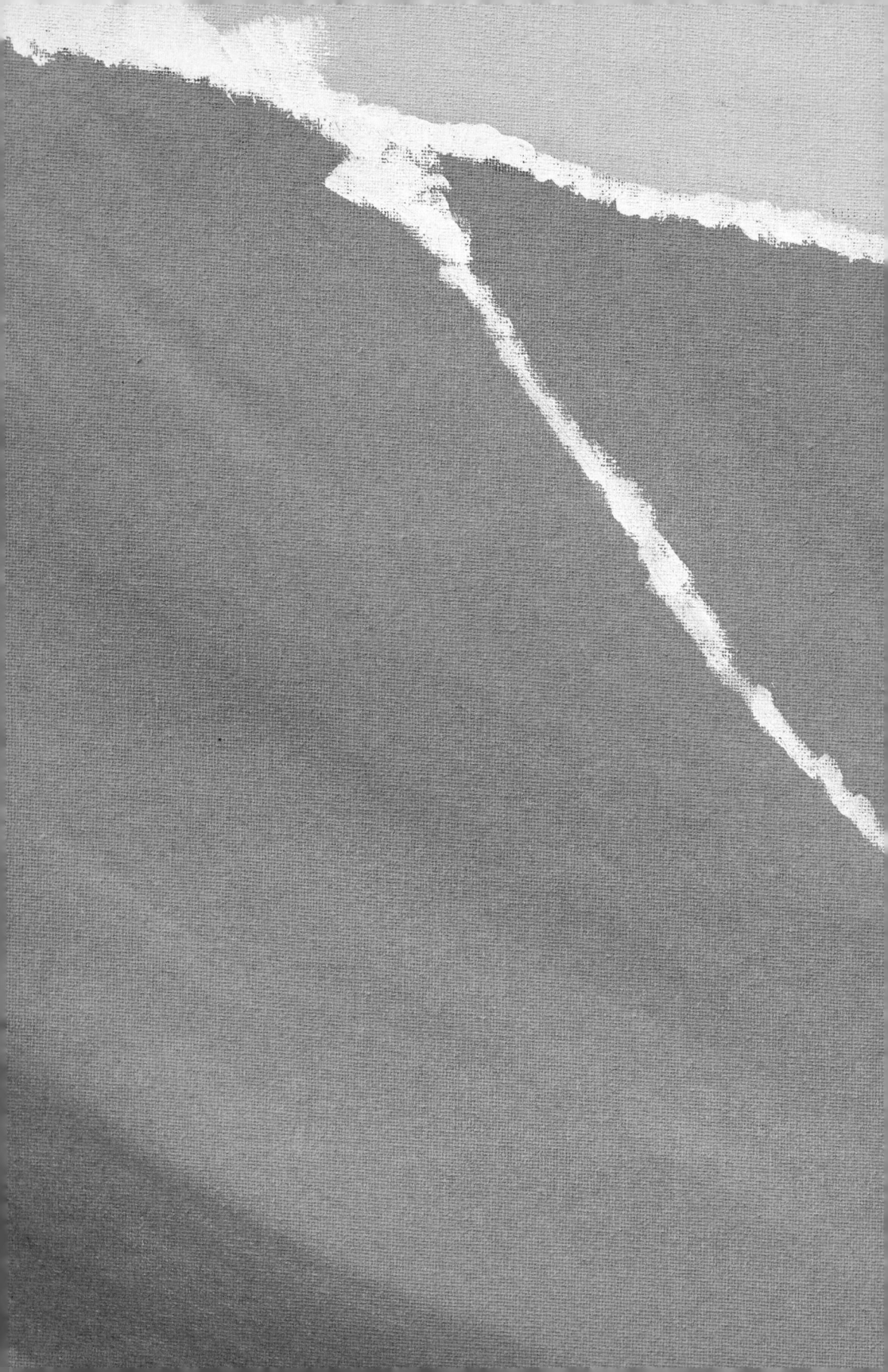

La vague

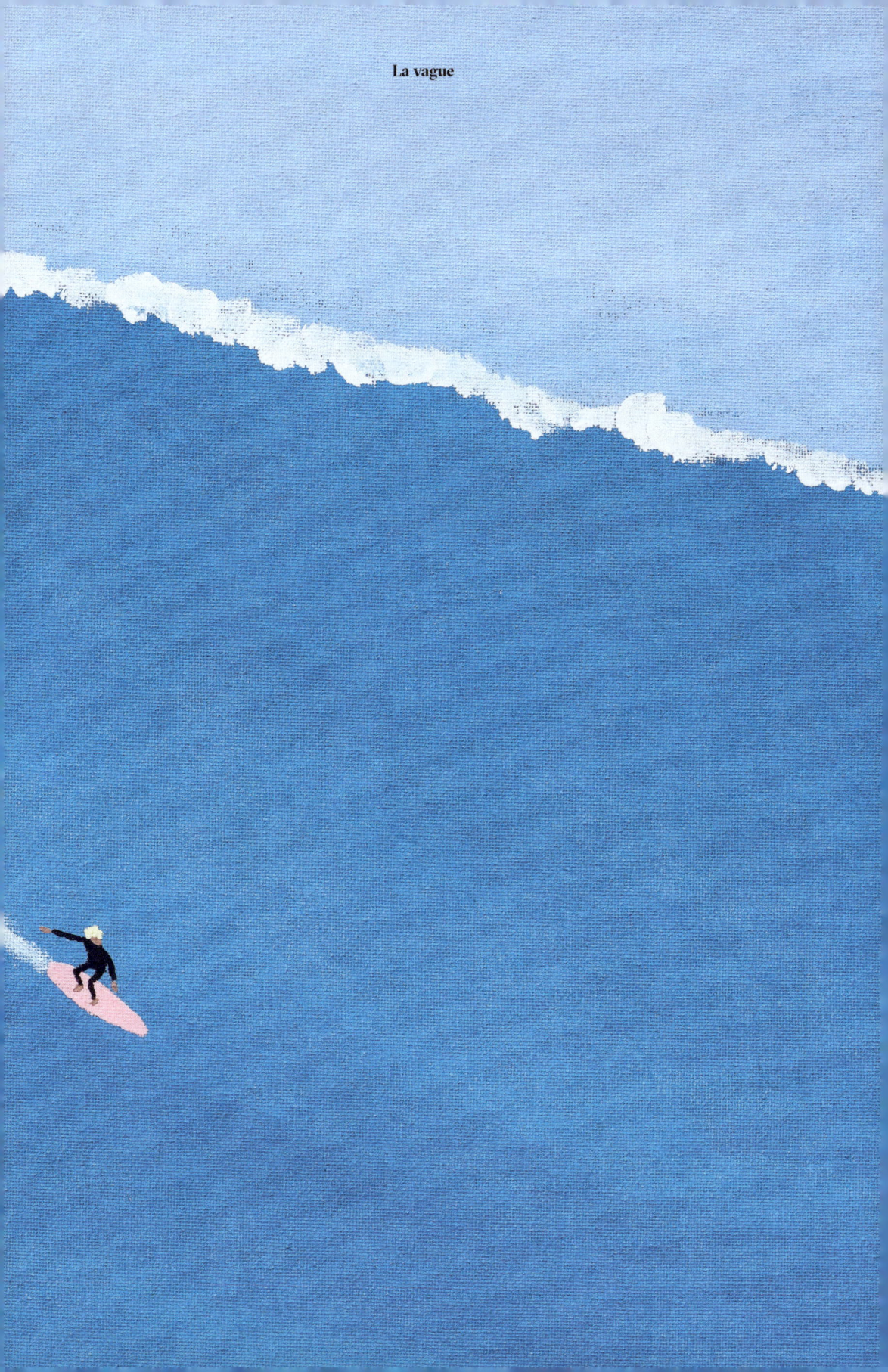

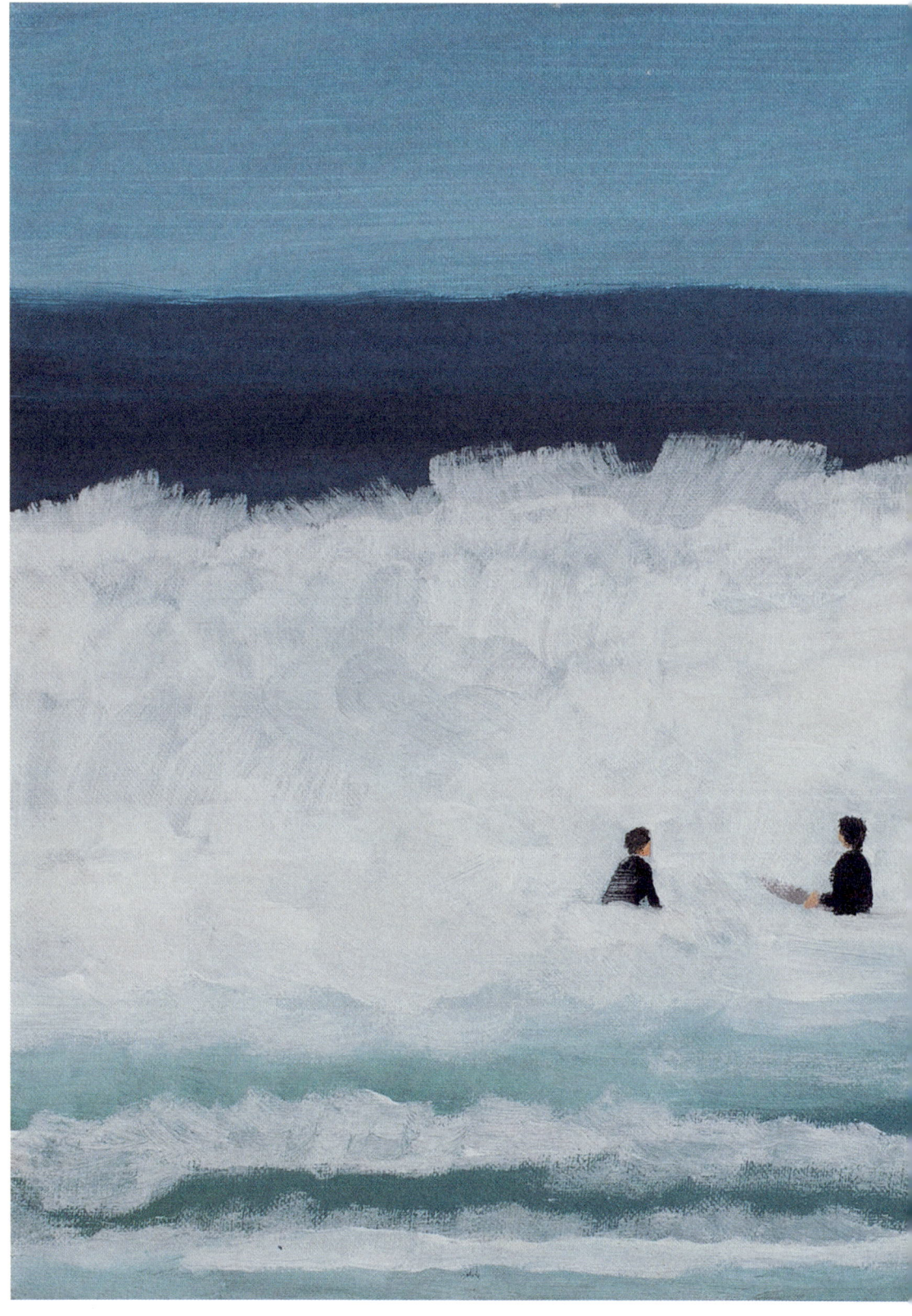

Étude pour la vague

I'd like viewers to feel a hint of narration seeping through my paintings

Q&A

Jean Jullien

Who is Jean?
A French painter and artist.
I live and work in Paris, but I often
return like a boomerang to the
place where I grew up in Brittany.
The sea beckons.

If you were to describe your art
in a few lines, you'd say…
It's bold, colourful, versatile
and playful.

How does the ocean influence
your life/work?
I find being in the water peaceful
and inspiring at the same time.
I love it. It makes me very happy.
Surfing has also changed my
perspective on painting. It made
me crave a slower way of life,
and this in turn is noticeable
in my work. I used to be obsessed
with a surfer's movements but I
let that fixation go.

When people look at your work,
what would you like them to feel?
Intrigued. I'd like them to feel a
hint of narration seeping through
what's being painted. I try to
capture a moment that made me
happy while giving hints of a story.

What kind of materials – paper,
paint or canvas – do you use
for your artwork?
For paintings I use linen canvas
and Holbein's acrylic gouache.
I like how matt it is, but at the
same time it's got the versatility
of acrylic. To get it almost chalky,
I mix it with gesso, which lends
a nice asperity to the surface.
And for paper, I usually like to
work on multi-recycled paper
with a black pencil brush.

Any painters that inspire you?
I don't know if they inspire me, but
I do like their work: I love Pierre
Bonnard, David Hockney and
Alexander Calder. He's not
a painter, but it doesn't matter.
Philip Guston also. And for sure
Henri Matisse.

How does it feel to have over one million followers on Instagram?
It's strange. It's overwhelming and touching that so many people are interested in what you do. I used to be quite freaked out by it and now I've just decided to focus on posting when I want to post, when I have something to show, and to create work not for social media but for me and the people that love my work.

You've worked for _The New York Times_, _Vogue_ and _Le Monde_. You've also exhibited in art museums and galleries from London to Seoul. And you have created your own monograph with cult publisher Phaidon. Is there something you still dream of as an artist?
A lot! Animation, for example. Or graphic novels. In general, I think the way I'm trying to veer towards doing more large-scale exhibitions and installations that can diffuse a sense of narration through immersion.

Can you recommend any other books about surf art?
Any decent Raymond Pettibon coffee table book. And the _Surfer's Journal_ magazines – they have a particular love for surf art.

Do you have a favourite quote that inspires or motivates you?
'C'est la vie.'

Where do you currently live or surf?
I live in Paris for various reasons and I also have a place in Brittany, where I grew up. It's near Lesconil and is home to my studio and all my surfboards. We usually go surfing near La Torche in the winter and other more secret spots in the summer. I find it very inspiring because I like how a cold sky can impress in colours. The same goes for dunes that are illuminated by the sun. The result is an ash yellow colour I really like painting and depicting. The water often shows the colour 'glaz', which is a Breton word for a tint somewhere between grey, green and blue. I will probably enjoy painting it forever.

Are you still dreaming of moving to Brittany, where you grew up?
I do. I mean, I love the scenery. I just know that it's quite austere in winter and that I also find a lot of inspiration from being surrounded by people and a busy life, so it's a bit of a schizophrenic situation. I just like both.

Are there other places in the world where you feel at home?
I love Japan. I feel very much at home there. Actually, I find myself comfortable in a lot of places where I can meet new people, and discover places to hang out, or surf, or paint. And then I always know that home is home. I'm like Ulysses.--->

Q & A
Jean Jullien

What would your dream surf trip look like?
I've already been there. I've been to Hawaii to surf and it was awesome. I'd love to go to visit family in Tahiti as well, even though I know that the surf is quite intense over there. But I quite regularly visit Japan for work and there's a spot in Zushi that is just magical. The waves are mellow, but the friends I take with me are the very best, so surf sessions are always memorable.

Are mellow waves your thing?
I love from mellow to mid-high. I don't really need the thrill of bigger waves. The best surf for me is medium chill. It's more about the moment, getting in the water, planning a trip, being with people that I love, in an environment that I find beautiful and visually inspiring. If I can perform – great. Otherwise, I'm just happy to be there. •

Has surfing given you anything in life?
Surfing gave me peace when I needed it the most. And perspective and a nice parallel to my art career. It also made me realise that the best things are not about performance but more about process.

What does surf culture today mean to you?
I think it's a multifaceted world. There's the mainstream, there's the indie, there's the core, there's the performance-based... Different aspects and all of them are interesting. There's a certain artistic philosophy to be found in surfing. I always see correlations with the world of surf art. My brother and I also love the vintage neon from the 1980s. Our uncle and auntie had a surf shop called Nova Fun in a place in France and it really filled our head with visuals from surf brands such as Gotcha, Hot Tuna, Town & Country, all of that stuff. It's vivid imagery in our heads.

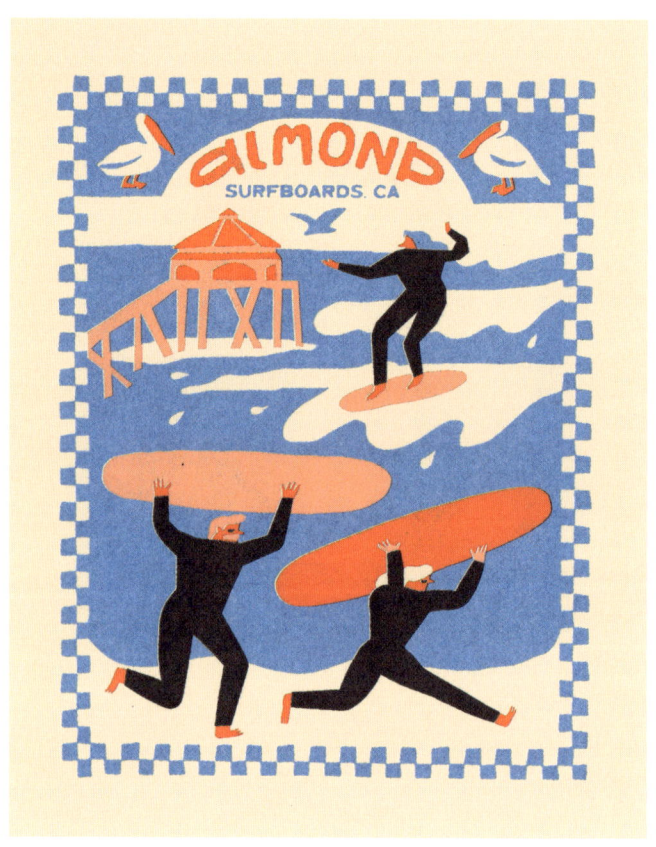

11

The pier

Cotton candy sunsets

Taisiia Kordiukova

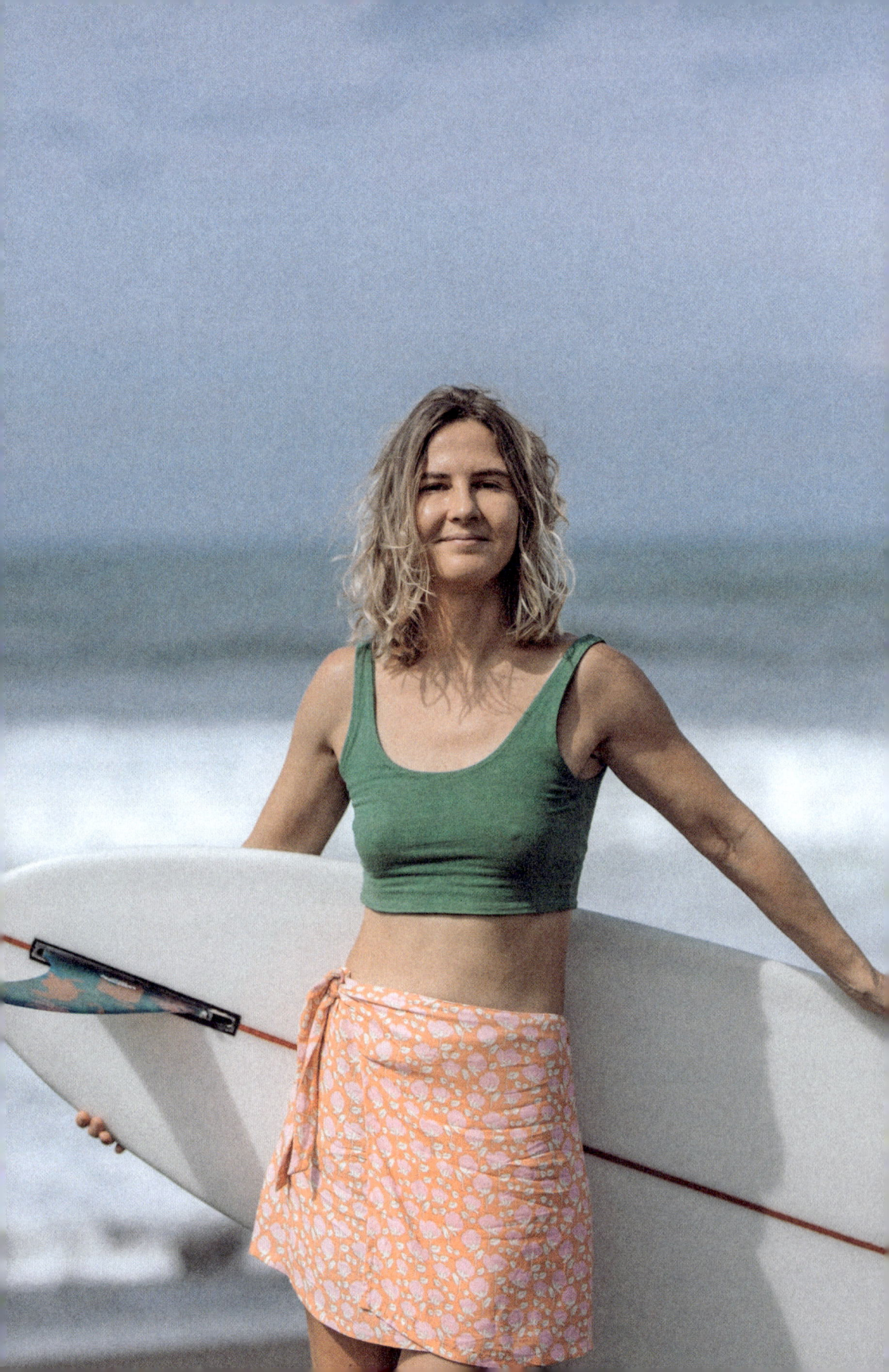

Taisiia is a Russian illustrator who ended up on an Indonesian island and now creates art with love from Bali. In her drawings she captures the few seconds when surfers become one with the waves.

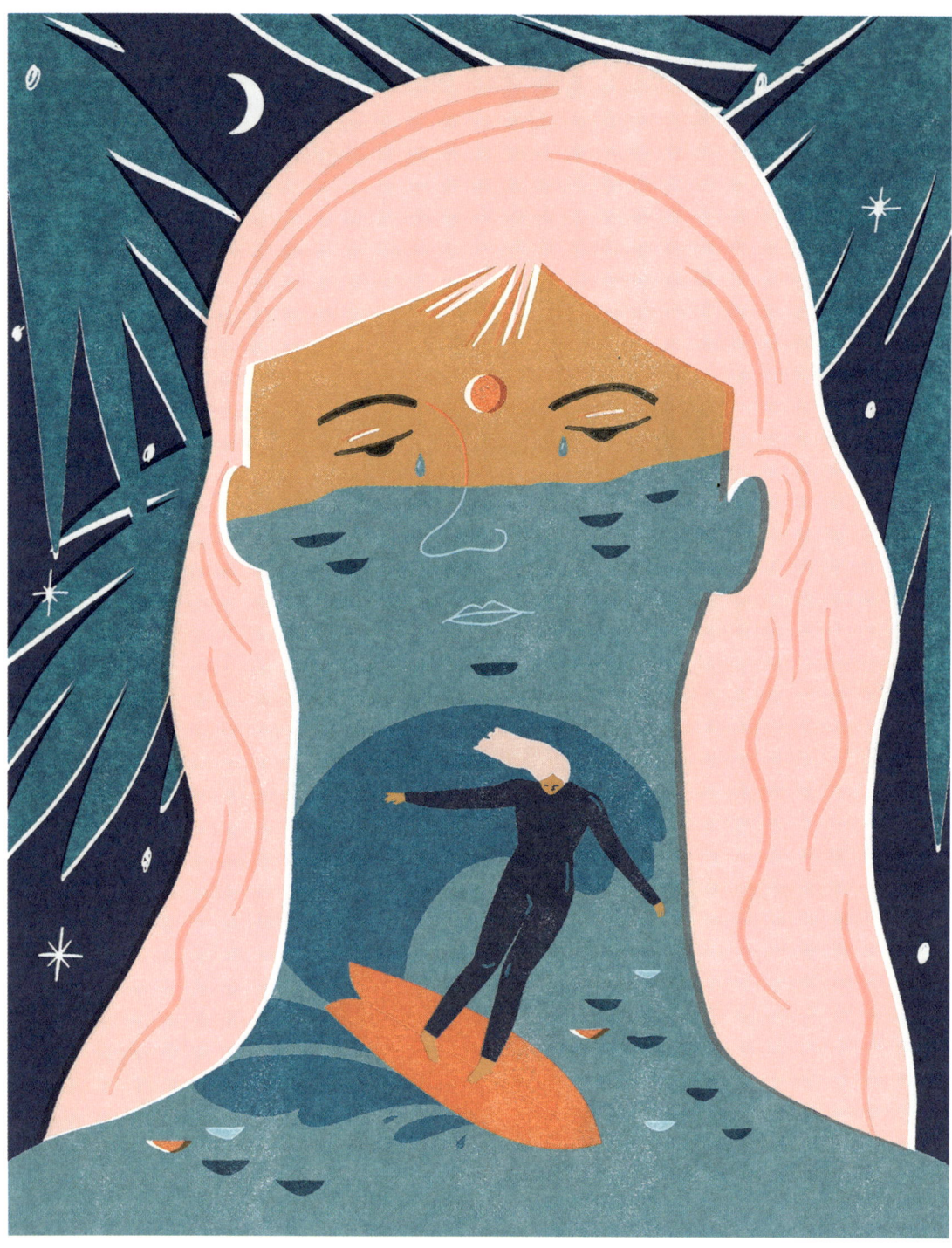

My forever medicine and joy

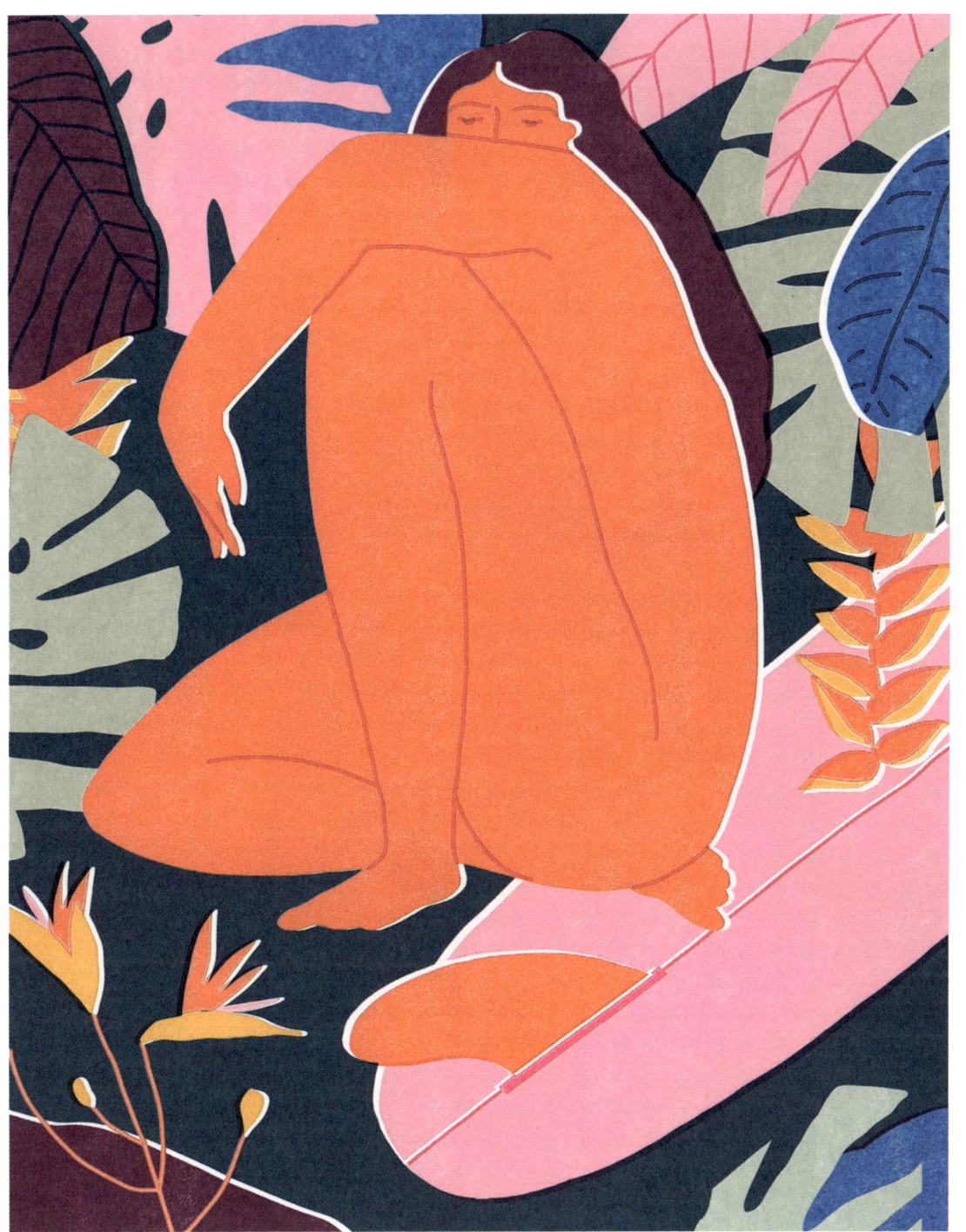

Island noon

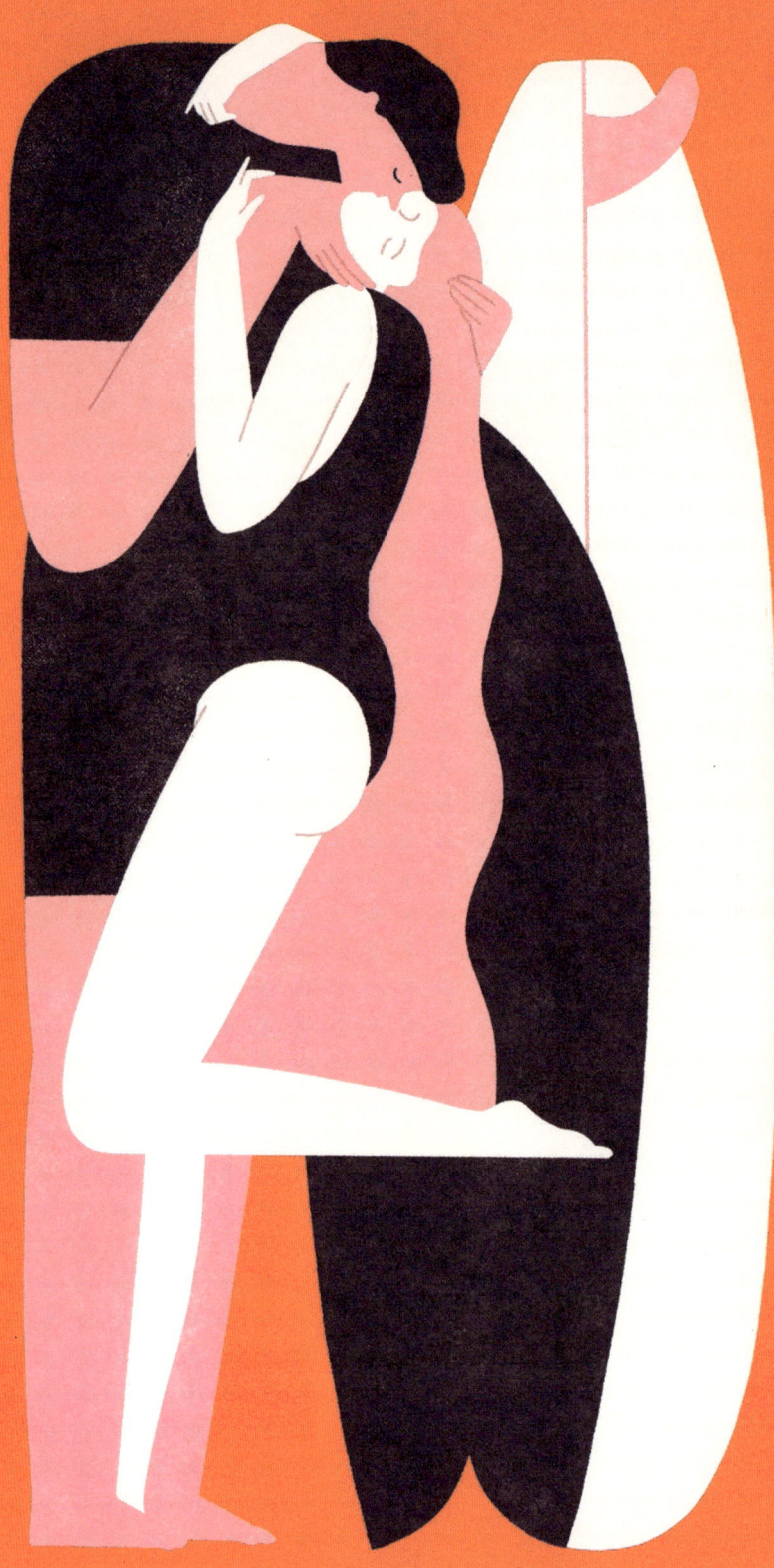

'Wave Lovers (below) is special to me because I drew it after I met my boyfriend, my partner for several years now. We crossed paths while surfing,' says Kordiukova.

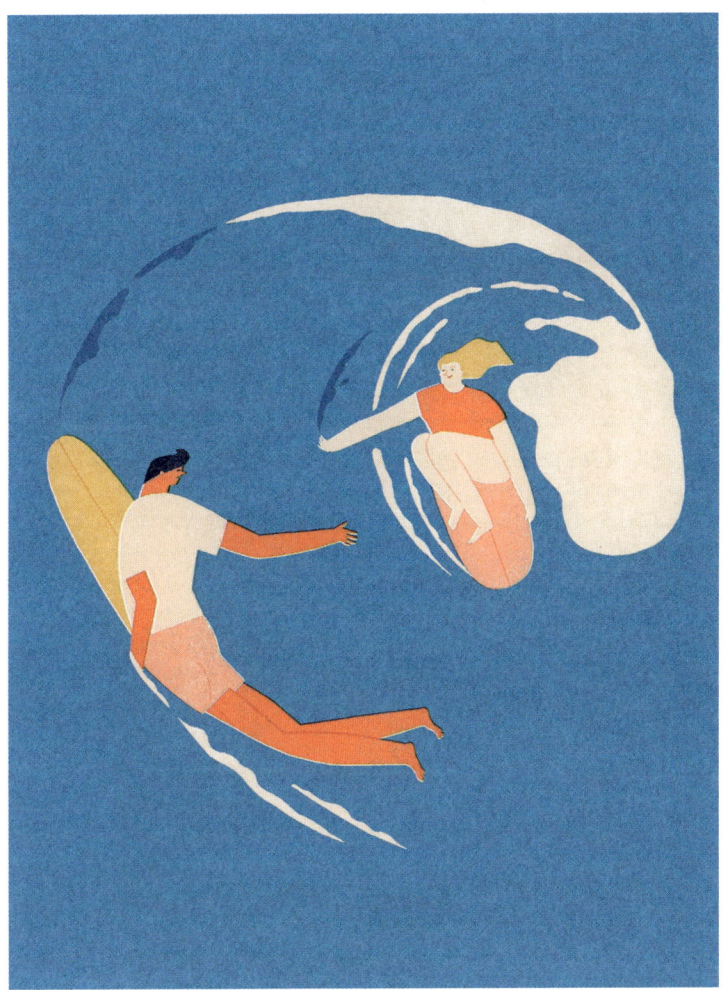

Q & A

Taisiia Kordiukova

Who is Taisiia?
I'm an illustrator, designer, surfer and cat enthusiast living on the island of Bali.

What came first: surfing or drawing?
Art came first: I've been into art since my childhood and later graduated in graphic design from the University of Arts in St Petersburg. Surfing entered my life much later, after years of travel and self-discovery. Eventually, I found the perfect means of self-expression through the synergy of surfing and illustration – a space where my two passions converged.

If you were to describe your art in a few lines, you'd say...
My art is a harmonious blend of joy, freedom and humour, capturing carefree scenes packed with all the colours of a cotton candy sunset.

Your website is called Kookumbra and your personal Instagram is Uhuhualoha. Are these words in a language we don't speak?
Haha, not exactly. Uhuhualoha is just my personal Instagram name, known in the surf and art community. Kookumbra represents a brand I created with my partner, offering various products like art prints, stationery, surfboard fins and T-shirts.

When did you first think: I can do this for a living?
I already knew before surfing entered my life. I was already drawing and found some success on platforms like Spoonflower, where people could buy fabrics with my designs, as well as on print shops like Society6. I also worked for different clients. When I moved to Bali, everything fell into place – my love for surfing and my previous experience in illustration.

How does your art come to life?
My creative process typically begins with raw and somewhat unattractive sketches. I then transition to Procreate, where I refine and bring the artwork to life. Finally, in Photoshop, I add a touch of beauty and infuse a retro look, crafting the final aesthetic that defines my pieces.

Is creating art meditative or does it feel like hard work?
Creating art is a truly meditative journey and it brings me deep satisfaction. However, tasks like preparing for print, managing social media, photography and correspondence are more challenging for me.

What clients do you work for? Any collaborations you'd like to mention?

In 2017 I did a significant collaboration with The Seea. I created a series of illustrations highlighting their recycled fabric line. The Seea was the first brand to notice my work on Instagram. And I recently worked on an exciting project with Almond Surfboards, creating a super cool T-shirt. Additionally, this summer my design won their art contest, resulting in a surfboard featuring my design.

Do you have a favourite quote that inspires or motivates you?

Perhaps one about it 'never being too late to have a happy childhood'.

Where do you currently live or surf?

I live and surf in Bali. Occasionally we embark on surf trips to nearby islands, such as Lombok, Sumbawa and Mentawai, exploring new horizons and waves.

How did a Russian girl end up in Bali?

I was born and grew up in St Petersburg, Russia, located on the Baltic coast, close to Finland. A city known for its stunning European-inspired architecture. But the weather is just awful. That was the reason why, after I graduated from university, I went on my first trip to India and haven't stopped travelling since. Bali was one of the destinations from my yearly travel cycle through Southeast Asia and Latin America. My love for surfing brought me back to the island again and again, so one day I just stopped travelling and stayed here.

Some people think Bali has changed too much over the years. Would you agree?

Yes, Bali has changed in some ways. There has been rapid development in some places, lots of traffic and crowded tourist beaches. But Bali is still special. It has changed, but at its heart it's still about love, peaceful living and a connection with nature. If you go a bit away from the touristy spots, you'll find the real, untouched beauty of Bali.

Do you remember how and when you fell in love with surfing?

I first tried surfing on holiday in Goa. It was love at first wave. With great enthusiasm, I visited the local surf club every morning, rented a board, and spent up to four hours in the water waiting for waves. Being a full-time surfer seemed like an elusive dream to me then. I couldn't figure out where and how people could live, earning a living to surf every day. The answers to these questions, I found in Bali.

What is a perfect surf session in Taisiia's world?

I wake up before dawn, paddle out in darkness, catch the first waves almost blindly, relying on intuition. I witness the sunrise while in the ocean, sharing the moment with a couple of friends to make it even more enjoyable. We have a blast until we're exhausted, and as a reward, a cup of coffee and a biscuit await on the beach.

Has surfing given you anything in life?

So many things! First of all, it gives me the opportunity to be surrounded by a community of people who share my passion. Surfing is about connecting with the ocean. Being synchronised with an energy that comes from inside the ocean, and for a few seconds you can become one with the wave and dance with it to the end. •

12

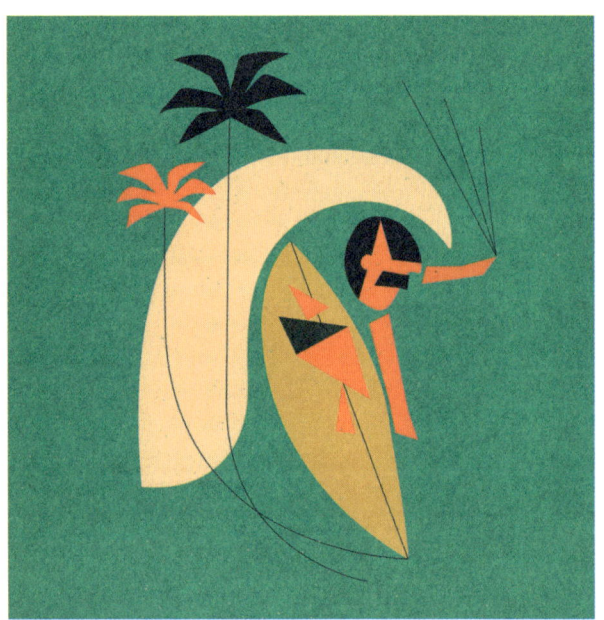

Tropical barrel

Vintage vibes

Nick
Kuchar

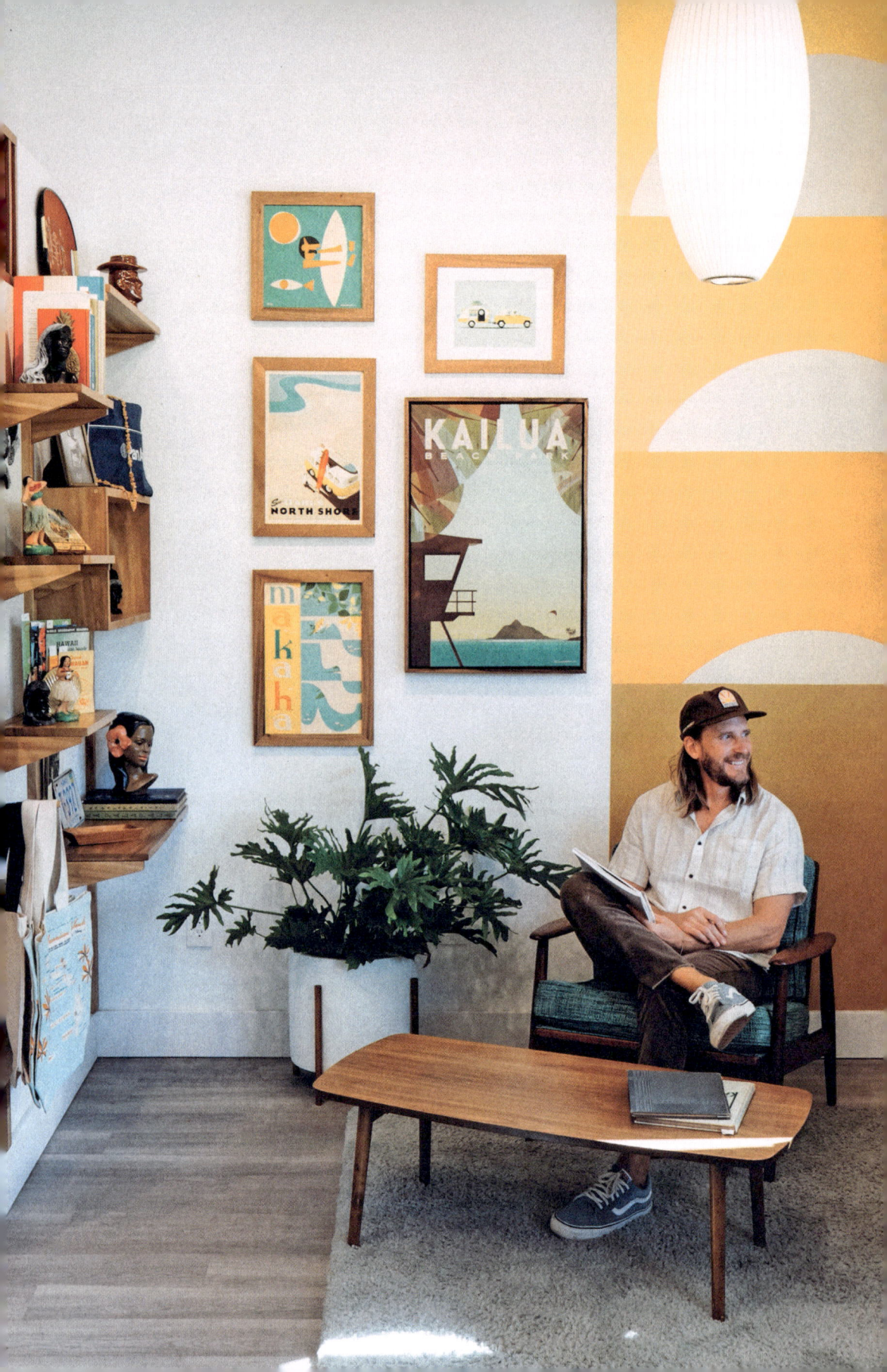

Nick Kuchar's vintage-inspired artworks make us feel nostalgic for the 1950s. By using muted aquas, yellows and burnt oranges, the Hawaii artist has created a distinctly recognisable style and a contemporary take on mid-century modern.

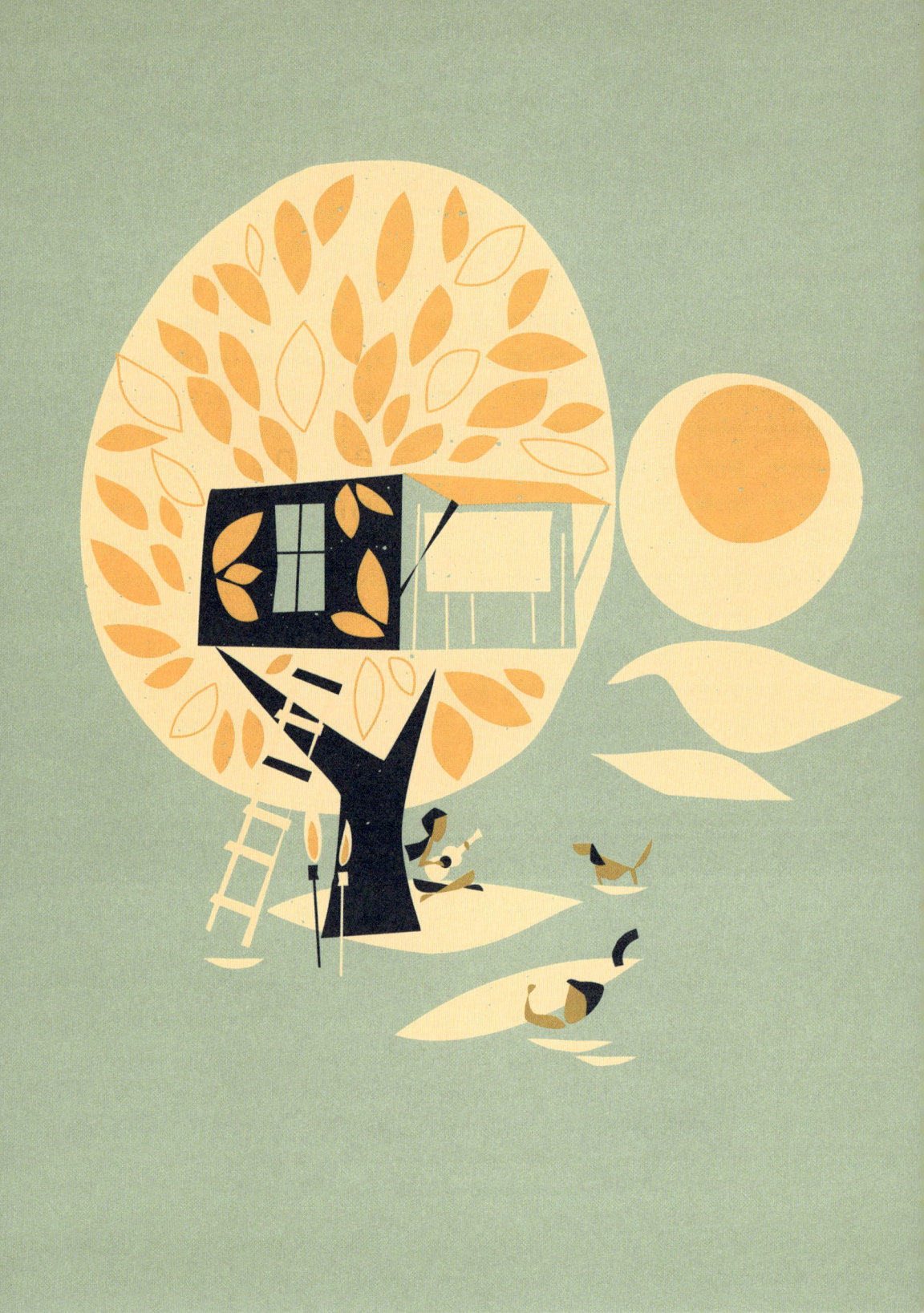

Treehouse

My style goes
back to the
mid-century
modern vibes
of the 1950s.
I find inspiration
in old billboards
and early 1900s
airline travel
prints

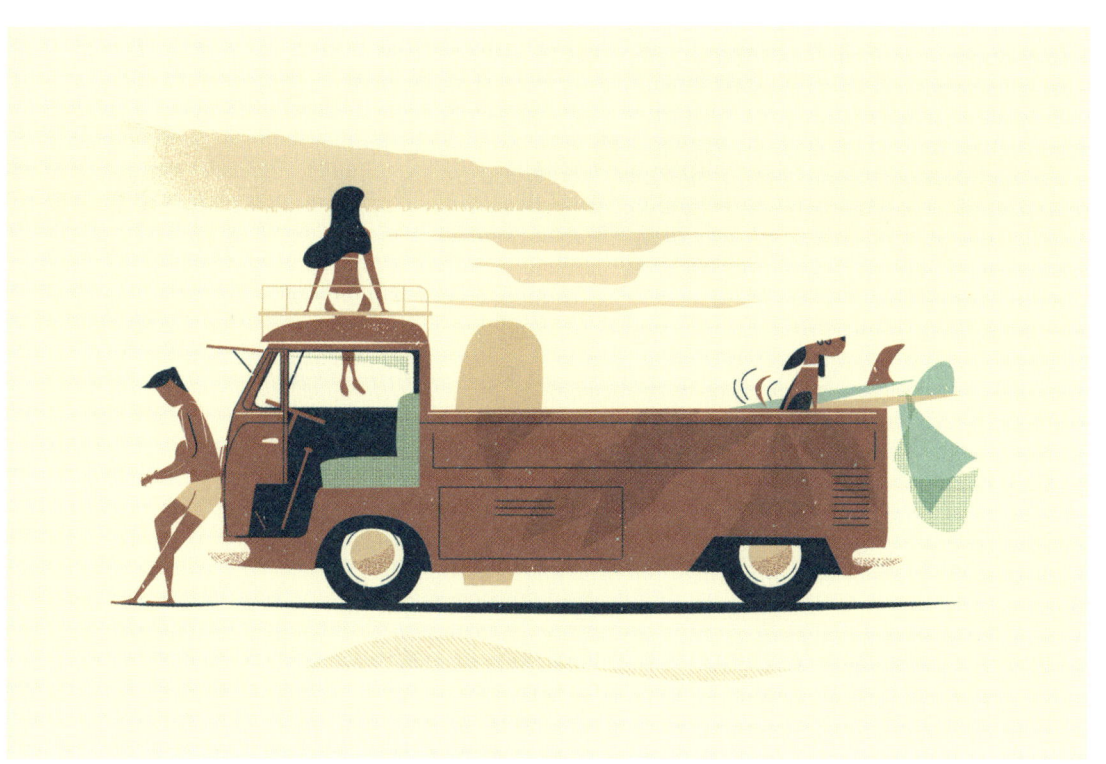

Ali'i Beach magic hour

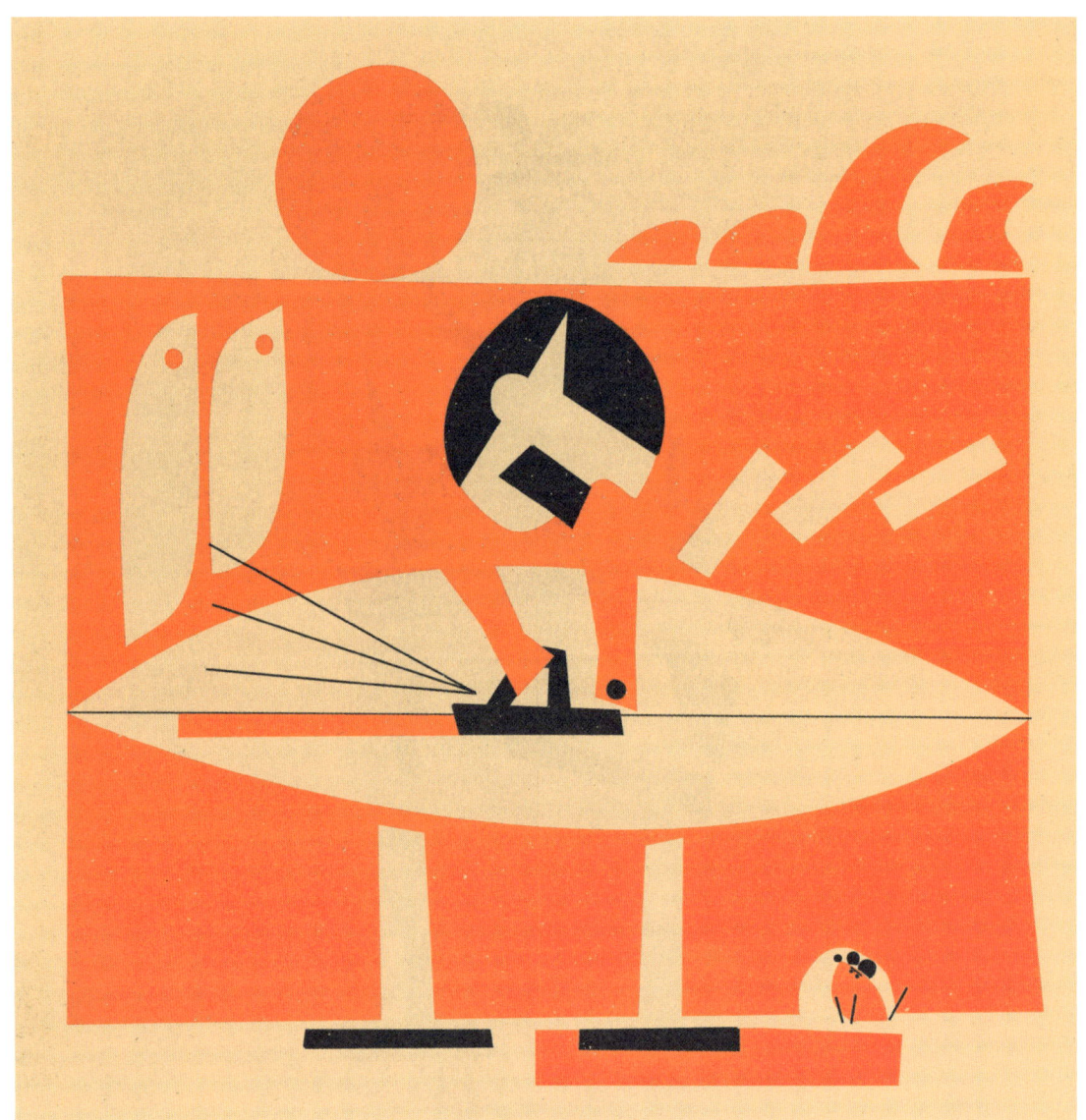

The creator

Both works are part of the Wave Slider series, where surfers are depicted within geometric forms.

Nick Kuchar seamlessly blends vintage aesthetics with contemporary flair.

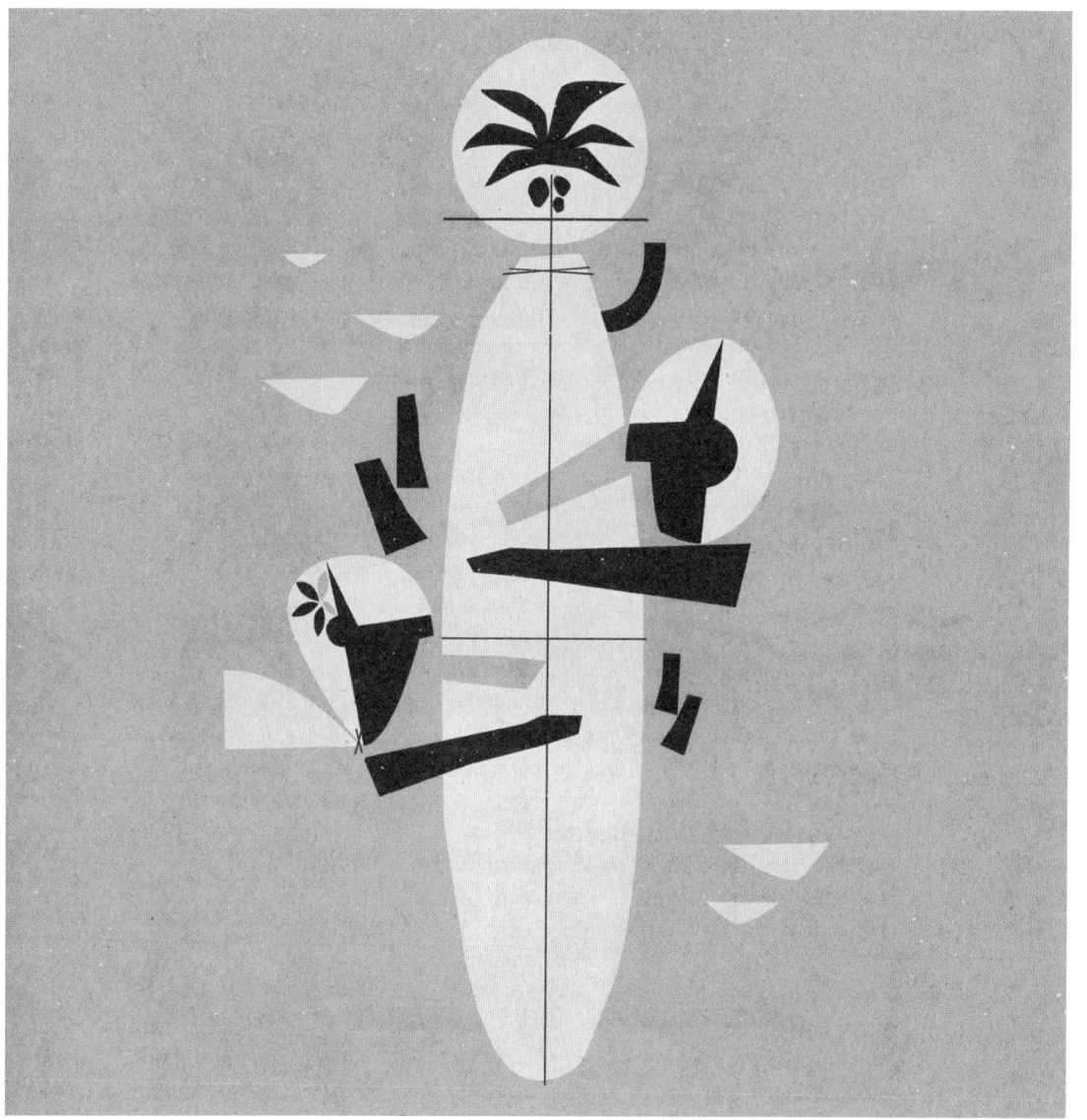

Q & A

Nick Kuchar

If you were to describe your art in a few lines, you'd say…
Anytime I approach a piece, I prioritise colour, composition and simplicity. I feel that's what makes my art recognisable. Those are the principles that make my style hearken back to the mid-century modern vibes of the 1950s. I find a lot of inspiration in old billboards and early 1900s airline travel prints.

It seems like you have a retro go-to colour palette?
Yes, the muted aquas, yellows and burnt oranges give the art a nostalgic sense and also make it approachable as decor in most home interiors.

Can you mention any painters or artists that inspire you?
I love Charley Harper (American modernist artist, ed.). He could illustrate animals and characters that were lifelike and simultaneously in a very simplified, stylish and beautiful design.

When did you first think: I can do this for a living?
My wife and I were searching for artwork to decorate our house, but couldn't find exactly what we wanted. That's when I began creating vintage-style maps and travel prints. She thought they turned out great and suggested I start an online store. So I took her advice, and within about a year, a few local shops noticed my work and started selling it. It's been a natural progression, and I feel blessed to be able to pursue my passion.

You were born in Florida. How did you end up in Hawaii?
We moved to Hawaii on a whim in 2005 and discovered a rich and vibrant community and culture to call home. We served tables for years before I got into creating artwork and turned it into a career.

Your career certainly kicked off. You even have your own store. Not too many artists can say that. Was it an important thing to achieve?
We opened our first brick and mortar in 2020 during the pandemic (were we crazy?). It's worked out well for us and I love it. To have all of my creations on display in one space is a dream come true. We built all of the display fixtures ourselves and curated the space with a selection of vintage Hawaiiana items like chalkware, books and pennants.

You also have your own podcast. What's it about?
It's called 'Secondary colors, with Nick Kuchar & friends'. Making art is fun, but making a living off of your creativity is difficult. The podcast goes behind-the-canvas to discuss the nuts and bolts of successful art, business and making it work. We invite friends to talk about pricing your work, for example, or the power of community.

What's it like to surf in Hawaii?
I grew up surfing in Florida, which was great but the amount of quality waves in Hawaii is pretty mind-boggling. There's definitely a crowd and an expectation to show proper surf etiquette. I view this as a great teaching experience for my kids in the line-up to equip them to be responsible and respectful surfers.

When people see your work, would you like them to 'feel' the islands?
I hope my art gives viewers some joy, while also bringing an appreciation for the locations I depict in Hawaii. Our surroundings are truly special, and I do try to feature their beauty through my creations.

What does your quiver look like?
Currently I'm surfing with my kids a lot around Oahu on my 9'8" Todd Pinder – a really talented local shaper. I have three kids under seven so I put them on the front of the board like a hood ornament and we have a blast tandem surfing.

What does surf culture today mean to you?
There's such depth to 'surf culture'. It's a sport where a lot of the charm is not even when you are actively riding a wave. It could be in between sets chatting with friends and enjoying the scenery around you. •

13

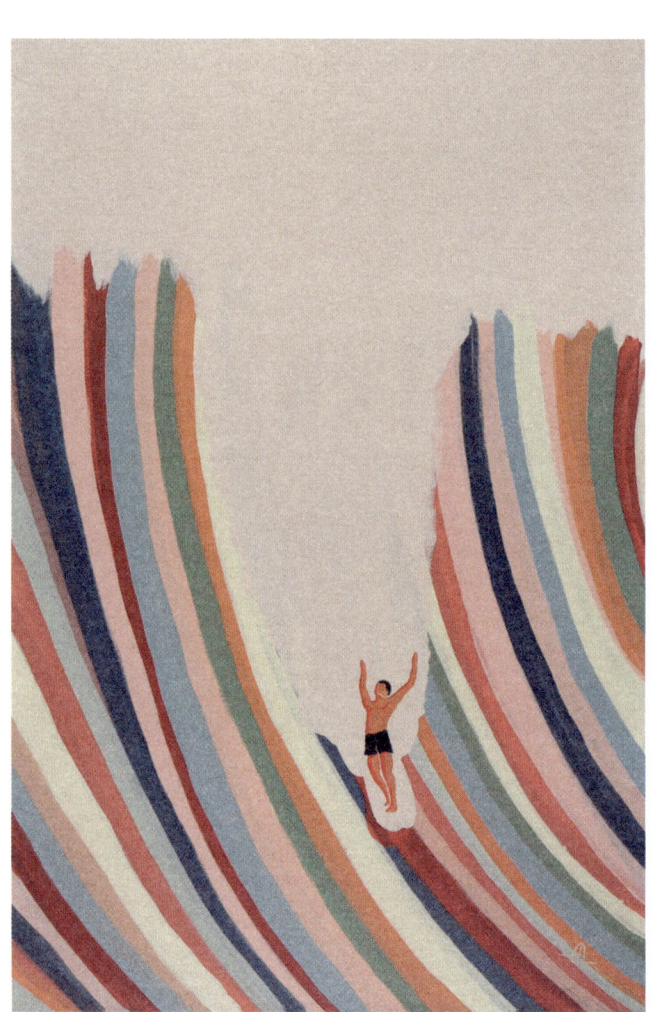

Hands in the air

New stripes

Fabian Lavater

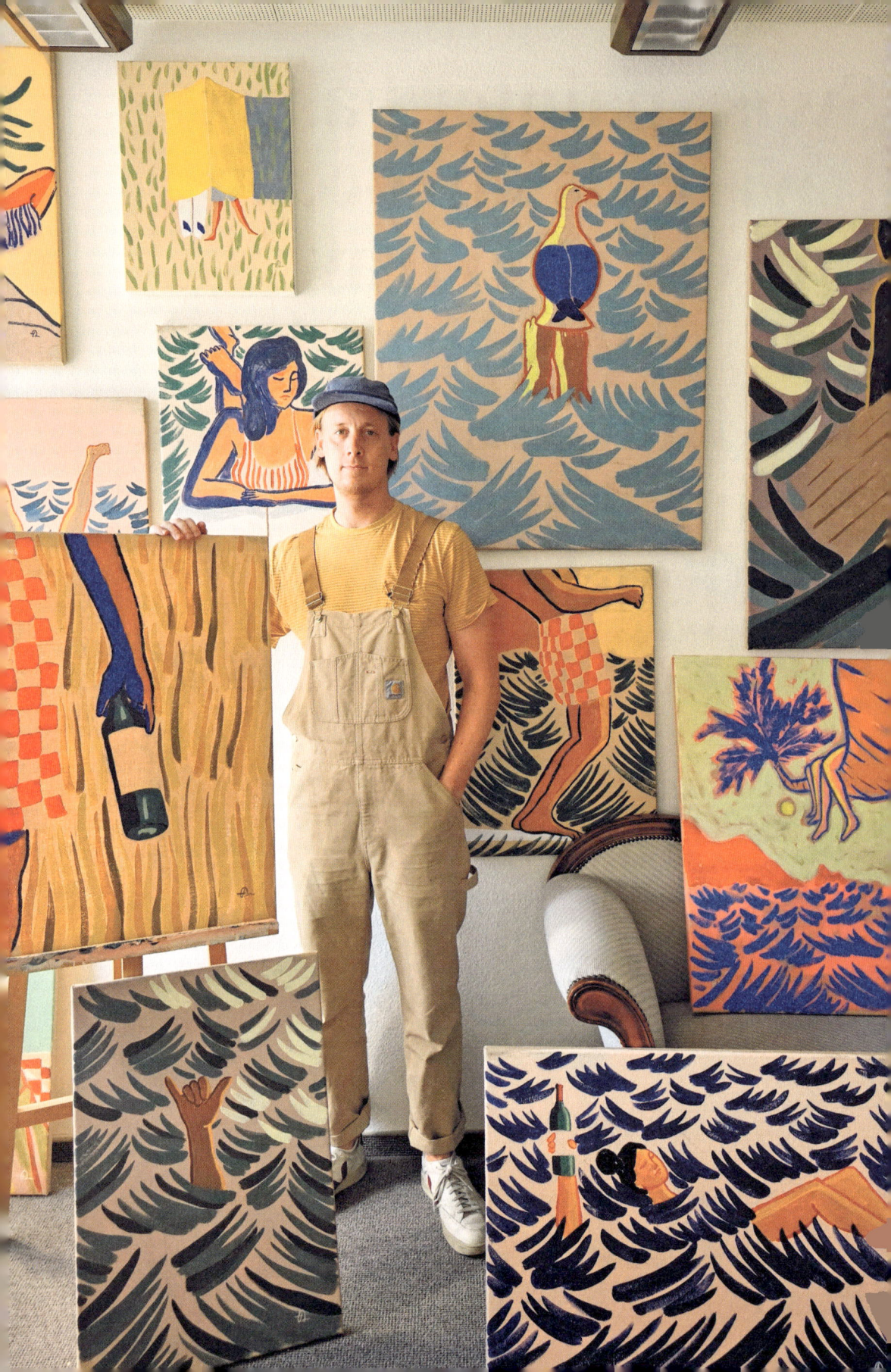

Swiss painter Fabian Lavater is an 'ocean tourist' who travels between Switzerland and Biarritz, enjoying a long-distance relationship with the sea through his art.

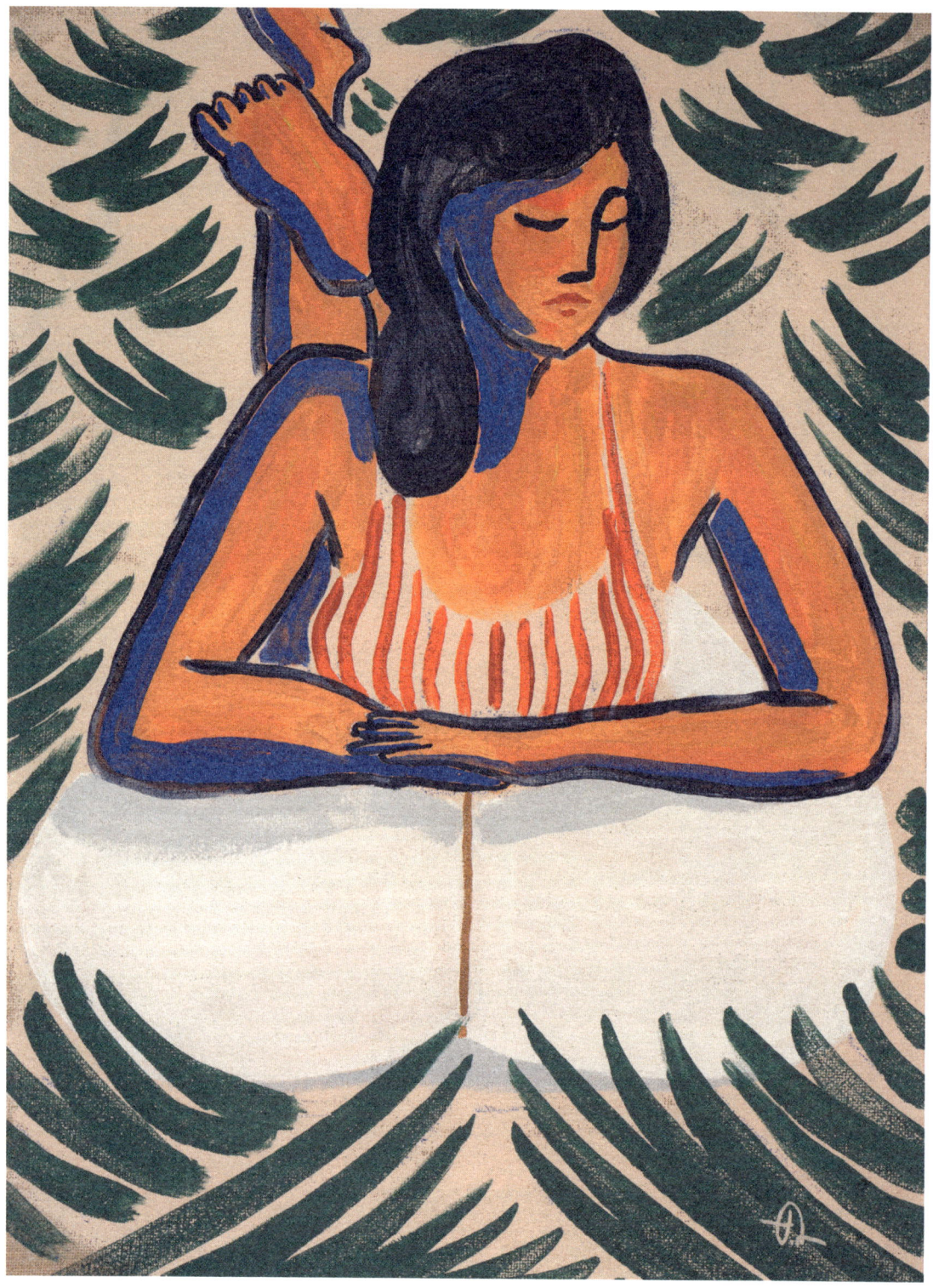

My kind of peace

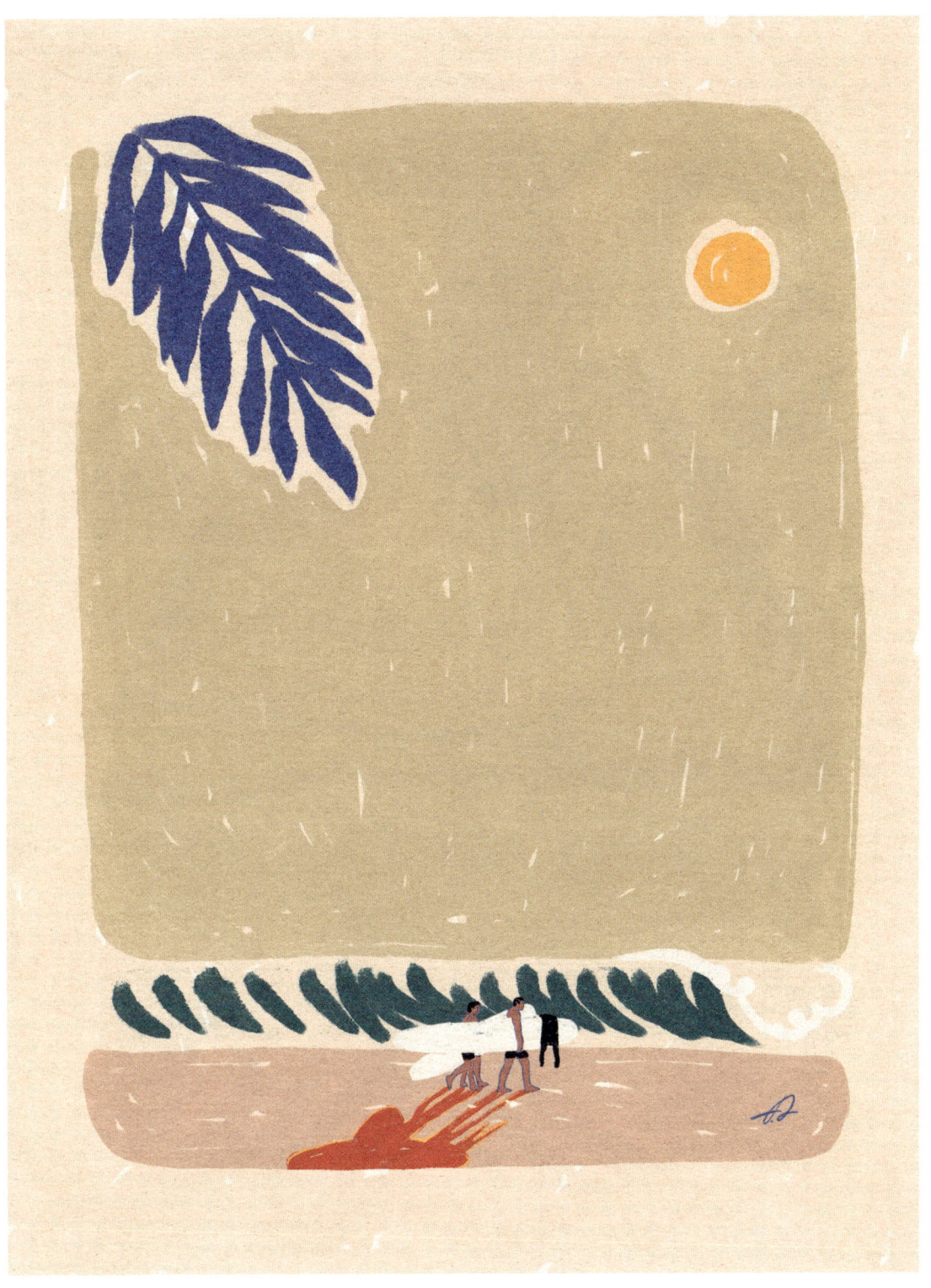

Too hot for wetsuits

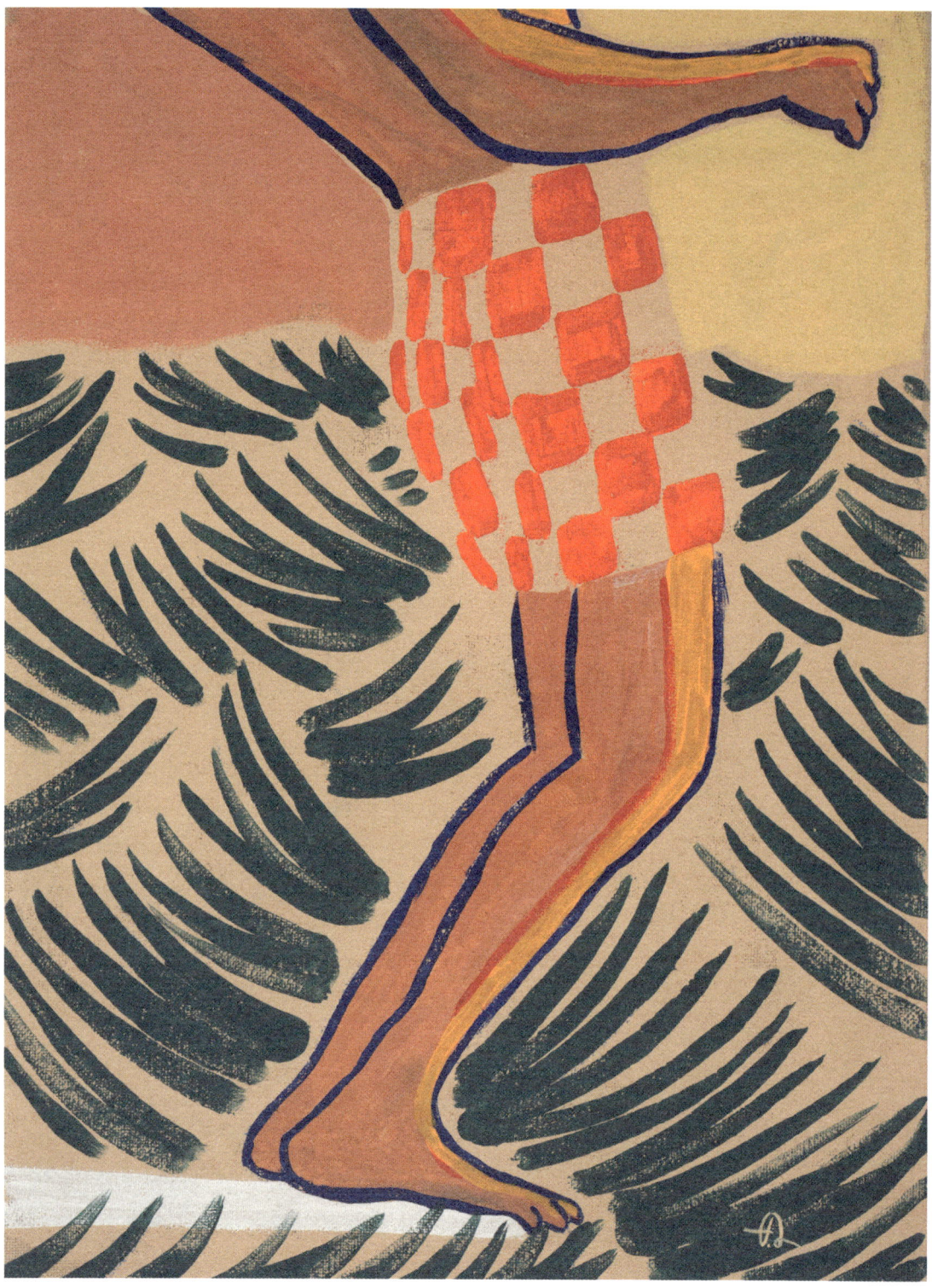

Hang ten and now

I try to capture the 'in-peace moments', which I personally experience when being outside. When daily struggles seem far away and you're just living in the moment

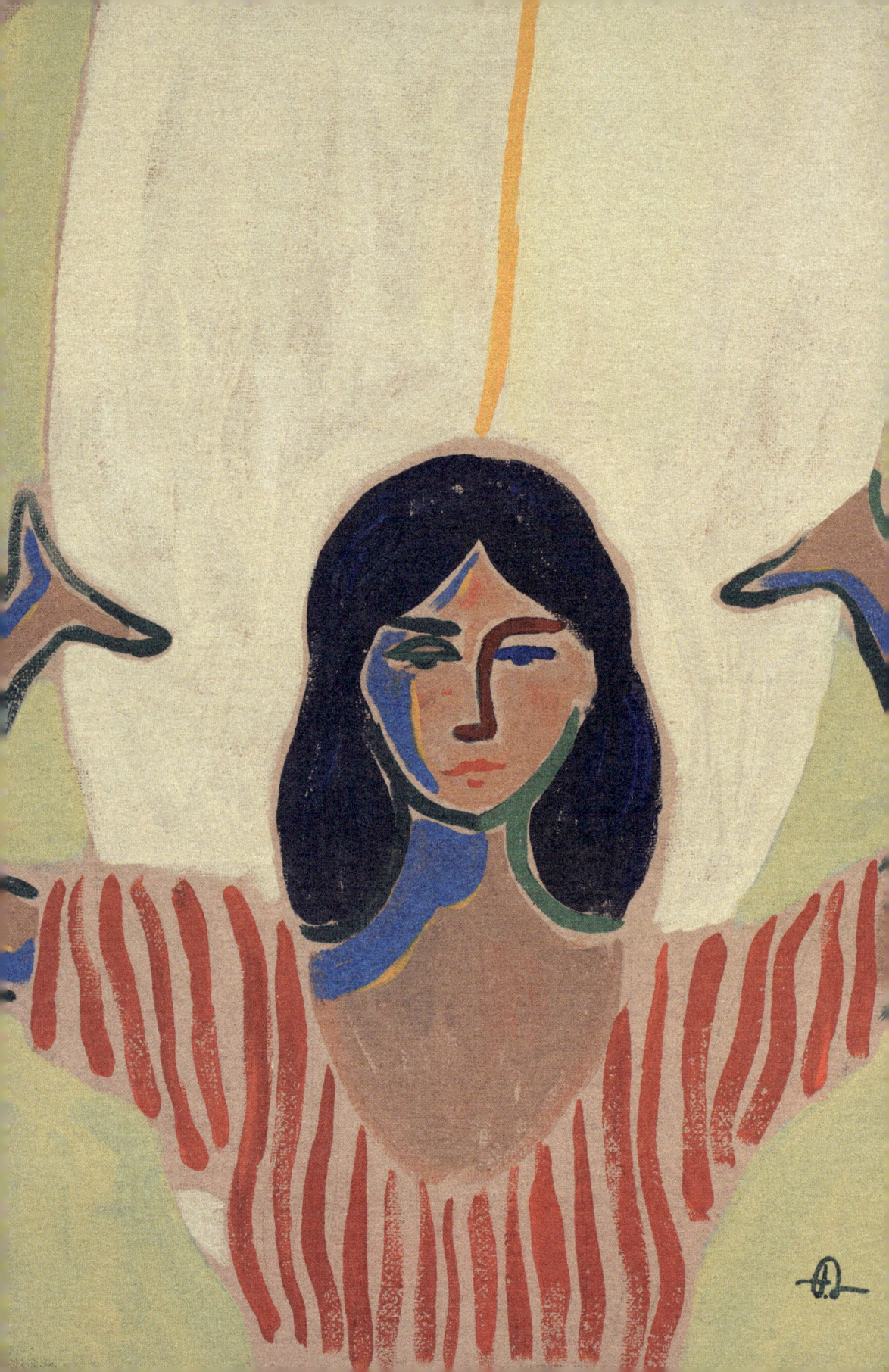

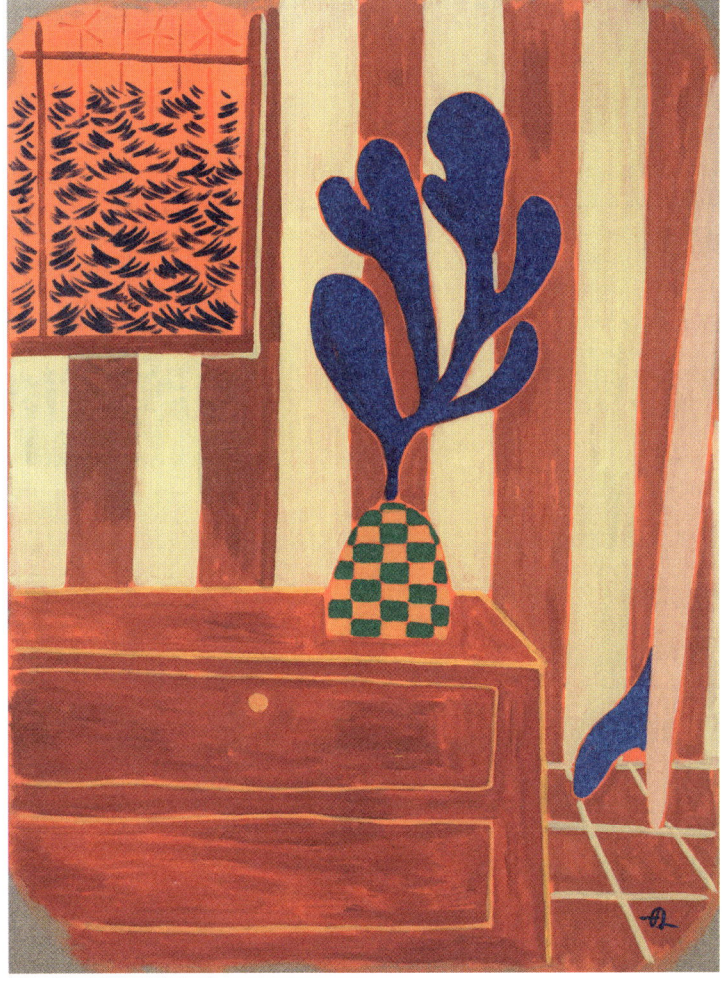

< The only luggage

In recent years, Fabian Lavater has shifted his focus from illustration to fine art, opting for acrylic painting on canvas instead of digital work on his iPad. This transition has naturally influenced his artistic style.

The room depicted below draws inspiration from Matisse, known for his paintings of interiors. Lavater titled the artwork 'Precious ocean'. The presence of a red wall could allude to climate change, while the vase is filled with sea corals. The inclusion of a window, reminiscent of Matisse's style, provides a glimpse into the surroundings.

Precious ocean

Q & A

Fabian Lavater

Who is Fabian?
I'm 33 years old and have a master's degree in sustainable development, but decided to pursue my lifelong dream of a career as an artist instead of going into the corporate world. Besides art, I'm most passionate about surfing, the outdoors and nature in general.

Your art has happy vibes. Would you agree?
I hope so. I'd say I'm a pretty happy and optimistic person in general, so it might shine through in my art. There's this narrative that good art comes from trauma and people who've struggled their whole life. I don't agree.

If you were to describe your art in a few lines, you'd say...
My art is simple yet playful, without too much detail in it. Topics are life by the ocean, surf culture and living outdoors. I try to capture the 'in-peace moments', which I personally experience when being outside. When daily struggles seem far away and you're just living in the moment.

How does the ocean influence your life/work?
I've always liked the ocean, but it was only when I started surfing that I felt this deeper connection with the sea, which I think over time has also transferred to other natural elements, such as a forest or the mountains. Having that relationship made me more conscious about nature in so many ways.

How does your art come to life?
The initial idea can come from anywhere really, be it a photo I see on Pinterest or a picture I took myself, a colour palette I like or something I experience in real life. Also, my own art can inspire more art. Then I would sketch on my iPad and play around with the colours and composition until I'm happy, before painting it on canvas or paper.

Do you have a quote that inspires or motivates you?
I don't think I have one. I believe in general not to overthink life. Life really is about the simple things, whether it be your favourite people, good food or being in nature. And also a healthy portion of doing nothing. Not trying to be productive or efficient every single day.

You contributed to the book Kleine Philosophie des Meeres. Can the ocean teach us life lessons?
The title means 'Little Philosophy of the Ocean' and it's written by Laurence Devillairs. It's about finding contemplation or calmness through the ocean, how the sea can show us an art of living that respects our natural rhythm. Originally published in German, it has now been translated in other languages.

Do you have an opinion on price setting in the world of surf art?
I have an opinion about price setting in the art world in general, where I think lots of people sell way under their value. I see artists selling prints for 15 euros, and I wonder how they can ever make a living from it. You also have to be aware that lowering prices is way easier than raising them once your audience is used to a certain price range. But I'm well aware that it's tough to find a good price range. I'm also not a fan of artists who sell their art in a way that is too exclusive, meaning the average earner would have to choose between going on holiday and supporting their favourite artist. I believe that art should be accessible to everybody, and I don't like it when artists basically make their art a luxury brand.

Where do you currently live or surf?
We lived in Biarritz for a while but had to move back to Switzerland because of my girlfriend's job situation. So as a 'replacement' we bought a van, which is awesome by the way. It allows me to come to the Atlantic coast and work remotely. The dream, though, would be to have the best of both worlds, meaning living in both the Basque country and Switzerland, since I feel very much at home in both places.

Do you remember how or when you fell in love with surfing?
I went to a surf camp 13 yearsago in les Landes. Mainly for the infamous parties, I didn't expect to particularly enjoy surfing. I was so wrong because I've been hooked ever since. Lots of my friends tried out surfing as well, but only a few continued pursuing it. To me it wasn't even a choice.

What would your dream surf trip look like?
Definitely with a bunch of friends and my girlfriend. I've been meaning to go on a tropical surf trip for a while now, so it would be somewhere on an island, picture perfect clean water, and waves for everyone to enjoy on their level. Personally, I don't need big surf. Let's say 4 to 6ft , with a small barrel section but also clean faces for manoeuvres.

Has surfing given you anything in life?
Definitely some sort of a purpose. Something to save money for, something that always makes me excited like a little kid. I get nervous every time I see a good forecast, I picture myself on the waves before going in and, when in the water, it forces me to be in the moment. It's just the perfect mix of a physical activity in nature that doesn't feel like sports at all and one that also calms your mind. •

14

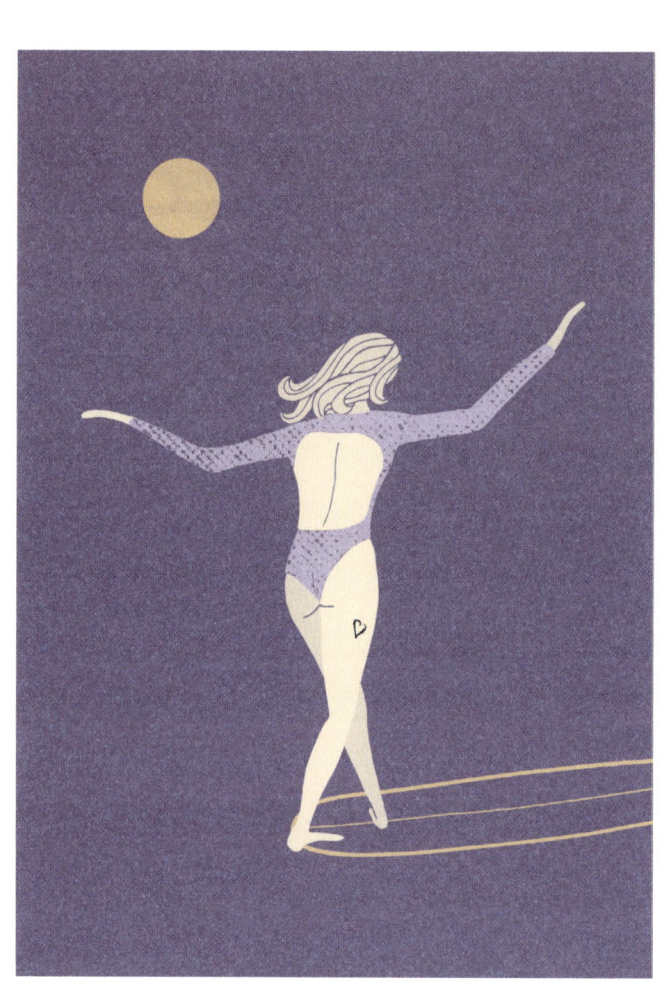

LOLA

Dancing queen

Lisa Marques

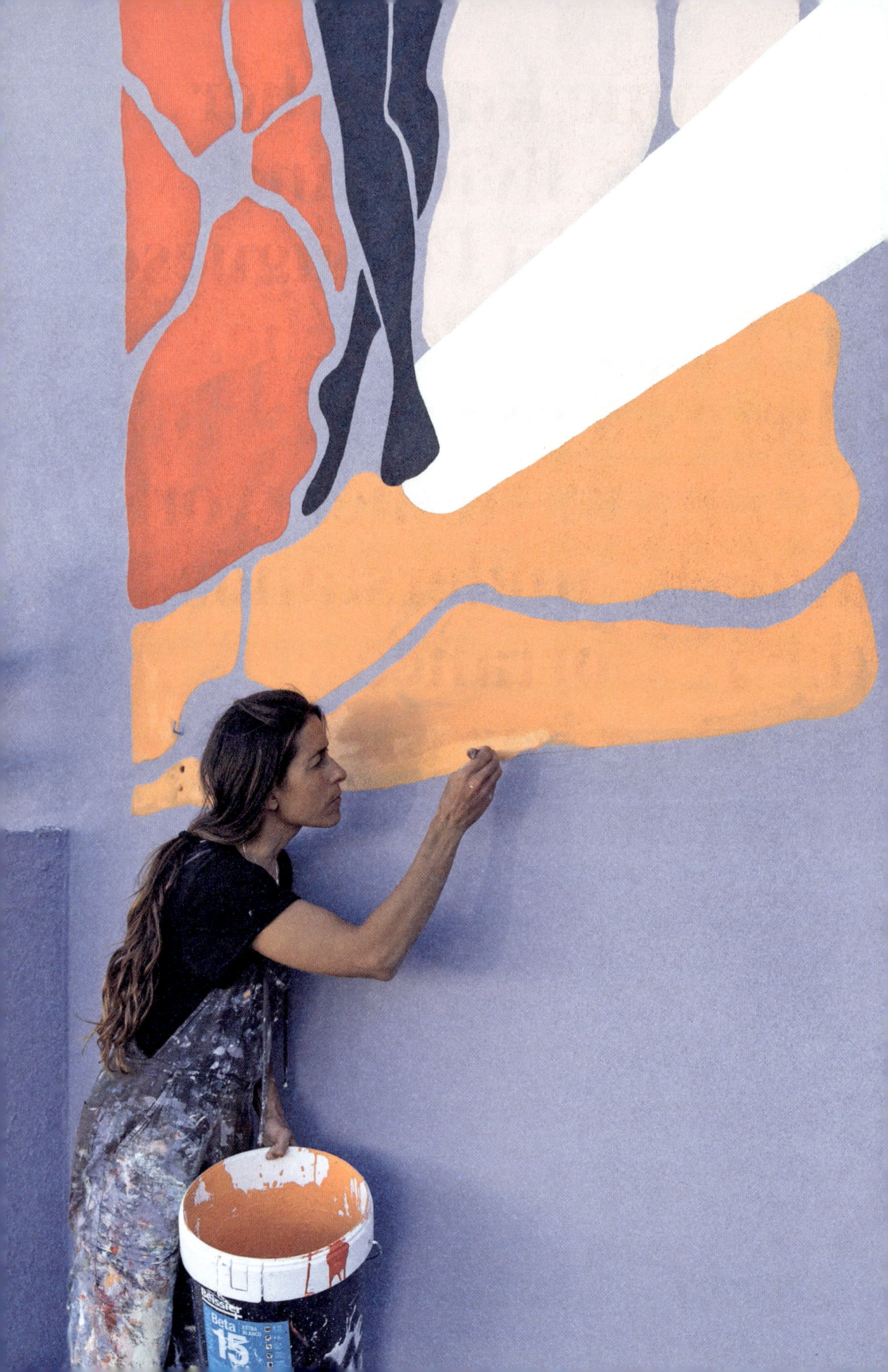

Everyone knows her as Lizzy, living and working in Portuguese surf mecca Peniche. There's a sense of femininity to her work and she understands the importance of using her voice as a female surfer.

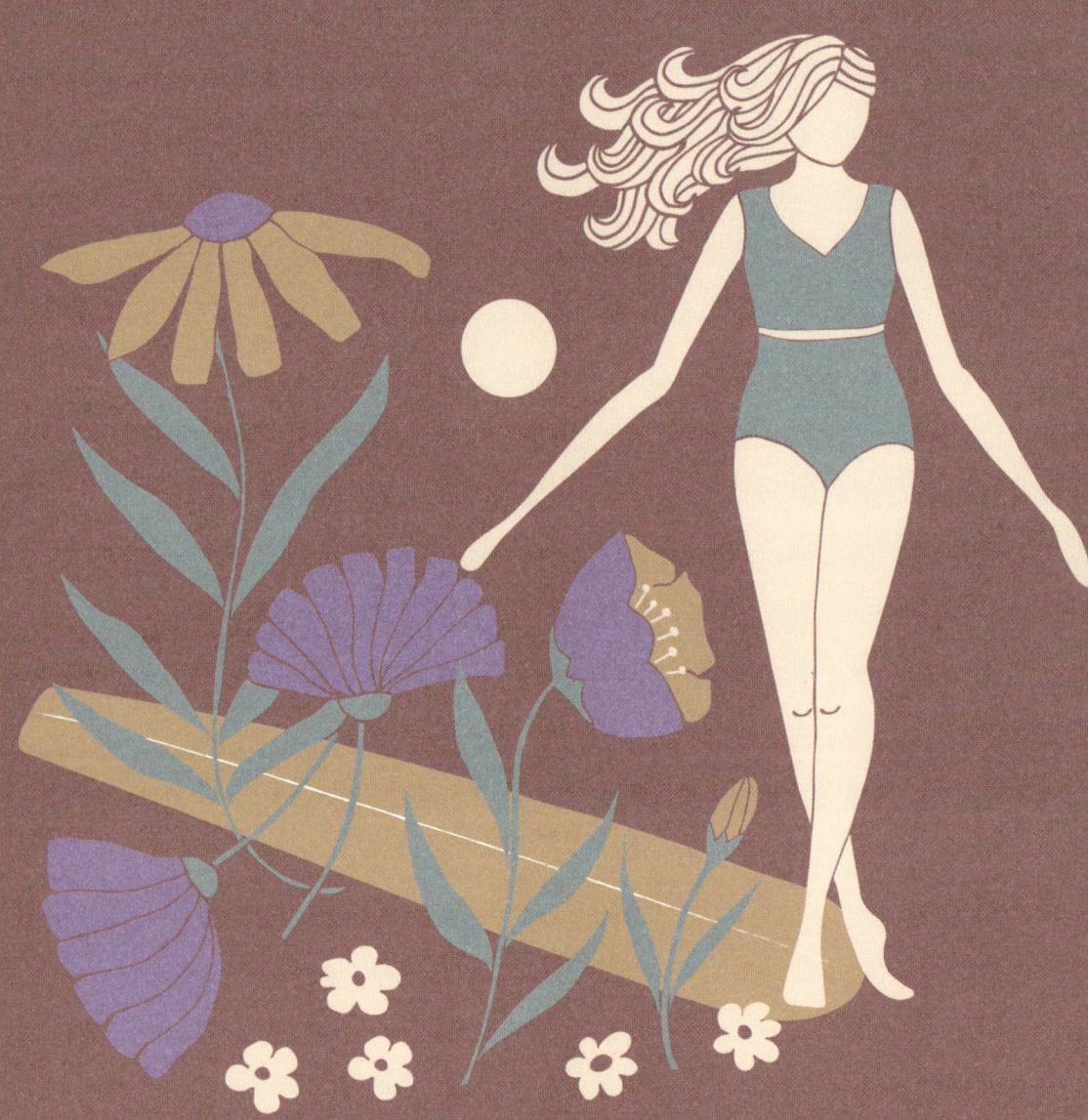

Thoughts and emotions can flourish like blossoms. 'To surf in Eden (left), you must learn to ride the currents of mindfulness', explains Marques.

'The art of surfing your own emotions requires a connection with our soul's tides,' says the Portuguese artist, who is training to become an art therapist.

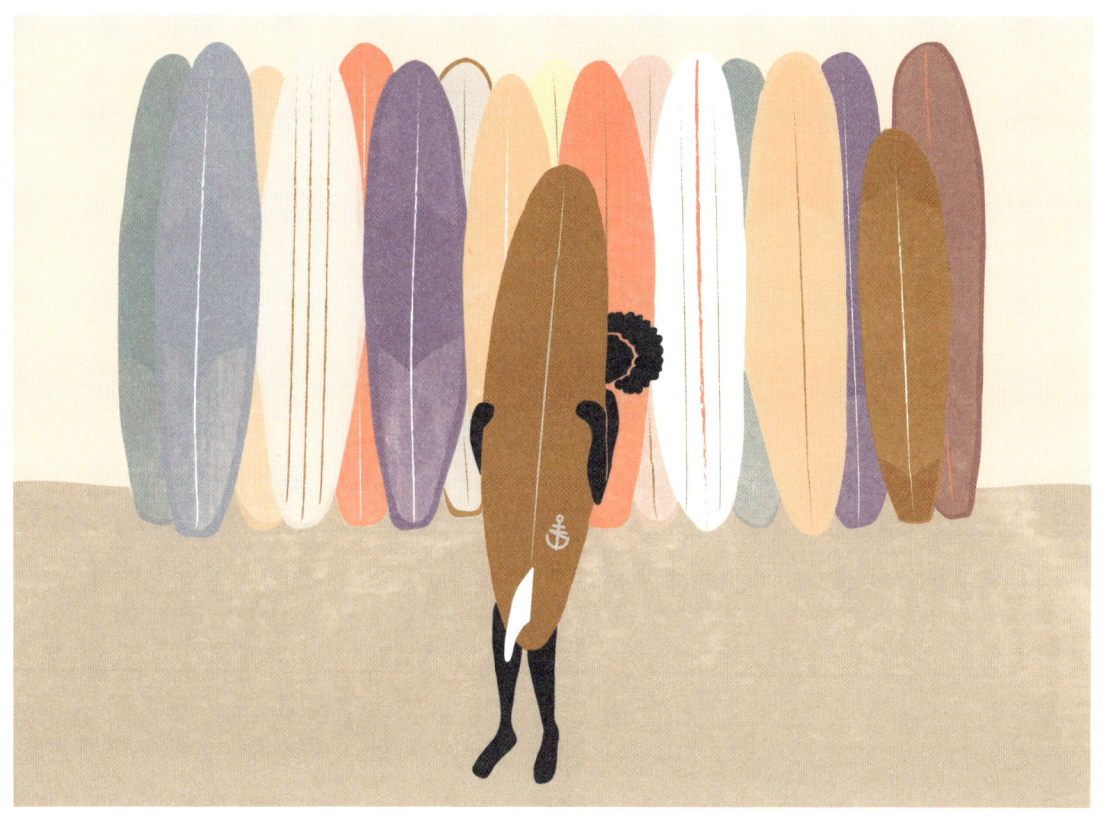

Surfing helped
me realise
that I can be
courageous and
graceful, radical
and quiet

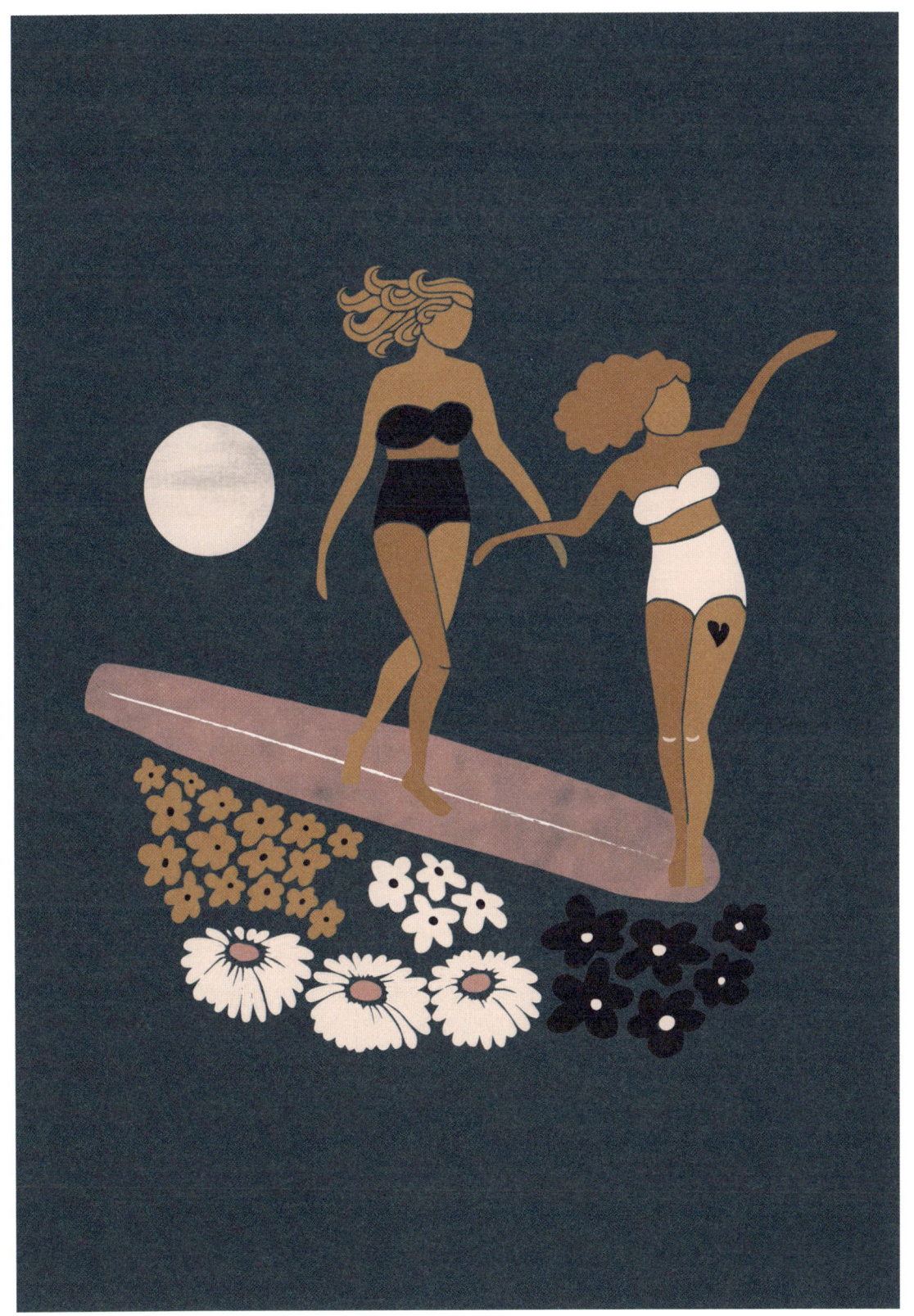

Malibu girls

Q&A

Lisa Marques

Who is Lizzy?
I'm an ocean lover, surfer and creative who likes to be close to the sea and nature.

How did you start drawing?
Drawing has always been part of my life. As a child, one of my favourite things was drawing and doing all kinds of crafts with my sister. We watched *Art Attack* on television and did all the creative challenges and activities. But it was only later, halfway through my master's degree in environmental tourism, that I looked at design from a more serious vision and as a business opportunity. And that's how a hobby turned into a career.

Your art seems to be quite feminine. Would you agree?
I agree! Surfing entered my life when I was a teenager, and the entire journey of learning to surf led me to self-discovery and I would even say the blossoming of my femininity. I realised that I can be courageous and graceful, radical and quiet. It also made me understand the importance of using my voice as a woman, of praising female surfing and salt-blooded women, not only for more representation in the surfing industry, but mainly to push the imagination of girls who can see themselves in my female figures dancing in the waves.

You're also training to become an art therapist. Do you see art as therapy?
My life took a big turn last year when I started building my new studio. It's a place where I intend to receive people, hold workshops, and start art classes for children. And yes, I'm also finishing an art therapy course. I think art can help us reconnect not only with our inner nature but also with the nature around us.

Where do you currently live or surf?

I live in Peniche, western Portugal. I moved here in 2006, when I decided that being part of the ocean was the only certainty I had in the long term. This fishing town has become a surfing mecca and even though I really enjoy travelling and surfing in different places, this is the place where I feel at home.

Do you remember how and when you fell in love with surfing?

When I was 13 years old, I saw someone surfing on television, and in that moment I decided that I wanted to become a surfer, and that lifestyle would be mine. It was my first decision as an individual. But my surfing has had several moments and phases, and I recently fell in love with surfing again when I started surfing a longboard.

Talking about longboards, what does your quiver look like?

Well, I don't have many boards, to be honest... I've been surfing mostly with a 9'4" longboard and a 6'4" single fin when it gets too big.

Can you pick a favourite surfing destination?

This is a difficult question, because I don't normally go on surf trips. I travel more for history, as I love ancient civilisations. So I'll choose Mexico and Peru, for their combo of history and waves.

Has surfing given you anything in life?

I often say I owe everything I am and what I have achieved to my relationship with the ocean. Surfing led me to rediscover who I am, to recognise and express myself with self-confidence, so my creations will always breathe from this connection. It influenced all my subsequent choices, and my life has been organised around the ocean. My career developed around my connection to surfing, the work opportunities, collaborations... They feed each other with the energy that flows between them. The ocean has taught me the greatest lessons of my life, always challenging my limits and fears, and testing my courage and resilience. She really is my greatest master. •

15

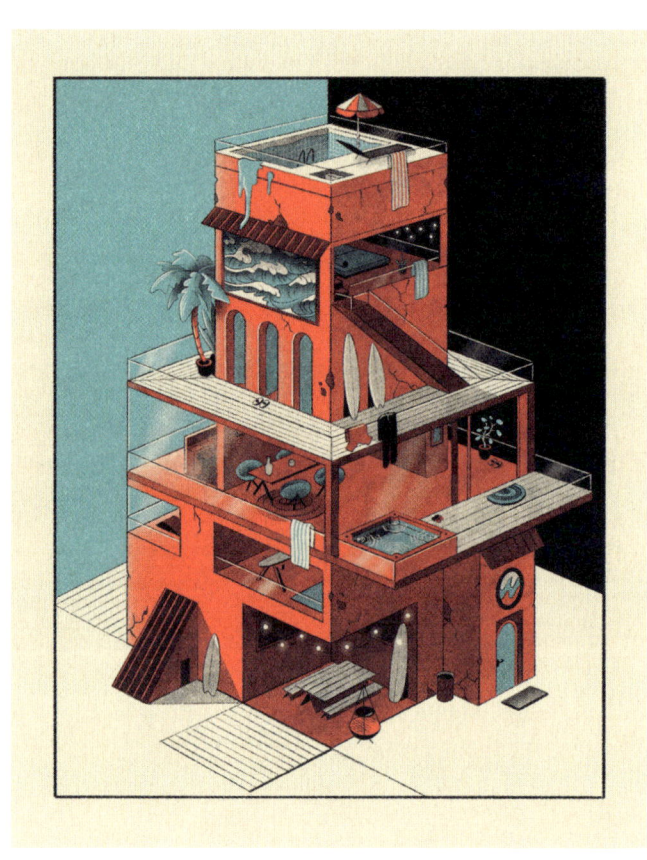

Comic style

Lennart Menkhaus

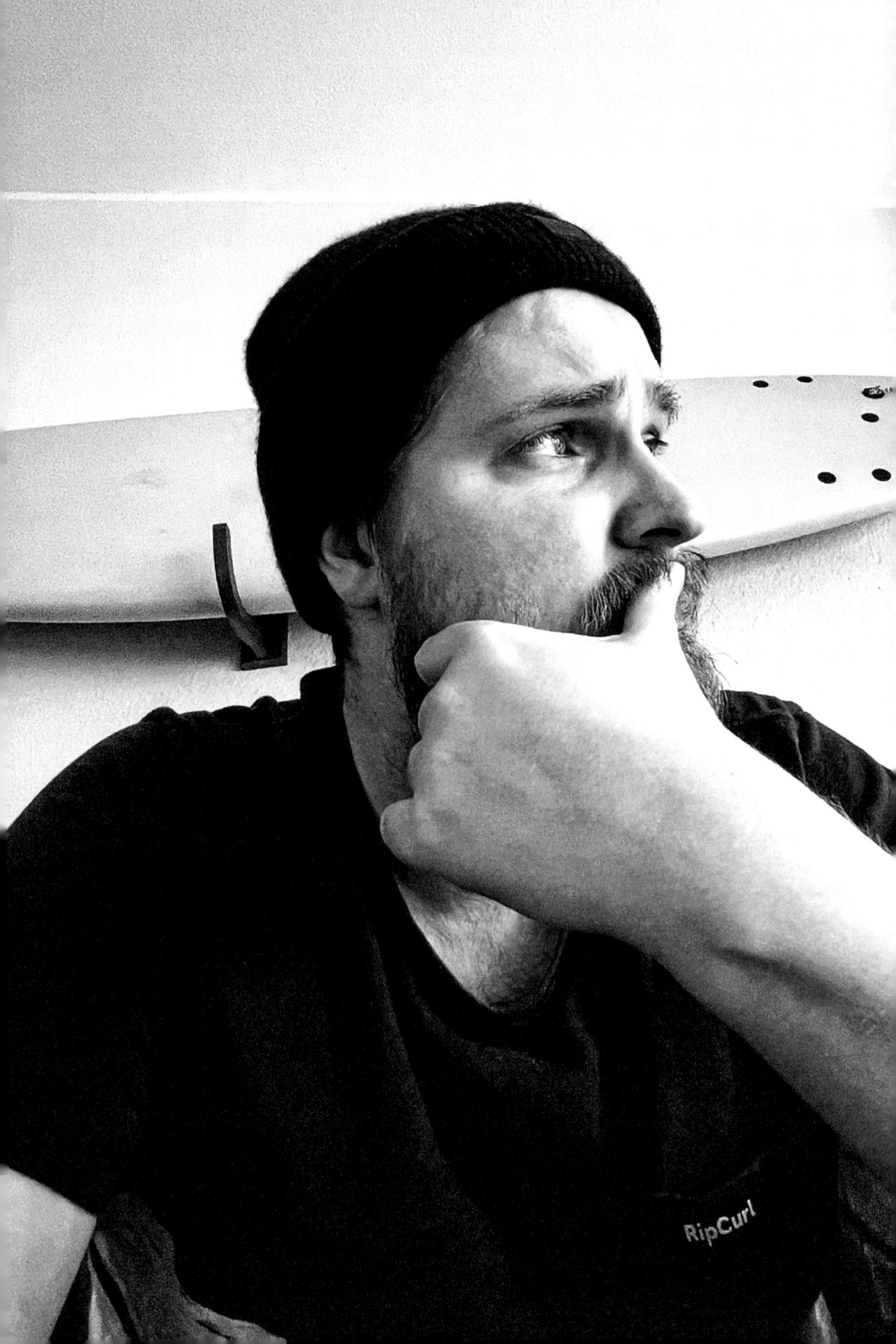

German illustrator Lennart Menkhaus mixes digital pencil drawing and comic style to create a whole other surf world.

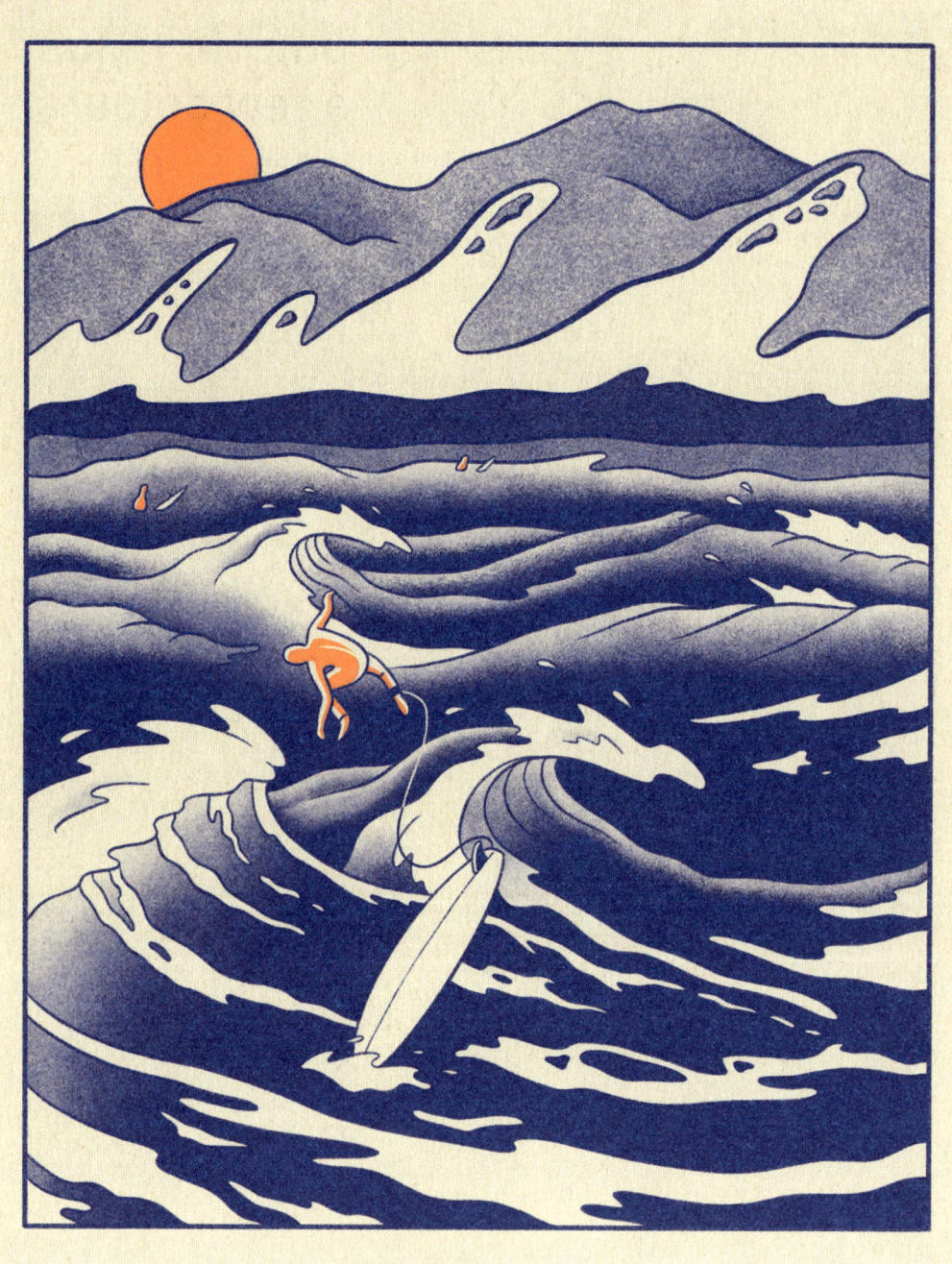

Cold Hawaii

I limit my palette to just a few colours. They don't reflect reality. I use them to give the artwork a bold energy

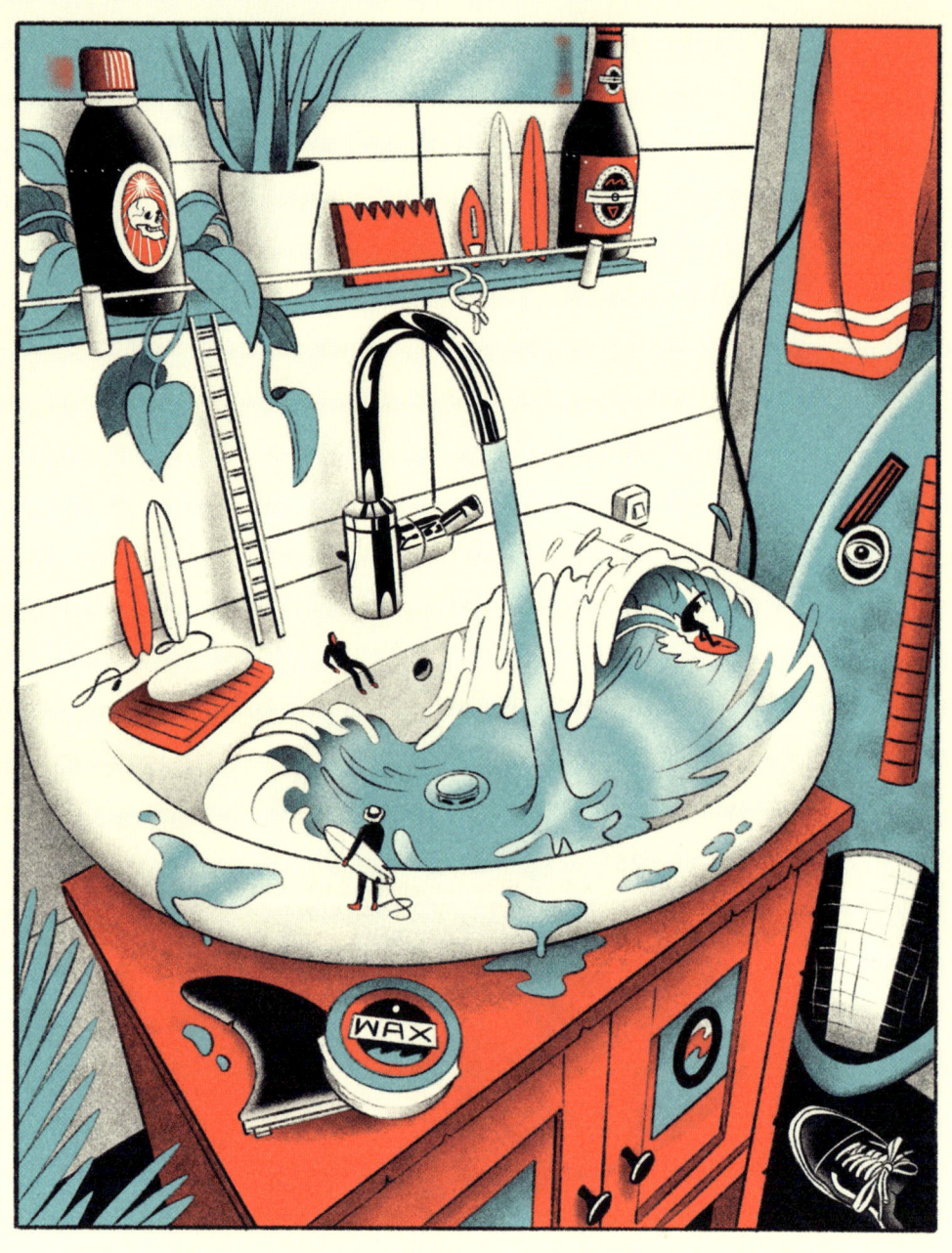

Sinkbreak

Menkhaus' style is almost incompa-
rable to that of any other surf artist.
Inspired by comics, he creates
fun little scenes featuring driving
sharks and sink surfers.

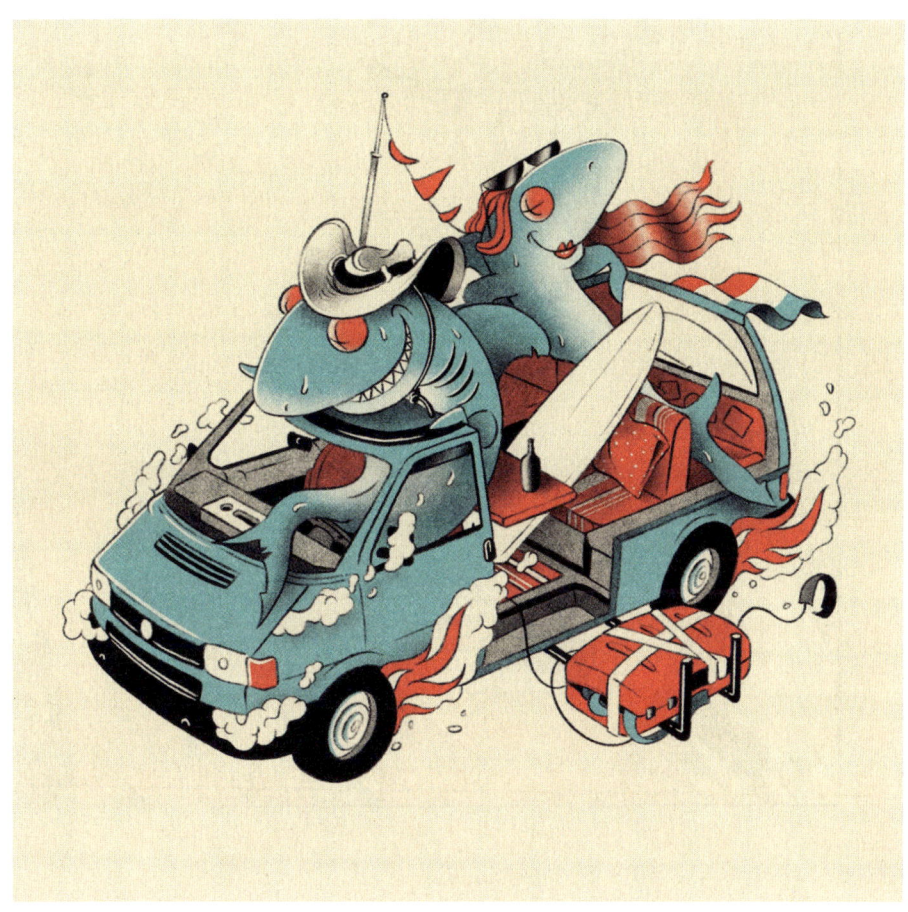

Q & A

Lennart Menkhaus

Who is Lennart?
A 32-year-old illustrator from Oldenburg in northern Germany.

If you were to describe your art in a few lines, you'd say…
My art is a mix of classic pencil drawing and comic style. I capture what inspires me and use only a few colours.

There seems to be something different about the colours you use?
I prefer using specific palettes with only a few select colours. Most of the time the colours don't reflect reality. They accentuate parts of the artwork or a certain feeling. I use them to make it brighter, darker or bolder.

Can you describe your drawing technique? Do you tend to create your work digitally?
Primarily, I draw on my iPad. It's fun because I get to be a lot faster than when I draw on paper. There are also more or different possibilities. I do tend to pick up my sketchbook anyway, but that's the art that people usually don't get to see from me.

Sometimes you draw about peace and ocean awareness. Do you feel you want to spread a message on those topics?
Definitely. I think it's the bare minimum in these current times to become more aware and spread that message. Especially if you have somewhat of a following.

Is there something you are particularly proud of?
I'm proud of the amount of art I've created over the past months and years. Sometimes I take my time and look through my old work, most of which can't be found online anymore. It makes me happy to see the progress I've made.

Do you surf yourself?
Yes, I surf. Unfortunately not for
that long yet and not as well as
I'd like. I try to pick holiday spots
where I can surf. Last year I was in
Denmark and the year before that
the south of France.

**You live in Germany, which is not
very well known for its waves.
Or am I mistaken?**
I live in Oldenburg, northern
Germany. Thankfully, the coast
isn't that far away. There are
a few secret surf spots on the
East Frisian Islands off mainland
Germany. But I can't say that
they compare to Hossegor or
Klitmøller, which is why I look
forward to my holidays so much.

**Can you recommend any other
books about surf art?**
I love the book *Surf, Skate & Rock
Art* by Jim Phillips. It inspires me
a lot. I actually collect all kinds of
surf books with great imagery. •

16

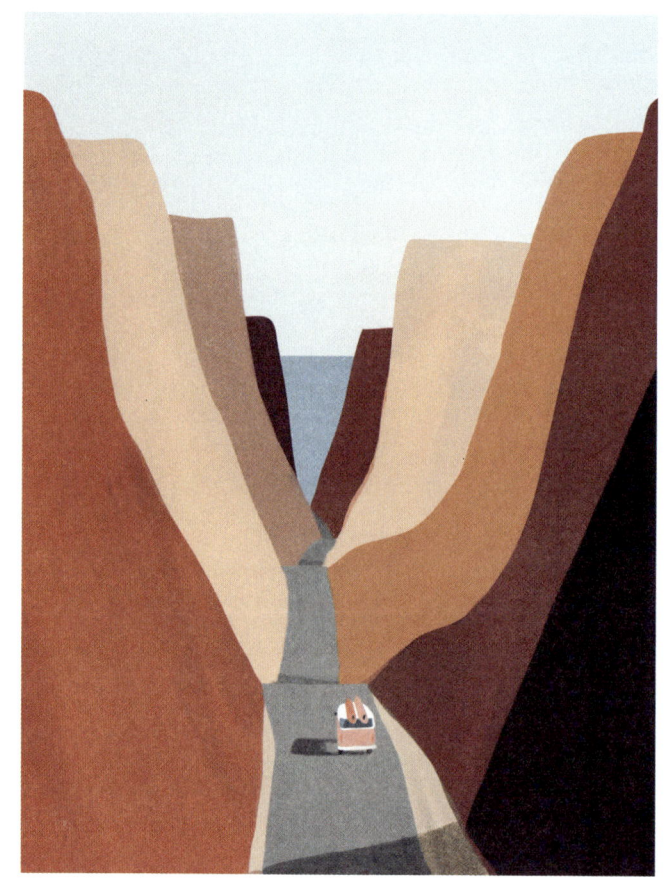

Eternity road

In-between realities

Quentin Monge

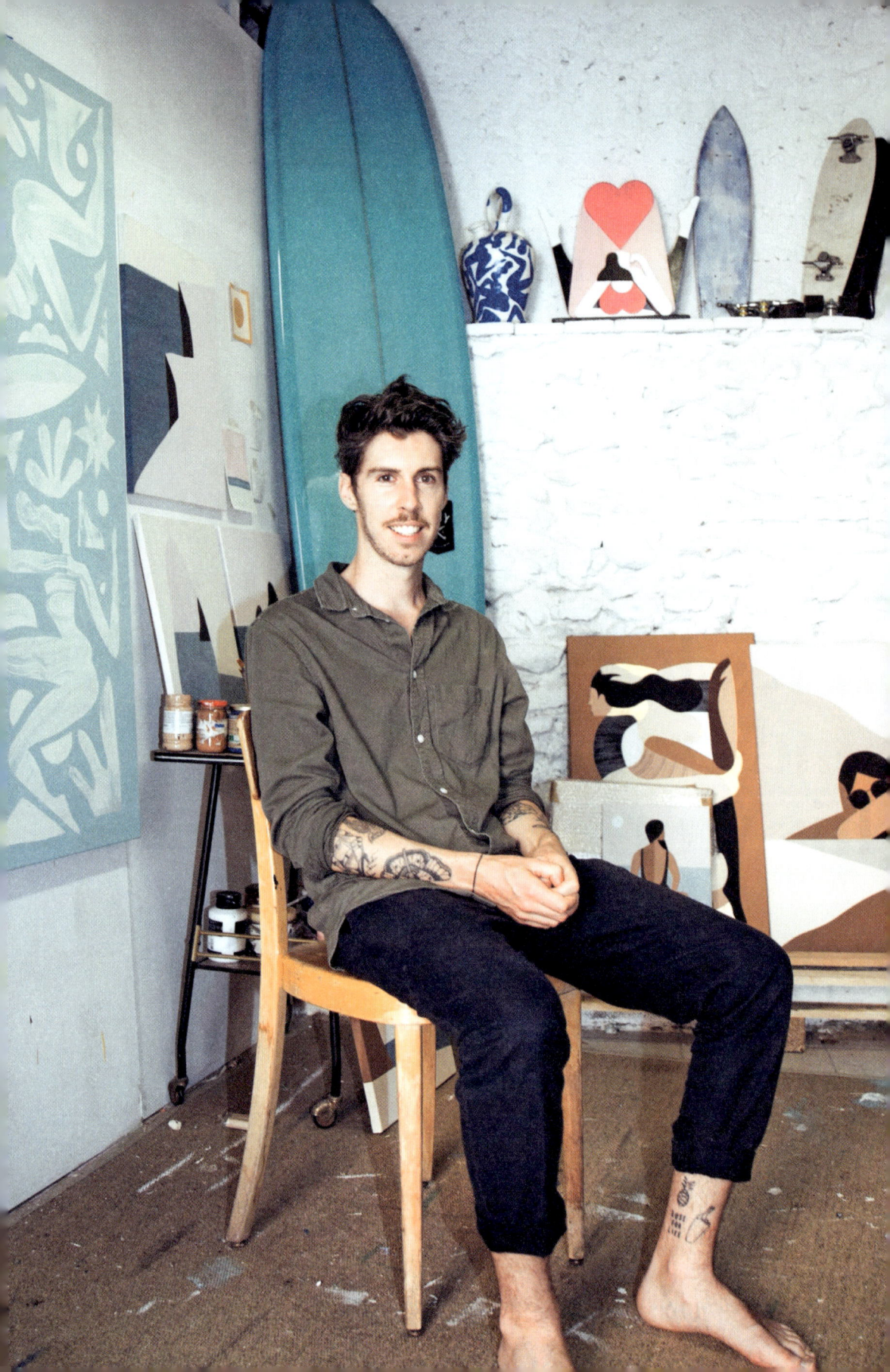

Based in Saint-Tropez, Quentin Monge can't surf as much as he'd like. Luckily, he can go wave-hunting in his own paintings. Warm hues and curved lines lend a softness and tranquility to his work.

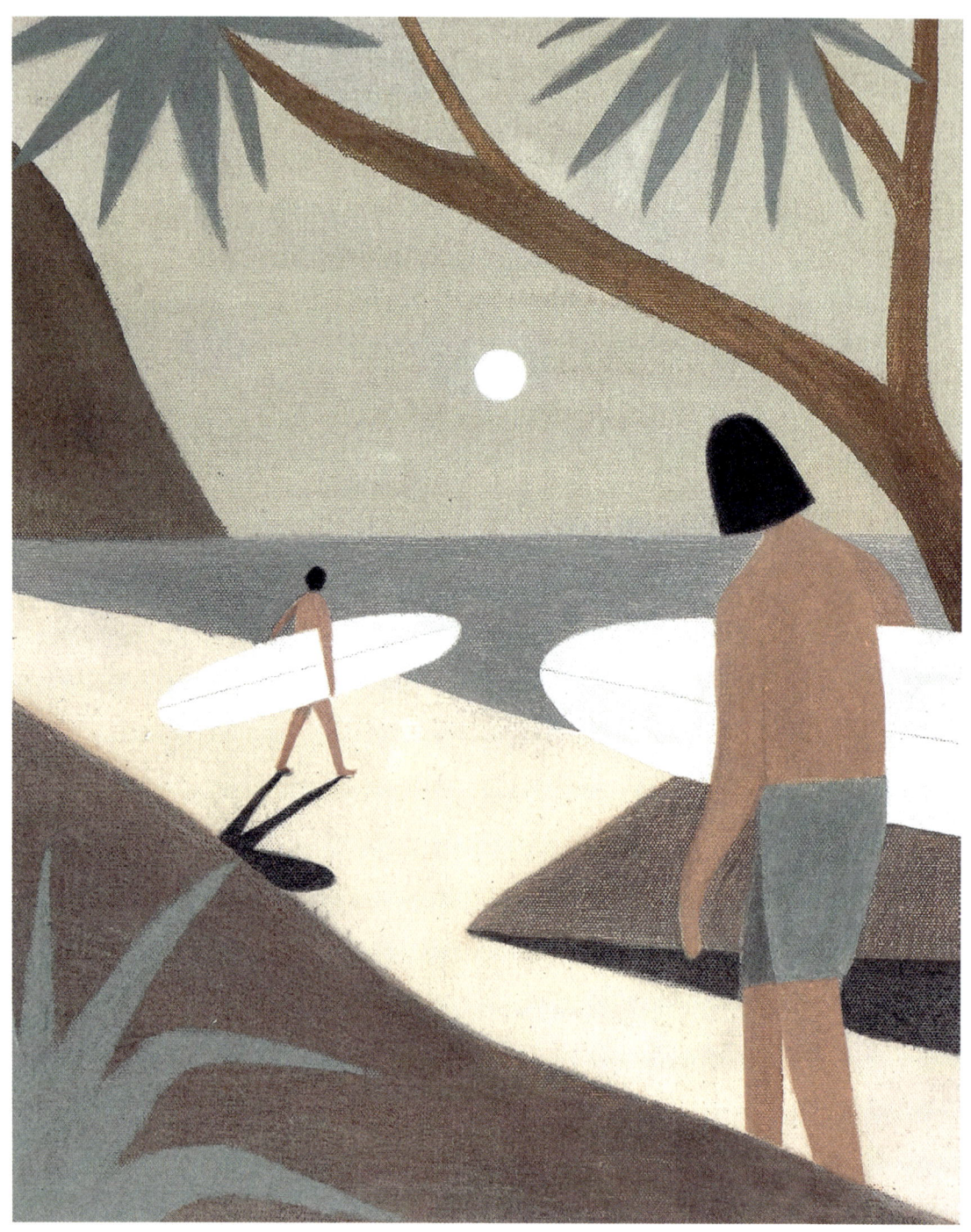

Late birds

Monge is an artist represented by Handsome Frank, probably the world's most exclusive illustration agency.

Over the years he has developed techniques and textures allowing him to create digital images that look like gouache or acrylic paintings.

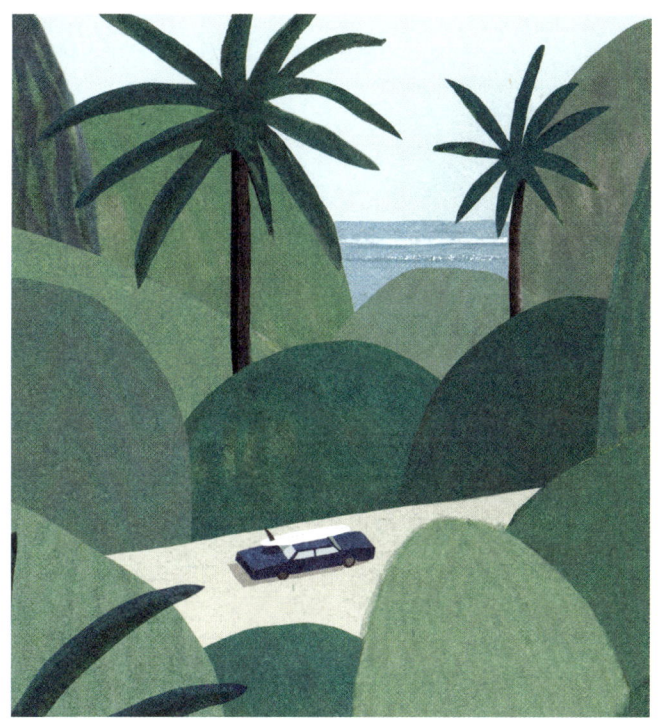

Once in the water, there's a lesson of humility

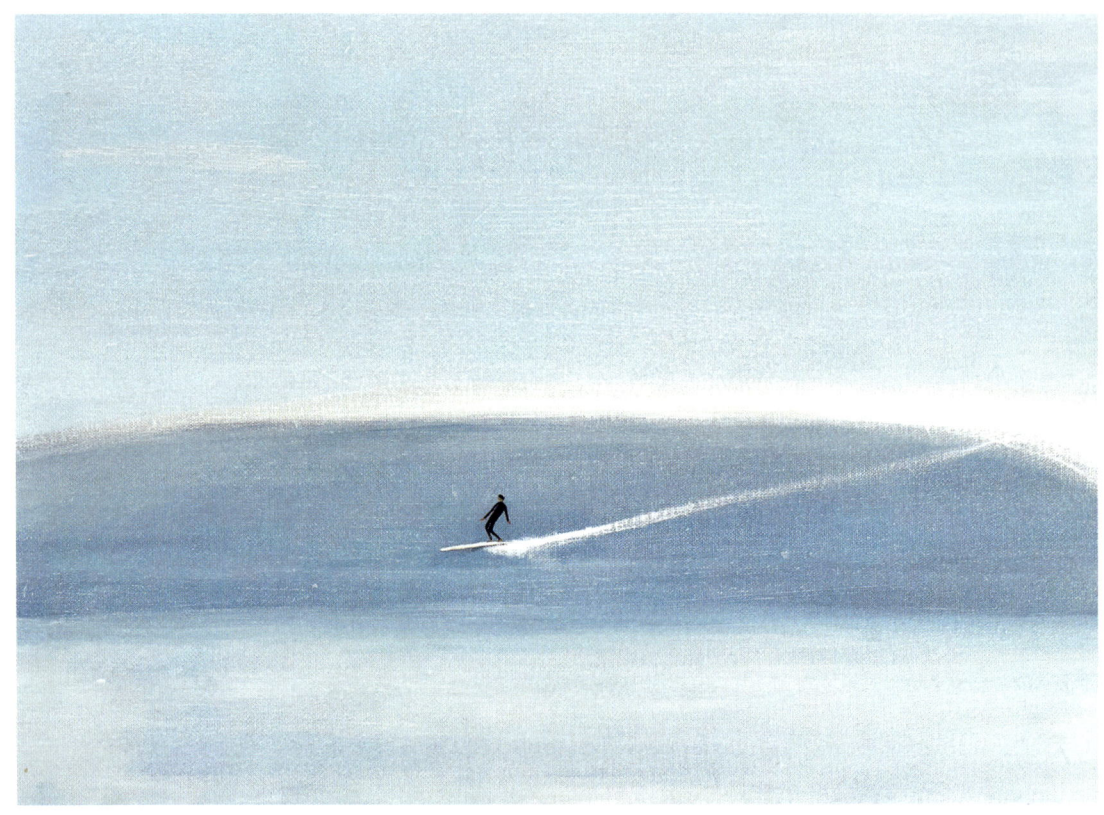

Floating truth

Misty morning

Q & A

Quentin Monge

Who is Quentin?
An illustrator from France
currently in the second father-
hood chapter of his life. I make
pictures out of memories,
dreams and observations.

**Your art has a dream-like spirit
to it. Would you agree?**
Yes, definitely, lots of composi-
tions come from my dreams,
or things I remember not
clearly, so my art is always
in-between realities.

**If you were to describe your
work in a few lines, you'd say…**
I try to capture the essence of
simple little things and moments
that make life bigger and
more beautiful.

**When did you start drawing
or painting?**
I often say that my first memory
is drawing in wet sand on the
beach as a kid.

**Do you have an opinion on price
setting in the world of surf art?**
I think it's a question of balance.
I personally consider it cool that
people value art so much that
they're able to pay a lot of money
for it. But I also like to do more
affordable projects to keep it
accessible for a wider audience.

**You've worked for famous clients
like Hermès, GQ and Airbnb
and you are represented by
illustration agency Handsome
Frank. How did these names
cross your path?**
A lot of assignments come from
social media, and indeed also
from my agents. I try to keep a
balance between my commercial
activity and personal practice.
I like how they can both influence
each other in terms of boundaries
and freedom.

What does surf culture today mean to you?

Surf culture gets so much attention these days. As a trend it comes and goes, but the ocean stays. For me it means that the sea should play a big part in our lives and in our fights. We should do everything we can to protect and preserve it.

Where do you currently live or surf?

I live on the French Riviera, in the Gulf of Saint-Tropez, which isn't very well known for surf. Beyond the bling-bling nightclubs, there is something really special about this place: the light and nature. Lots of the Impressionist painters came here because of this light. My house and studio are right in the heart of a forest of oak and pine trees. And also 10 minutes from the sea. I love the idea of having those two environments very nearby.

Do you miss the surf?

I grew up here and now I've returned to live and work by the sea. We don't have much surf, but when it works, everything revolves around that and we get to enjoy some nice sessions with very few people.

What does your quiver look like?

I really like my 5'4" retro fish that I got in Bali and also my custom Bastille board from Atelier Bleust, which is a great 7'6" single fin shaped by LUTA Surftoys. But I also love longboards, and even softboards can sometimes be quite fun.

Has surfing given you anything in life?

I think not having waves on a regular basis makes you enjoy it even more when the swell turns on. Any conditions/waves will suit me – I just enjoy what's given to me. I think that it's a valuable life lesson. And once in the water, the lesson of humility is even bigger.

What would your dream surf trip look like?

Every year I try to go to the west side of France. I also try not to take the plane too often, even if I have a lot of dream trips in my mind. They might just remain dreams, but can still happen in my paintings. •

17

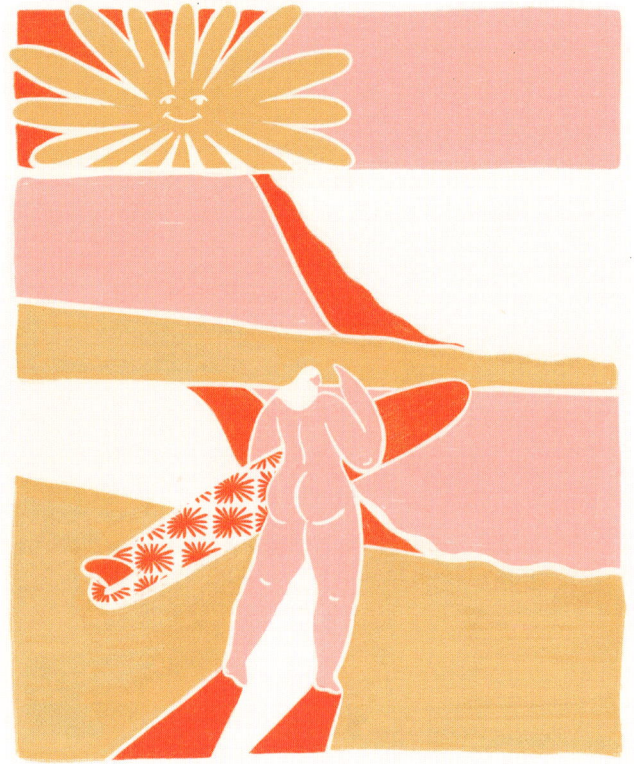

Not so scary waves

In the nude

Jessica
Soparlo

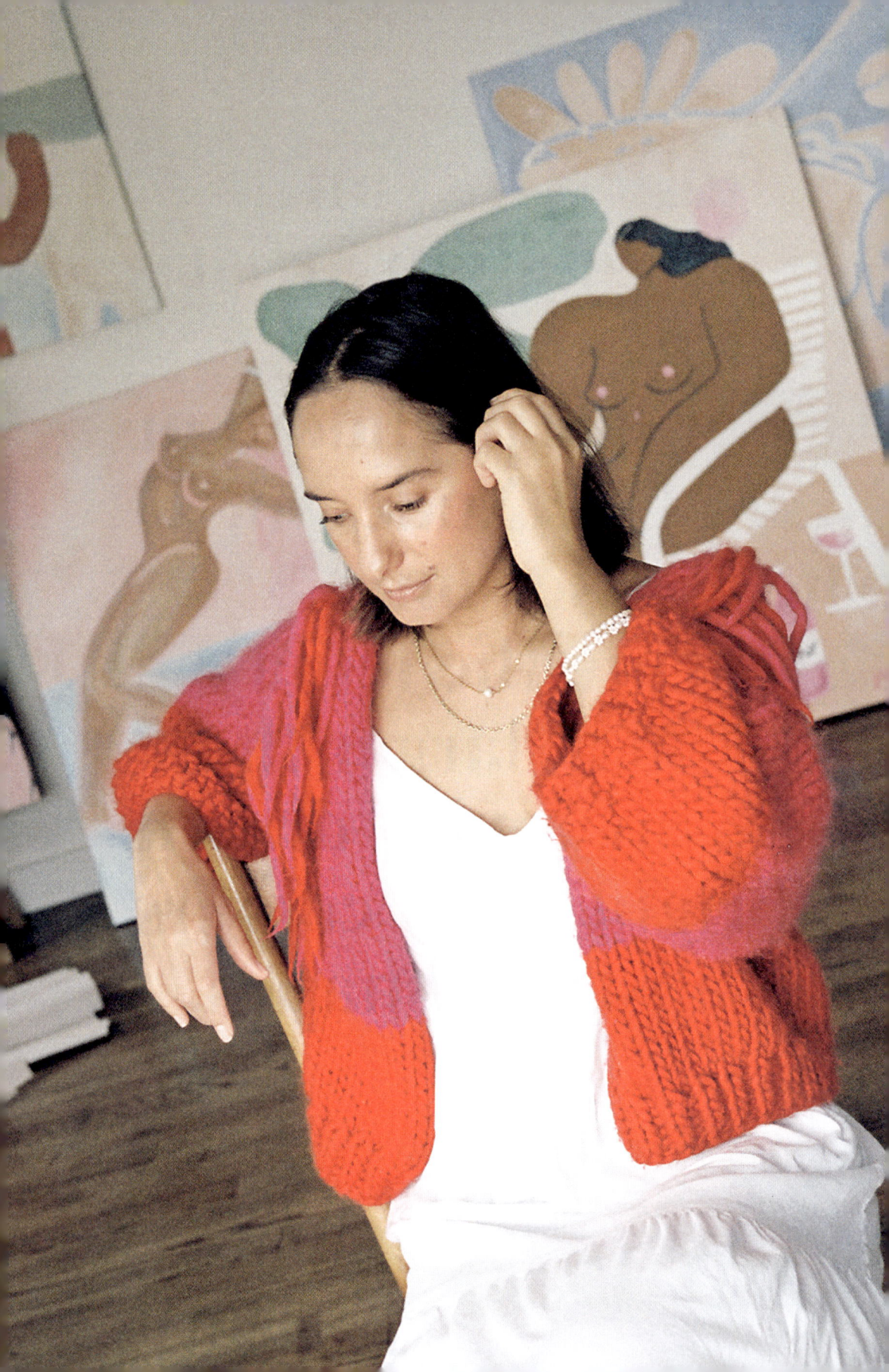

Women make surfing more fun, says Canadian artist Jessica Soparlo. Under her pseudonym Would Be Nude Not To, she focuses on featuring the female form in a 'larger than life' way and is drawn to bright, bold colours and abstract shapes.

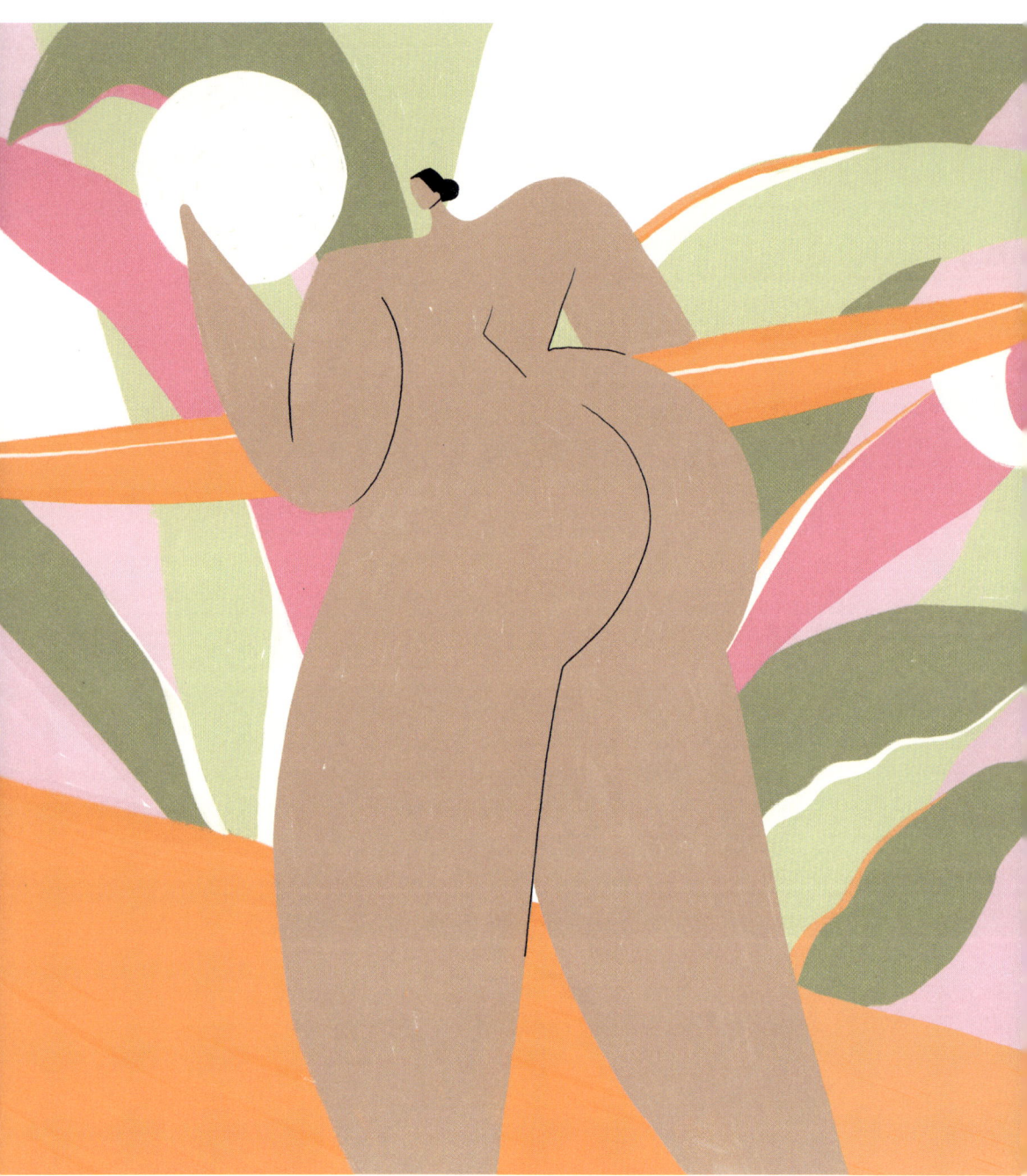

Hips don't lie

I'm sure there
are some 'rules'
when it comes
to painting,
but I try not
to think about
technique too
much and focus
on having
fun with
the process

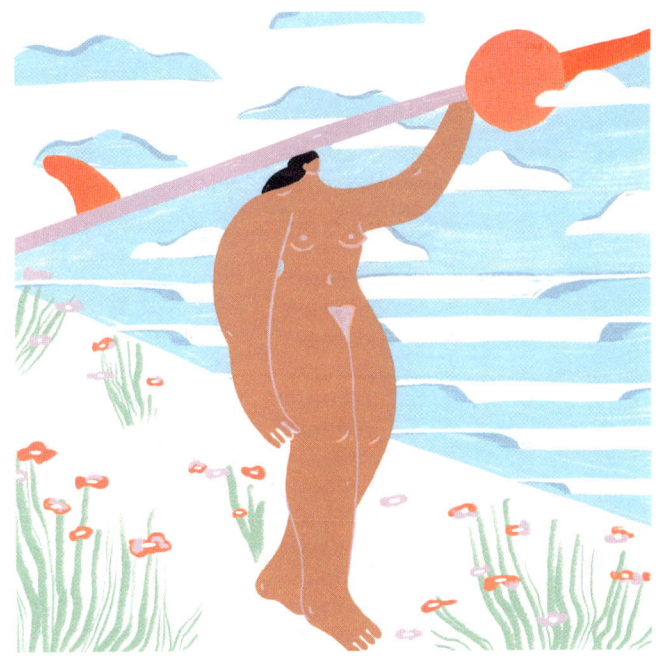

Brains carry boards

Q & A

Jessica Soparlo

Do you have a go-to colour palette?
I don't think so, but looking back at my work I'm definitely drawn to pinks, corals and bright, fun colours.

Who is Jessica
I am a freelance graphic designer and artist from the West Coast of Canada.

Your art is quite feminine. Does it share a particular message?
There isn't a specific message. A lot of my work is inspired by personal experiences and things I am working through. Being a woman who likes to participate in different sports comes with a lot of emotions and I like to draw my experiences.

When did you first think: I can do this for a living?
I have a pretty bad case of imposter syndrome, so it took me a while to commit to my design and illustration work full-time. When retail stores started approaching me and asking if they could wholesale my work, I definitely felt a huge confidence boost to pursue my art full-time.

How did you come up with your artist name Would Be Nude Not To?
I had a friend that used to say 'it would be rude not to' a few times a day. When I started drawing my little naked ladies and it was all I could draw for a couple of days, the name just kind of popped up.

How does your art come to life?
Most of my favourite pieces happened when my sketchbook or iPad were nowhere in sight. I find being outside, trying new things, snowboarding, surfing and even just walking through new neighbourhoods or cities provide ample inspiration. Afterwards, I often rely on memory or hurry home to find my sketchbook to get the idea out of my head and onto paper.

Do you think we need more women in today's surf culture?
Of course we do! Whenever I paddle out and I'm surrounded by men, the vibes are always a little weird. But when you paddle out and see a bunch of smiling female faces, you know you are going to have a great time. Women make surfing more fun.

Can you describe your painting technique(s)?
I've never had any formal training as a painter, it's just something I've done almost my whole life. I'm sure there are some 'rules' when it comes to painting, but I try not to think about technique too much and focus on having fun with the process.

Can you mention any painters that inspire you?
There are so many. But some that really stick out are Amber Vittoria, Laura Berger and Filippa Edghill. All three of them have their own particular way of portraying femininity.

Is there something you are particularly proud of?
I'm proud of myself for waking up every day and choosing my art! I have yet to do any serious damage to my surfboard, a 9ft longboard shaped by Altered Blade… I treat her like the princess she is.

Last year you opened the Always Sunny Shop with your sister and this year a second one. There's a lot going on in your life?
I hate to say it, because to me it's a boring answer, but my life is very busy right now. Last year my sister and I indeed opened up a small second-hand clothing and home goods store called the Always Sunny Shop, and just this week we officially opened our second business together, which is a small art gallery, pop-up shop and event space called Soft Studio. I have a logo project, and a couple of illustration projects going on, plus a painting commission. Managing three small businesses was not something I thought of for myself but here I am!

You seem to embrace a 'let's just jump' philosophy?
I have a favourite motto. It's not from a book, I'm not even sure where I heard it but I scribbled it down in a notebook: 'Those who fear, fall first.' I usually say it when I'm scared of doing something, but deep down I know that if I do it I will be proud of myself. It's helped me in business, snowboarding and surfing.

Can you pick a favourite surf destination?
I've been to the East Cape in Baja a few times and I adore the waves and sunrises there. But honestly, Tofino in Canada has got to be one of my favourite surf destinations. It's hands down one of the most beautiful places in the world.

Has surfing giving you anything in life?
Definitely. My relationship with the ocean influences all aspects of my life. It gives me inspiration for my art, amazing memories with friends and family, and a way to enjoy spending time with my partner. Basically, it has been a sort of north star in my life. I am constantly thinking about when I can get to the surf next, what I can draw to make up for my lack of surfing lately, and how I can spend all my hard-earned money on my next surf trip.

Can you often surf at home?
I currently live in Squamish, Canada. It is a smallish town that is surrounded by mountains and water. It is not a surfing town and if I want to surf, I have to take a ferry to Vancouver Island and drive either five hours or two hours to the nearest break.

Dedication! Probably no need to ask but surfing is part of your DNA?
For sure. I was a small mountain town kid who dreamt of being a Roxy girl and my first time surfing was in Hawaii when I was 12. I've always loved the idea of surfing, however I didn't start to surf consistently until I was 30. I'm 34 now and have been trying to prioritise surfing as much as I possibly can. That means lots of ferry rides, many hours in the car, and I am definitely poorer because of my surfing habit, but I wouldn't have it any other way. •

185

18

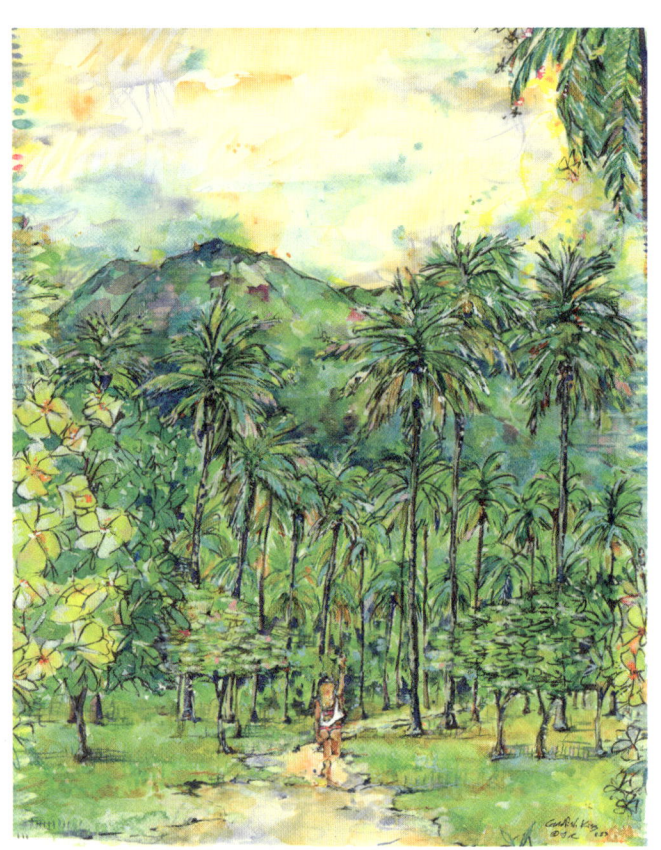

Walking in sunshine

Princess of fresh air

Rebekah Steen

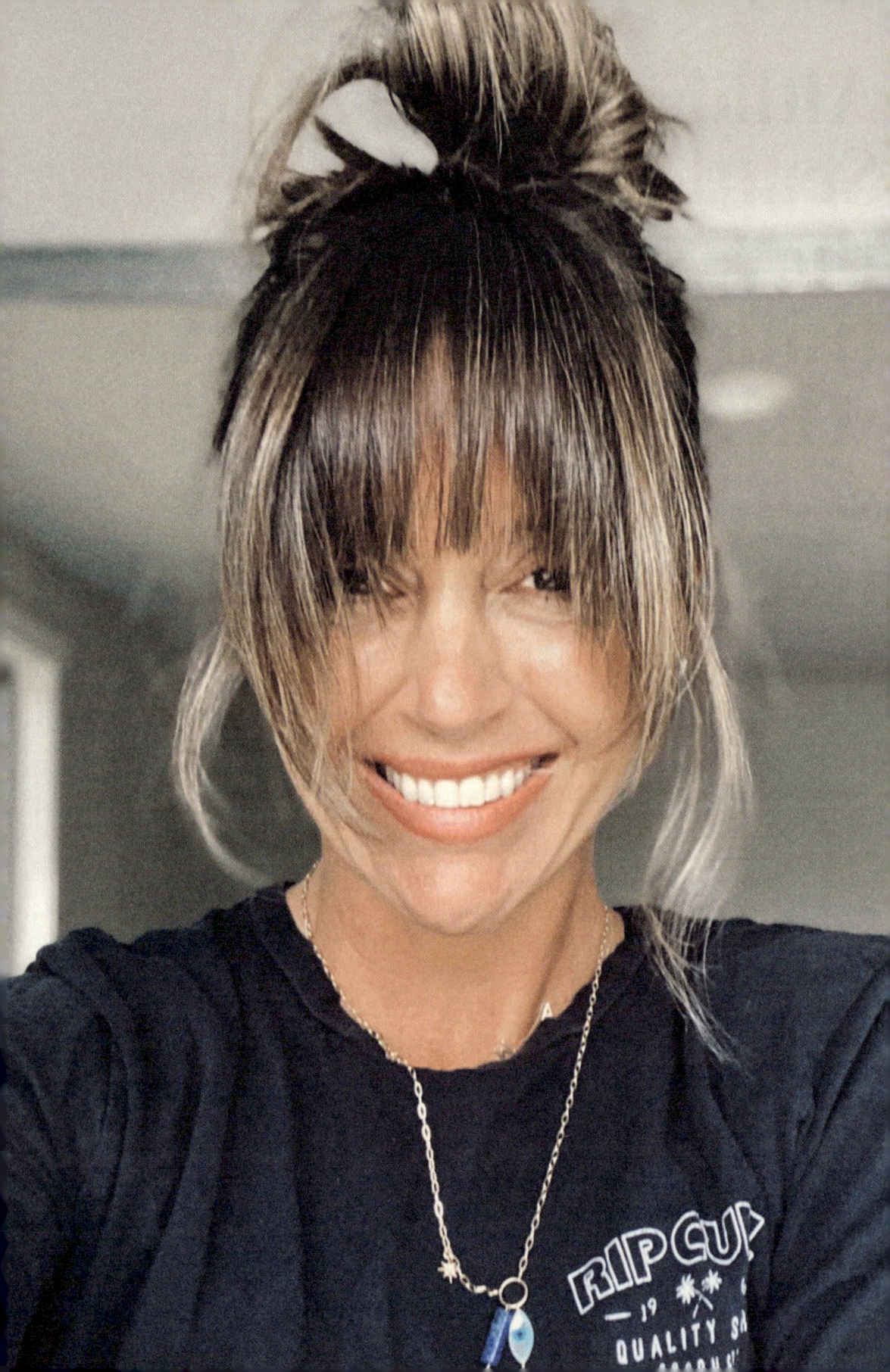

Although she lives near Seattle in the north of the USA, Rebekah Steen transports us to places where the sun always seems to shine. Bright, free, salty and tropical vibes galore.

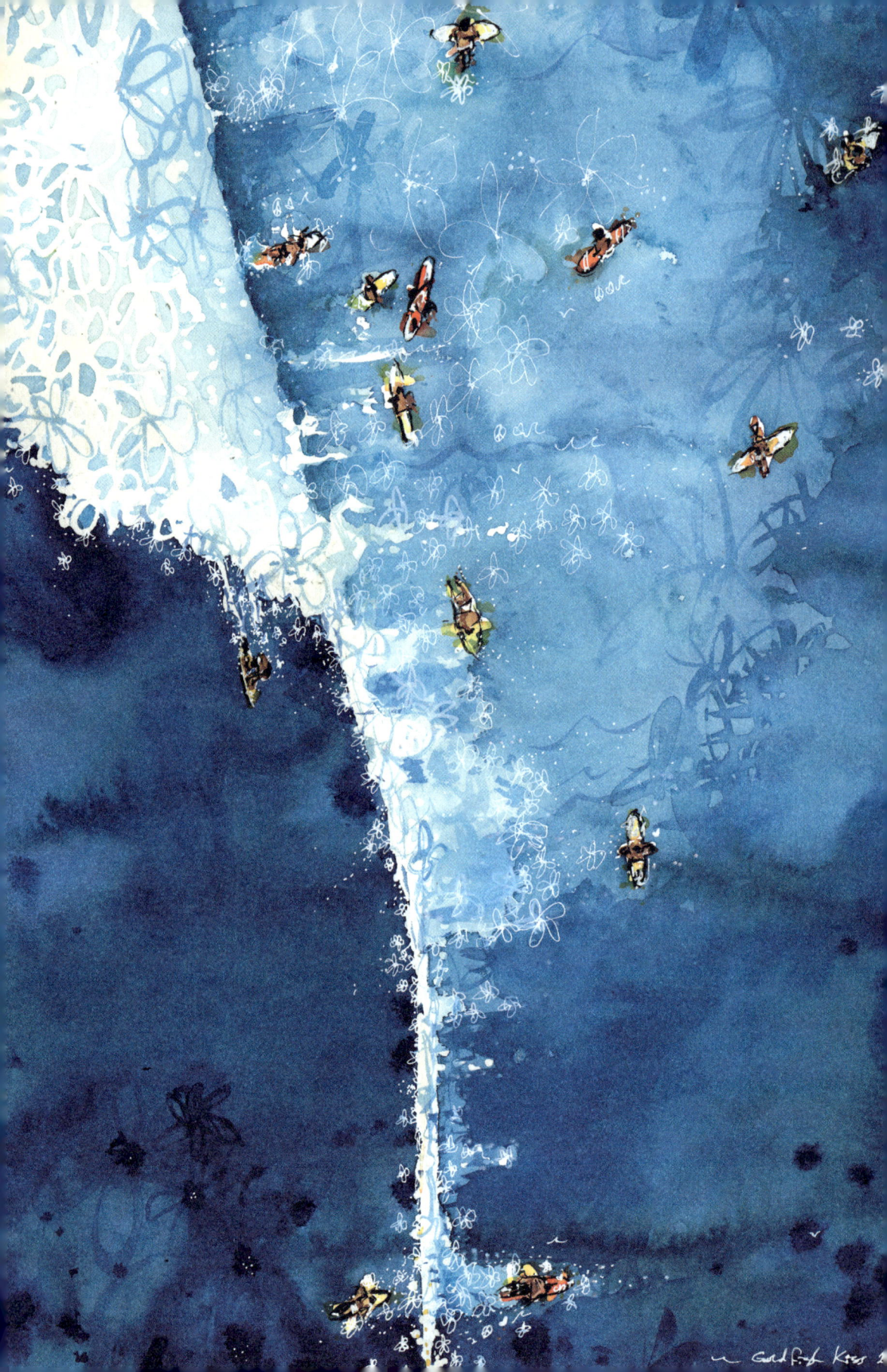

Goldfish Kiss

Steen blends her formal training as a painter with watercolour techniques.

'I am my own harshest critic', she says, 'and each painting is a cycle of self-doubt, experimentation and perseverance, then knowing when to stop.'

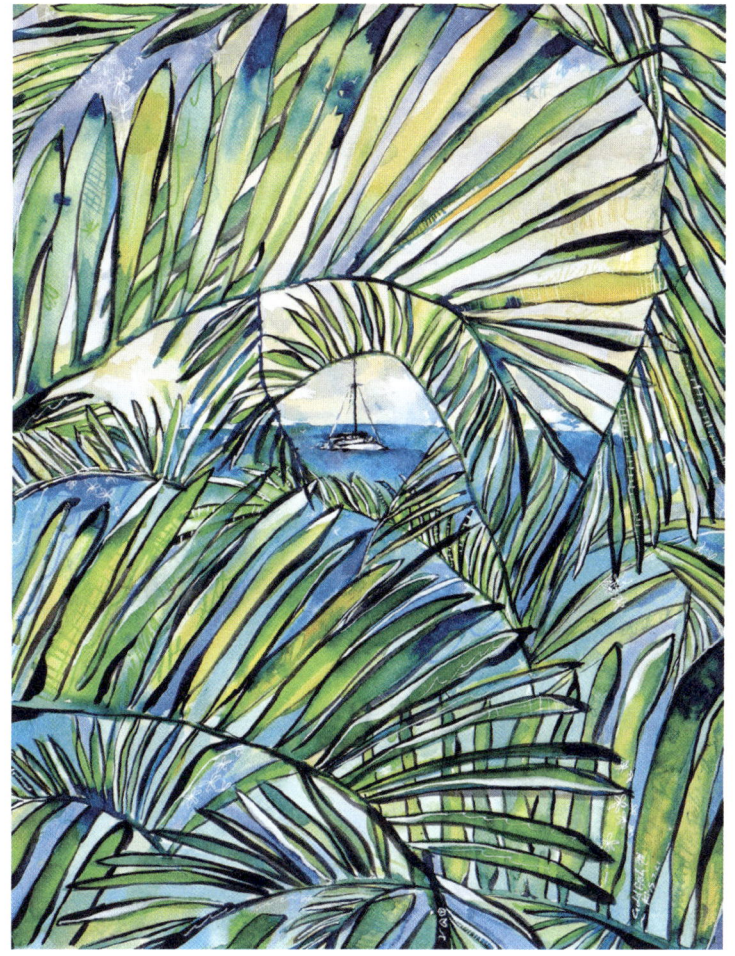

Some of the places I paint are real, and some are real in my dreams

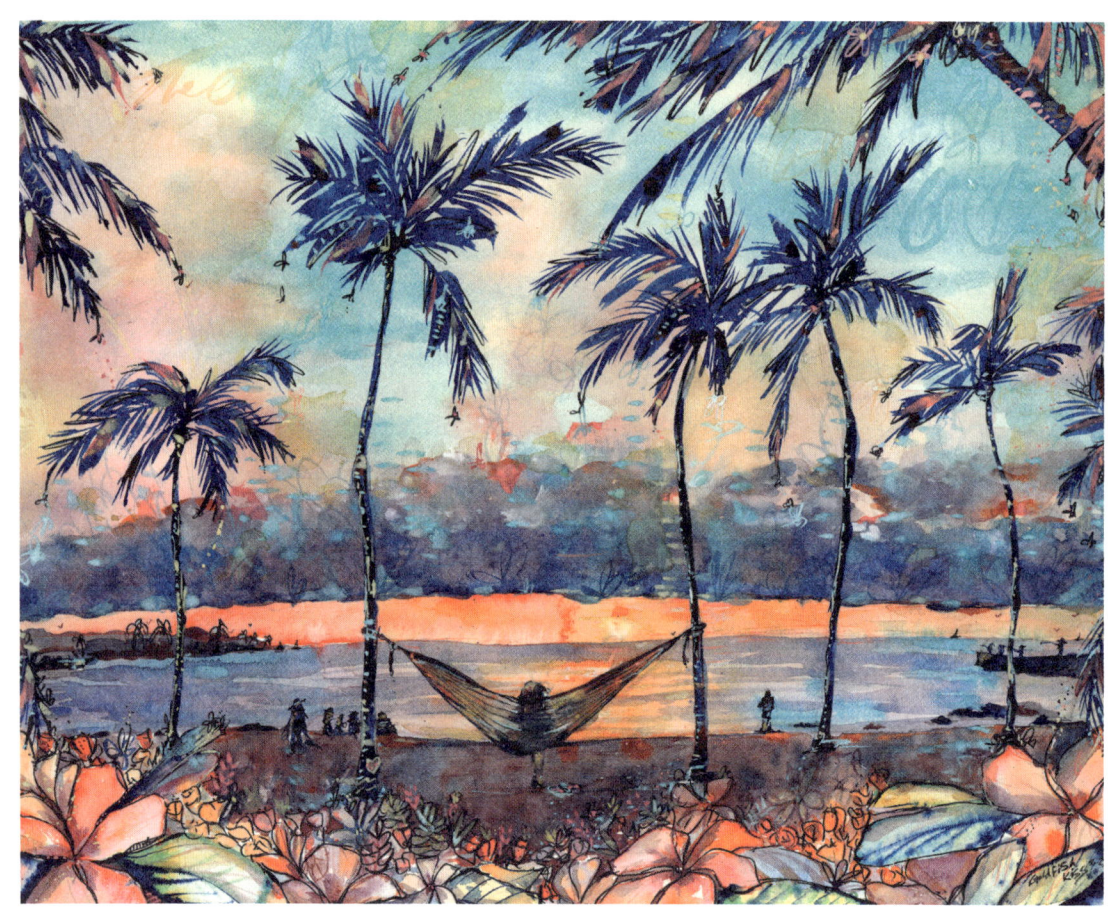

A-Bay sunset

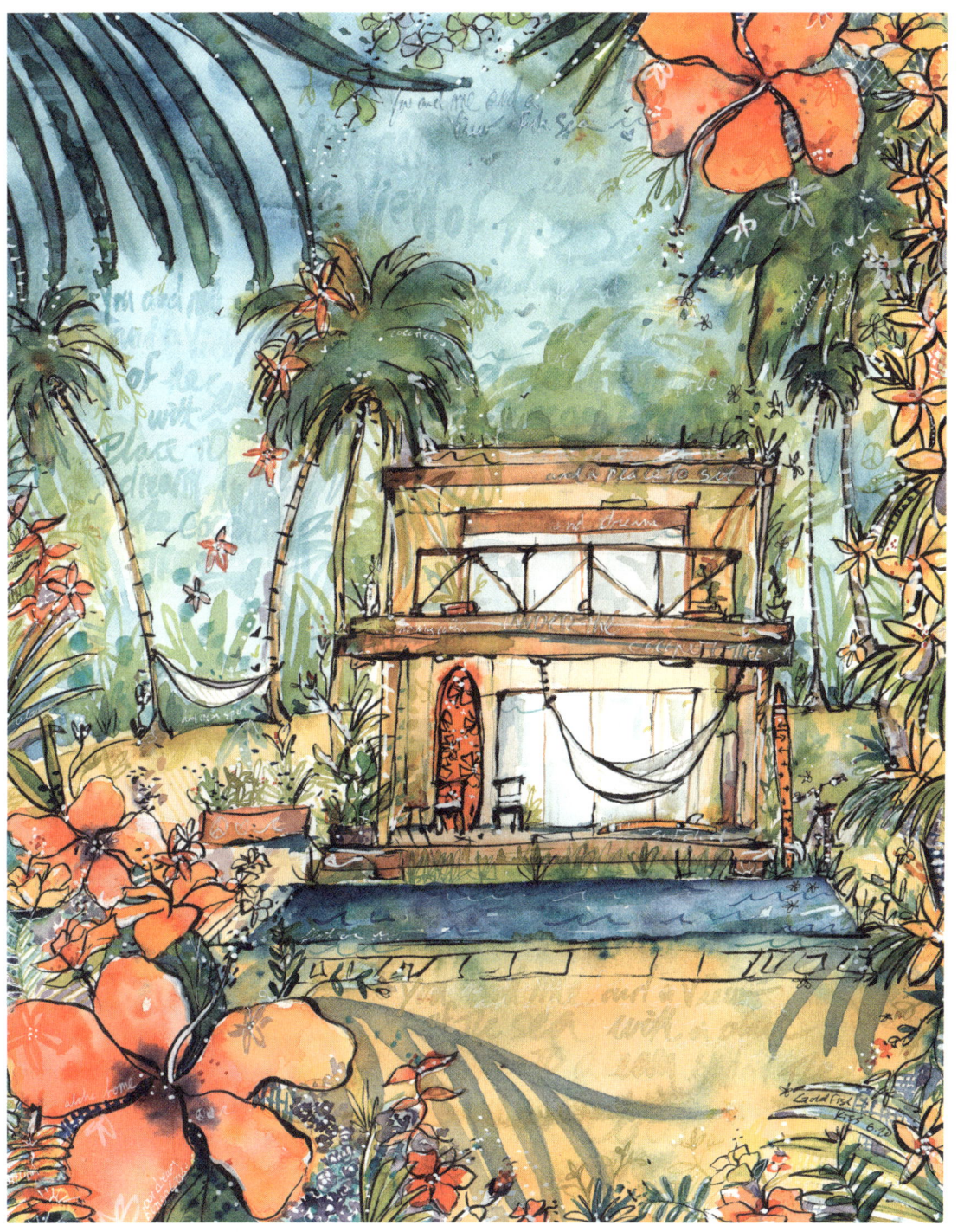

Dream house

Q & A

Rebekah Steen

Who is Rebekah?
My mom pretty much named me
SuperBek – mainly because I've
always been a girl with many
talents and interests, and I kind
of go all in when I find something
I love. I'm an artist, writer,
designer, wife, mom and all-round
creative… and a gal who loves
the fresh air.

If you were to describe your art
in a few lines, you'd say…
I'm embracing the mess and
painting what I'm craving.
Bright, free, salty and tropical
vibes galore.

Can you describe your
painting technique(s)?
I had quite a bit of training in the
Impressionist style of painting, so
that's where my lines and brush-
strokes tend to veer towards.
All my formal schooling was in
oils, and I am now doing water-
colours – a medium where I am
constantly learning new ways
to play with pigments, how the
colours bleed in different ways,
and layering to create dimension
effects I can't replicate. So I guess
free and experimental techniques.

Do the places in your paintings
actually exist? They look dreamy,
I want to be there!
YES! Most of them are places I've
been to and then I tweaked them
quite a bit. So some are real,
and some are real in my dreams.

What does the name of your brand
Goldfish Kiss refer to?
The top of the very first bikini
I owned showed two goldfish
kissing. I was two at the time and
still have the pic of me wearing it.
I always thought it was a catchy
name, and started a blog using it,
and for some reason I prefer signing
my name with that vs. my real name
since the blog is where I started
sharing my art and grew my
audience of art fans because of it.

Do you think creating art
can be therapeutic?
Yes, yes, a thousand times yes. But
what's interesting: as relaxing as it
can be, it is so nerve-wracking as
well. I am my own harshest critic,
and each painting is a cycle of
self-doubt, experimentation and
perseverance, then knowing when
to stop. But the whole process of
putting a juicy brush filled with
pigment on a thick piece of paper
is so soothing, it's remarkable.

When people look at your work,
what would you like them to feel?
Sunshine. I'd like to think it
brightens up their day and takes
them somewhere warm, which
is what it does for me when
I create it.

What kind of paper or paint do you use for your artwork?
I love Arches hot or cold press paper, depending on what I'm painting (hot-pressed paper tends to have a smoother texture than cold-pressed paper, ed.). Then my Sennelier watercolour palette is my base for paints. I fill in with some liquid pigment by Dr. Ph. Martin's. Lukas paints have my favourite turquoise, and I also use Daniel Smith watercolour sticks.

Do you have a favourite quote that inspires or motivates you?
'Get rich each day in ways that don't count at the bank.' It's from Gerry Lopez, at the end of the *Waterman* surf documentary he did a while ago. I pretty much tattooed that on my brain, and even wrote a poem about it.

Do you surf yourself?
Yes, I surf and constantly crave being on a wave or just able to grab my board and drive down to the beach and go catch a few. That was part of my life at one point, but not anymore. I live a bit too far now. The fire is still fuelled, and I get moody if I haven't paddled out in a while.

Where do you currently live?
I live just outside of the Seattle area in Washington. Not too far from the sea, so I can still get to the beach, but I'm about a 3-hour drive from the nearest consistent surf spots. And there aren't really any cams, so it's hard to know for sure what it'll be like once you get out there. I just can't stand driving. It's weird – I'd fly 20+ hours to go surf somewhere for a few days, but a 3-hour drive to surf is painful for me. The area where I live is gorgeous in all seasons, rugged, and there's so much to do in this region. I hike a ton, spend time on the lakes and rivers, and still get outside whenever I can, rain or shine.

Are there other places in the world where you feel at home?
As long as I have some big body of water near me, I feel quite at ease, but I definitely had a connection to Costa Rica last time we were there. Living in Hawaii was a dream, and the place we lived in Florida was a gem. I don't know, I feel like some place I haven't visited yet might hit the jackpot.

Is there something you are particularly proud of?
It's really cool to look at the first painting I ever did, compared to the last few. There's been so much growth and transformation that can only happen from hours and hours and late night after late night of putting brush to paper and never settling, calling it quits or letting my self-doubt get the best of me. I'm super proud of my son, too. He's such a cool kid. And I guess I'm half responsible for that. •

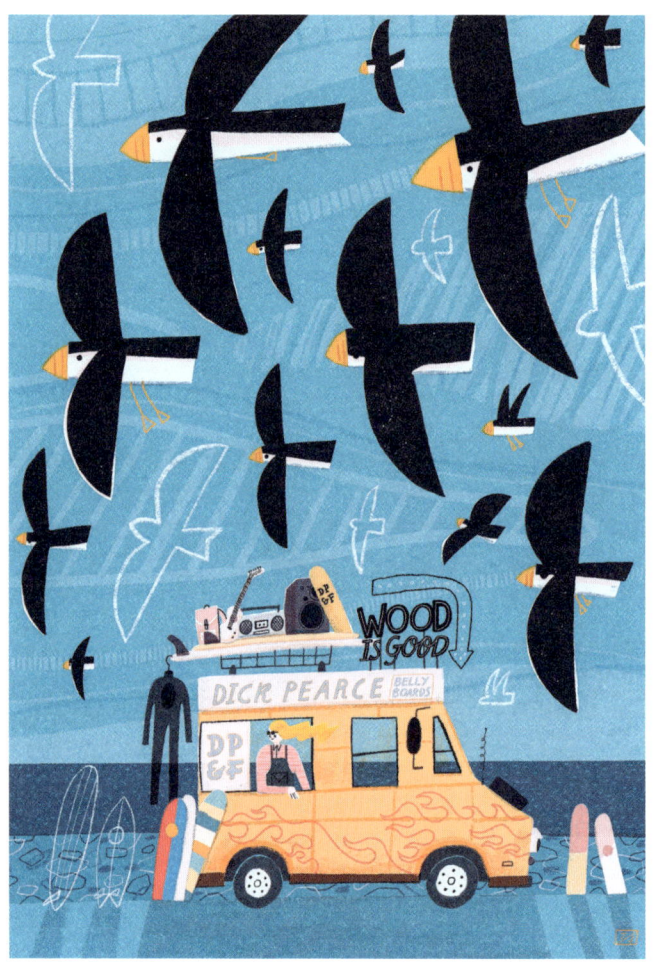

19

Dick Pearce Bellyboards

Seaside nostalgia

Jonty Storey

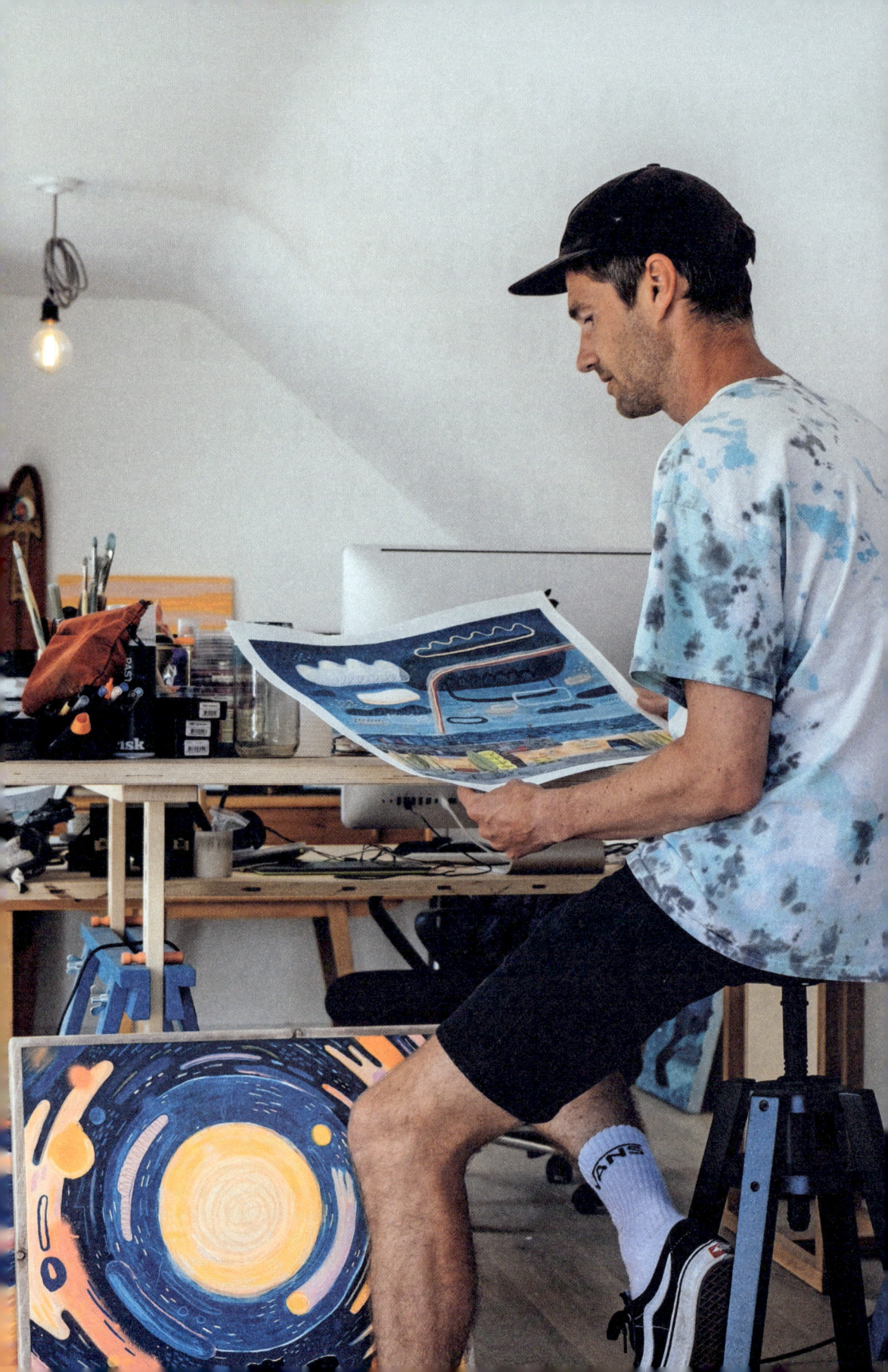

His artwork is a subtle nod to the past, but Jonty Storey keeps the seaside nostalgia contemporary with modern and bold colours. The ever-changing colours and moods of the ocean help him escape from daily life in Wales, just as his paintings do.

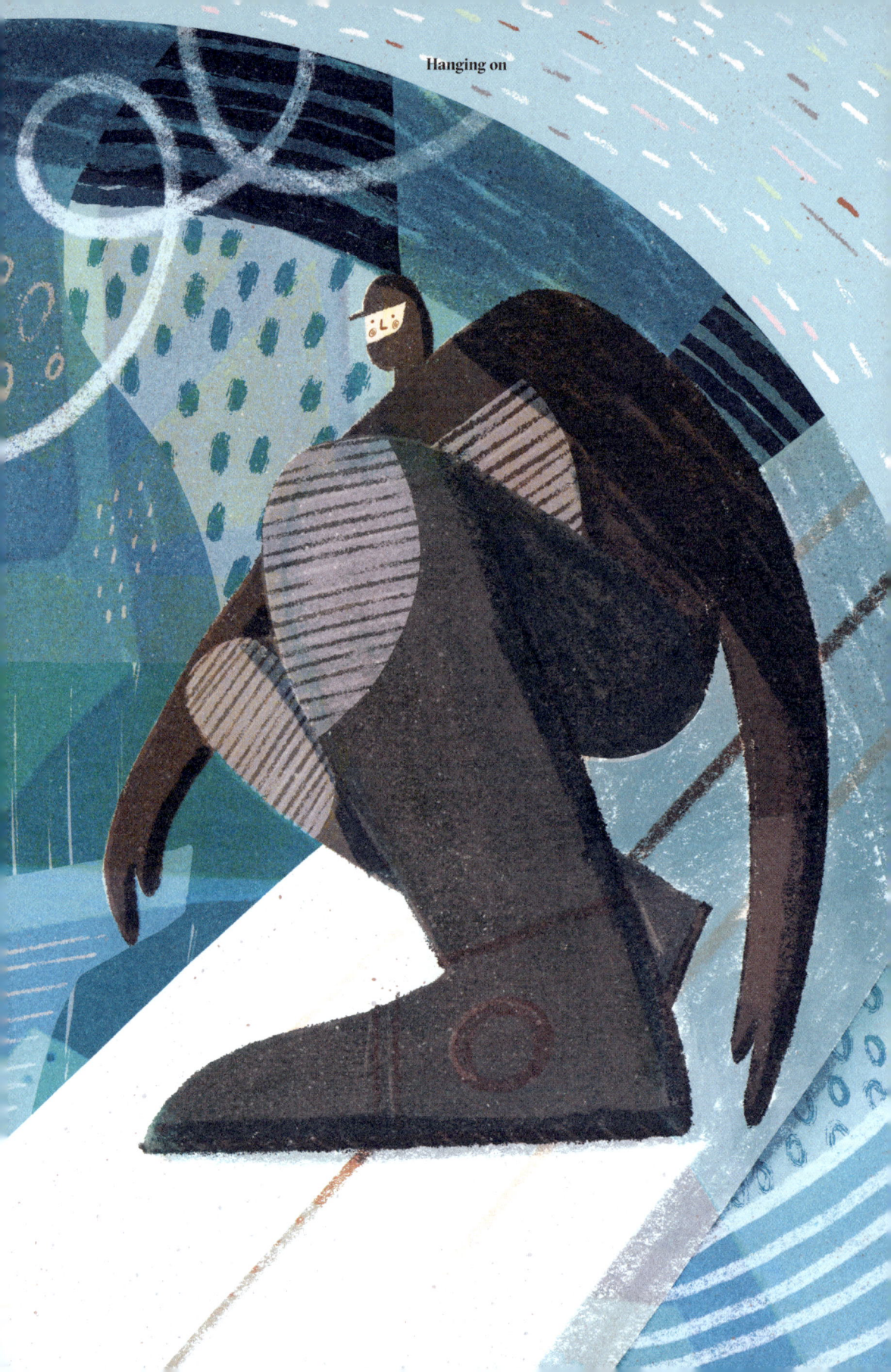

Porth Neigwl (below) is one of
Jonty Storey's local breaks in Wales.

'It's a 15-min walk down to the reef
from the road. The sun has got a
little bit of warmth back in it after a
long winter and spring is beginning
to show up. All the colours seem
vivid and new. You're doing the
half run, half walk thing. The waves
are cooking and you can't get in
fast enough.'

'That is what this painting is about.
It seems to connect with a lot of
people. I guess we all know that
feeling.'

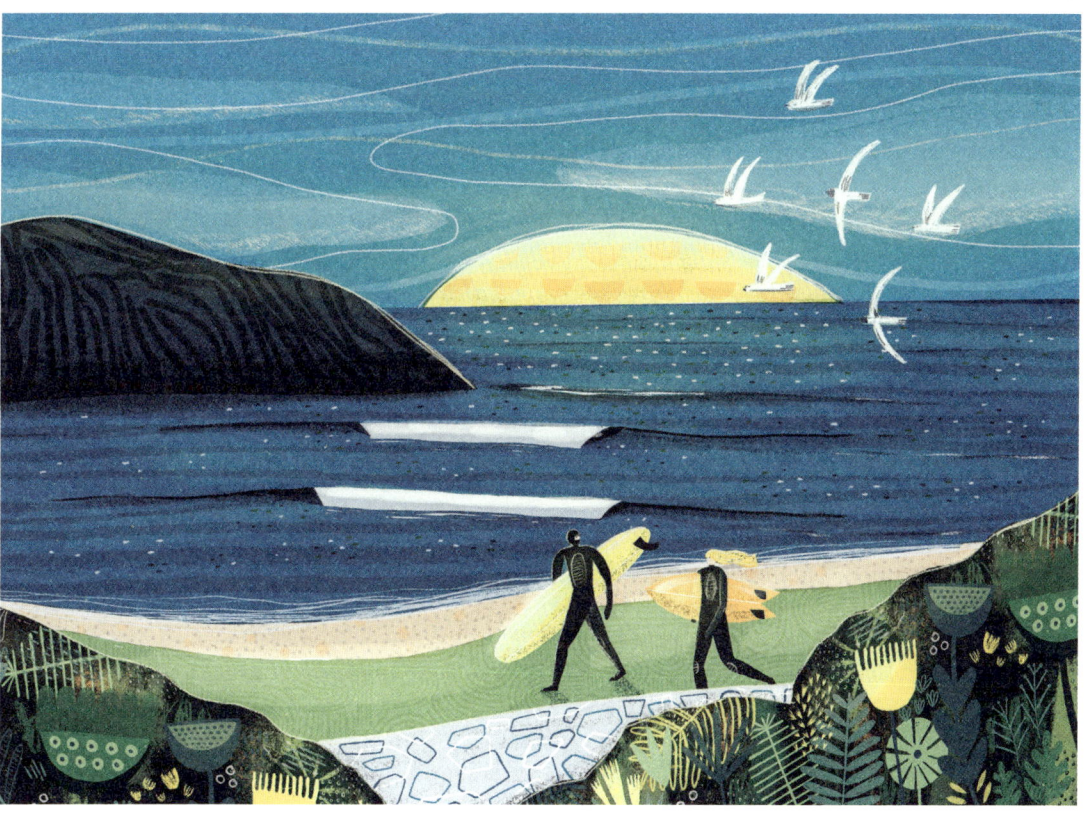

Porth Neigwl

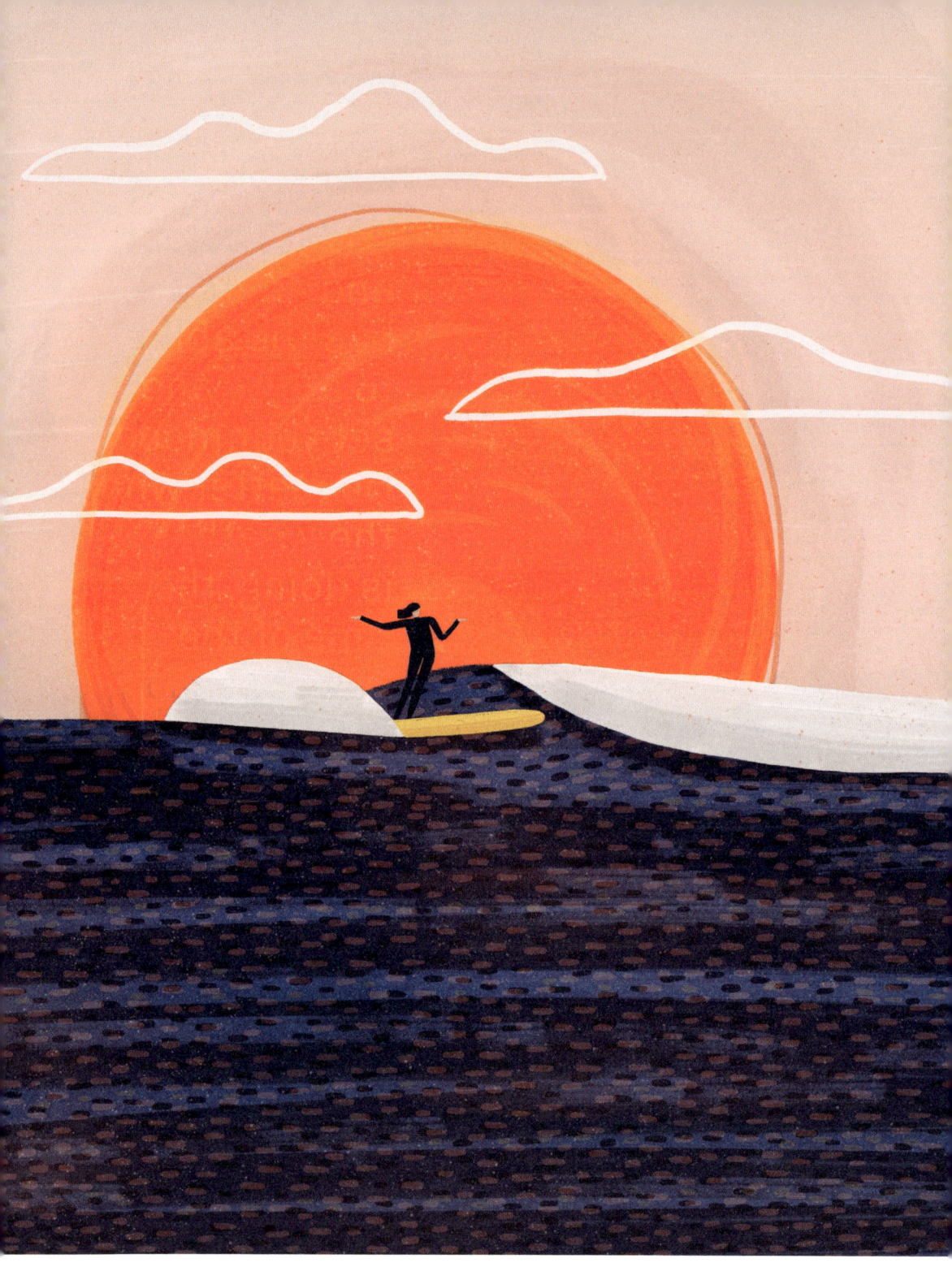

Sundowner

The ocean is a
constant source
of inspiration
and its colour
and energy
has the ability
to affect and
set your mood.
No matter what
the weather
is doing, the
time of the
day or season,
it's always
beautifully
different

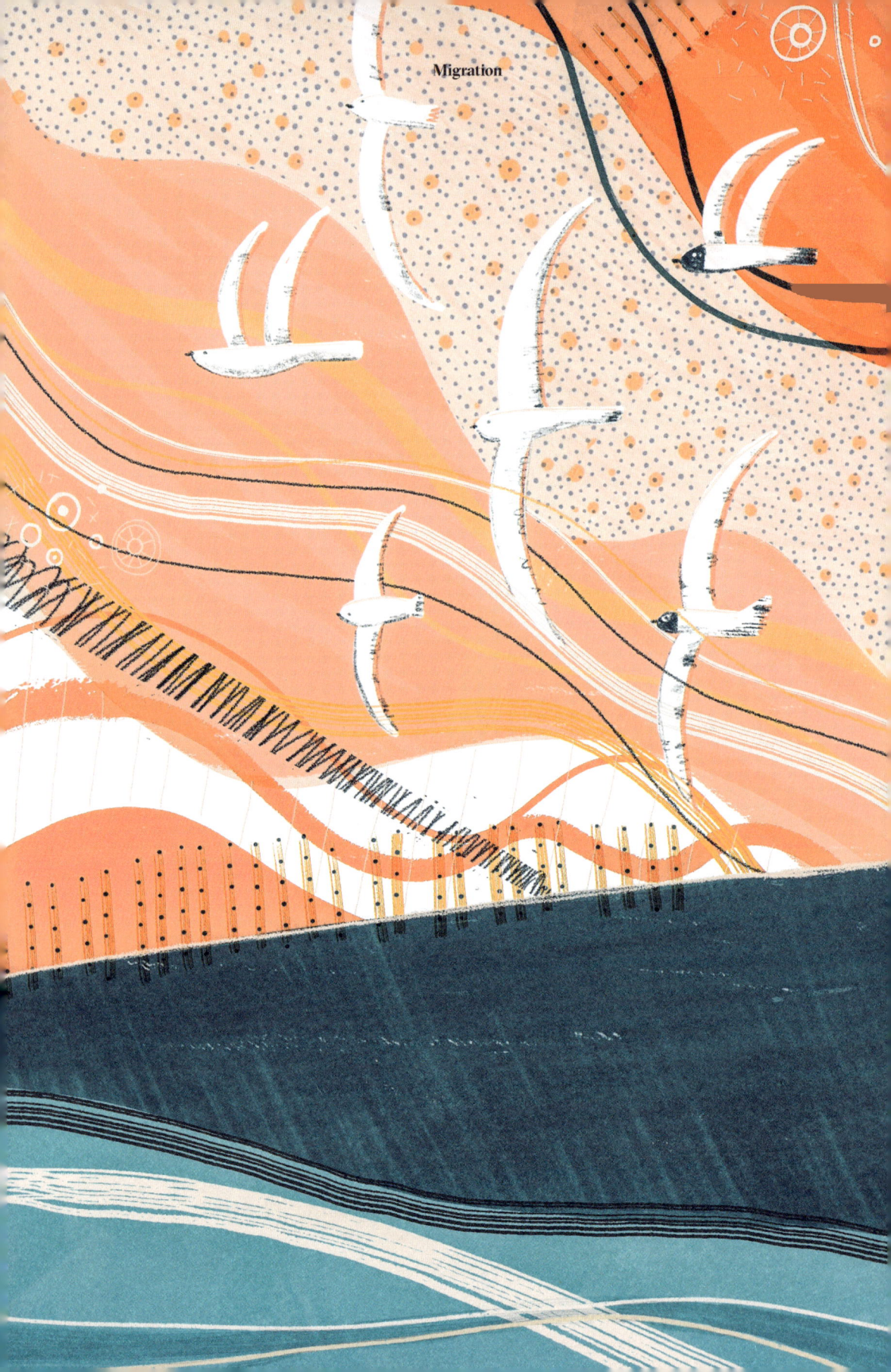
Migration

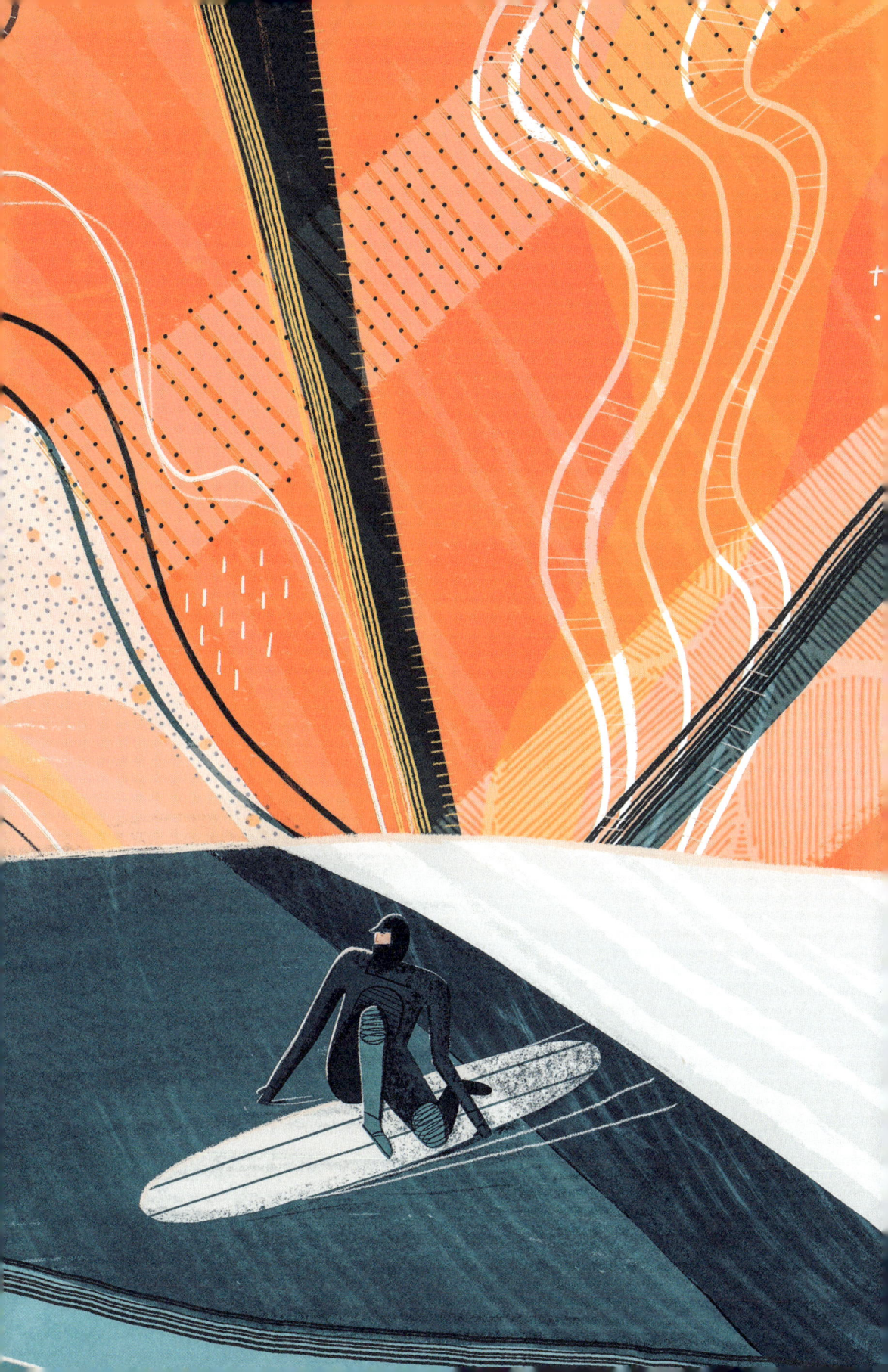

Q & A

Jonty Storey

If you were to describe your art in a few lines, you'd say…
I'm rubbish at this type of question. But I'd say a big influence is old nautical folk art and seaside nostalgia. I love to play with the juxtaposition of rural coast life here in the UK and the rebellious, anti-establishment surf and skate thing. A discreet nod to the past, while using a modern and bold colour palette.

Who is Jonty?
I'm a designer, illustrator and photographer, based by the sea in sunny Llanbedrog, North Wales, with my wife, two kids and tiny dog Beti.

What came first: surfing or drawing?
I've always liked drawing, ever since I was a kid, but I didn't really start surfing properly until my mid-20s. I guess that's when my design career started up too, working for a local surf brand here in Wales.

It seems like you have a go-to colour palette?
Not really. But I guess, looking at my work, there's a consistency of bold, punchy colours. Everything always comes out brighter and bolder than I want, to be honest. It's something I'm always trying to improve and work on. I'd like to have the confidence to be a little bit more subtle.

You use different techniques in your artwork: from risograph to paper cut and collage art. Do they complement each other?
I've always loved that paper cut style. No matter how hard you try to be neat and precise, it's impossible. I think you get some pretty amazing results when you start playing around with pattern and texture. It can transform something pretty boring into something quite special. Even when I'm working digitally, I always want to make it feel organic and analogue. Using a variety of techniques – I feel – gives my art a bit more depth and richness.

You often work with gouache, a water-medium paint using natural pigment. Why does it appeal to you?

It offers a high level of opacity and lends itself to creating vibrant and solid colours. I love it. It also offers a really matt and flat colour, allowing you to work over the top with pencils, pastels and pens.

I think you also have a thing with boats?

It's true! One of my first jobs was driving a little speedboat all summer while towing wakeboarders, ringos and inflatable bananas. I've actually been volunteering on the lifeboat in Abersoch for the last 10 years, which is great fun. It feels good to give something back.

How does the ocean influence your life?

The ocean is a massive part of my family's life, so I'm not sure we could be away from it now. It's a place to unplug and be close to nature. It's a constant source of inspiration and its ever-changing colour and energy has the ability to affect and set your mood. No matter what the weather is doing, the time of the day or season, it's always beautifully different, which amazes me. I find it humbling, terrifying and calming, all at the same time.

I feel like the ocean is almost tangible in your work.

I draw the ocean and surf a lot because I love it. It gives me a feeling I don't get from anywhere else. An escape from the daily grind. I do hope this comes across in my work.

What clients do you work for? Any collaborations you'd like to mention?

I've got some great regular clients including breweries, restaurants and surf shops, but recently I've really enjoyed working with Finisterre, Fjällräven and the Royal National Lifeboat Institution.

What is happening in your life right now?

Life is good: I have two beautiful kids who keep me busy and in check. They both love the sea as much as me, which is amazing. Watching them find their way in and on it is special. I'm also working on my first solo exhibition!

Where do you currently live or surf?

I live in Llanbedrog, almost as far north and west as you can get in Wales, on a little peninsula called Pen Llŷn. It's a bit of a tourist hotspot in the summer when it can get quite hectic, but most of the year it's pretty chilled. Away from the busy tourist villages, it's very rural with rolling hills, windswept cliffs and beautiful, quiet beaches. We get waves in the winter but they're generally cold and pretty fickle. There are a few spots that get good when all the conditions come together, which makes it even sweeter. The best thing is it's quiet – shhhh, don't tell anyone. Most of the time it's just you and a few mates sharing some waves, which is very special. --->

Q & A

Jonty Storey

What does your quiver look like?
I've got a garage full of old boards that I can't bear to throw away but the ones I surf the most are my 9'1" pin tail log for the small days and when the waves are good, I have a 6'6" Middy', which absolutely flies.

Do you have a favourite wave in the world?
I'd say the best surfs I have are at home with just a few of my mates. Like I said, it has its moments here in North Wales when there's only three of you out and it's good. I'd take that over boardies and a crowd.

Are there other places in the world where you feel at home?
I probably wouldn't say I feel at home, but I love the Caribbean. We recently sailed around Grenada and the Grenadines, and that was epic. Also loved spending time in south-west France. They have it pretty sorted there: wine, cheese and waves. All you need in life.

What does surf culture today mean to you?
I'm lucky living where I do because I think the surf culture here is pretty timeless. Everyone's generally quite nice in the line-up and most of the time we're all stoked to be out surfing and sharing waves. When you don't get great waves all the time, I think it gives you a bit more appreciation when they do come. I always have a shock when I go surfing on holiday, or I'm in a different line-up. I hate the agro, everyone hassling the shit out of each other for waves — I'm not sure I'd be surfing much if it was like that. But I don't want to dwell too much on the negatives. Surfing's fun, isn't it?

Can you recommend any other books about surf art?
When I was a stoner kid at art college, me and my pal were obsessed with David Carlson's *End Of Print*. Definitely what got me into design. I just grabbed it off the shelf now and got an instant hit of nostalgia. His *Transworld Skate* and *Surfer* mag stuff was so original and rad, you can still see its influence today. I guess that's maybe where the 'cutting things out' came from in my work.

Has surfing given you anything in life?
I have a pretty addictive personality, so I think surfing gives me some kind of anchoring. Definitely something to keep me busy and out of trouble. I can pretty much guarantee, even if the waves are poor, I'll always be happier when I come out of the water. I get so much joy now my kids are surfing, even when my son is snaking and dropping in on me. I think I've had some of the happiest moments in the surf with my two kids, and I know there will be many more to come. •

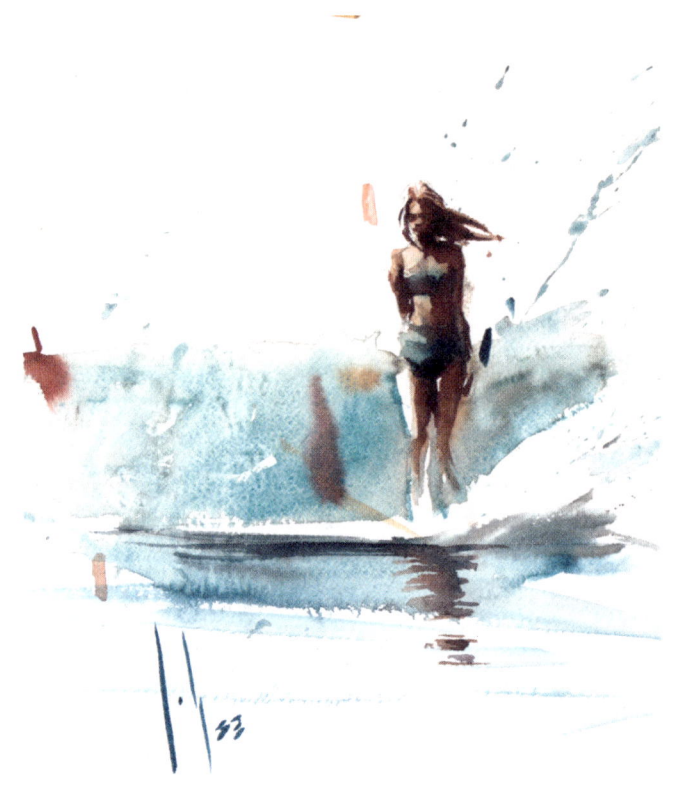

20

Surf bless

Watercolour dreams

Johny Vieira

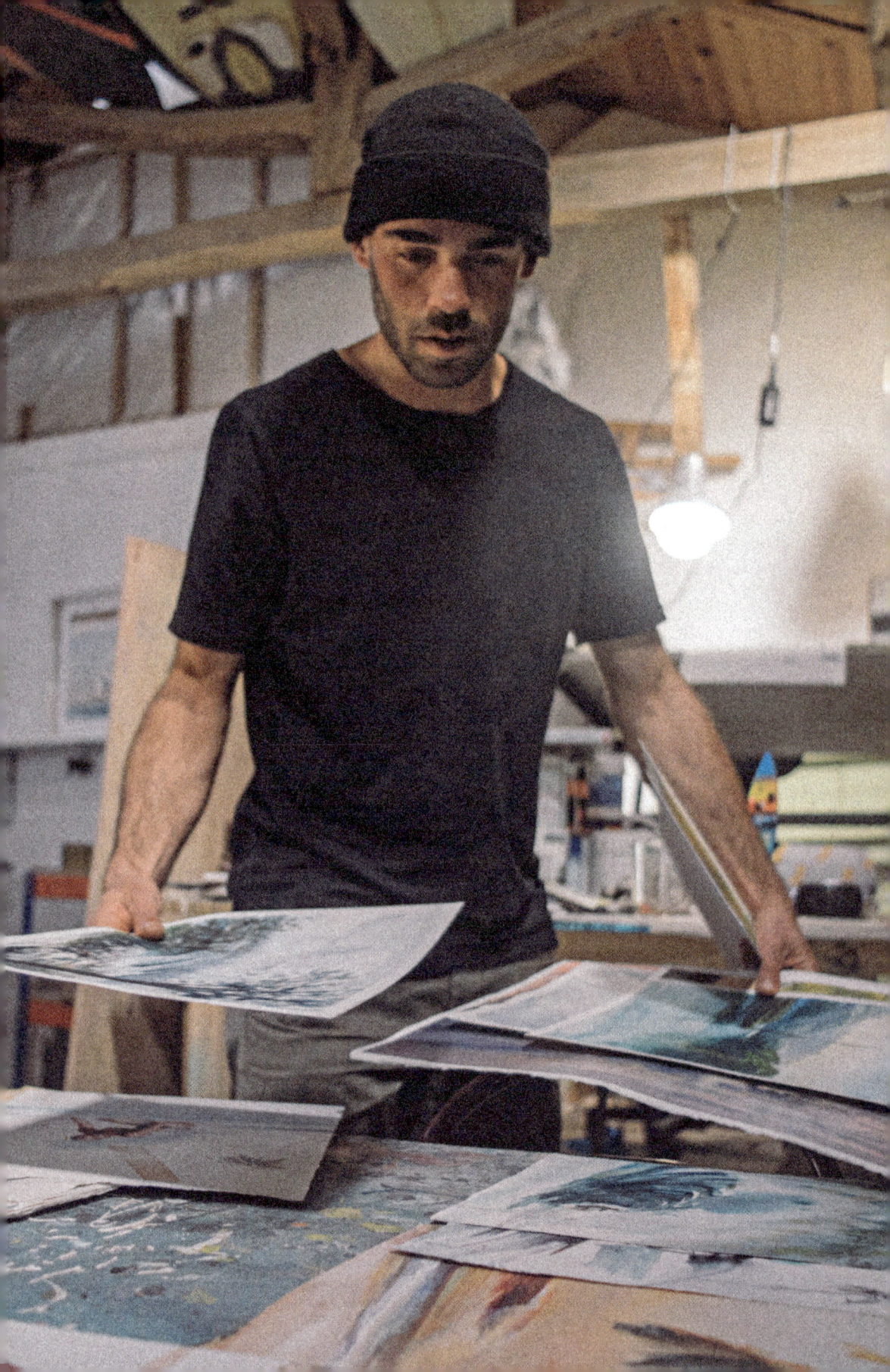

Living a nomadic life in his camper van, somewhere between Spain and Portugal, Johny Vieira captures surfers' moves in an almost poetic way and creates watercolour paintings that make us daydream.

Daydream

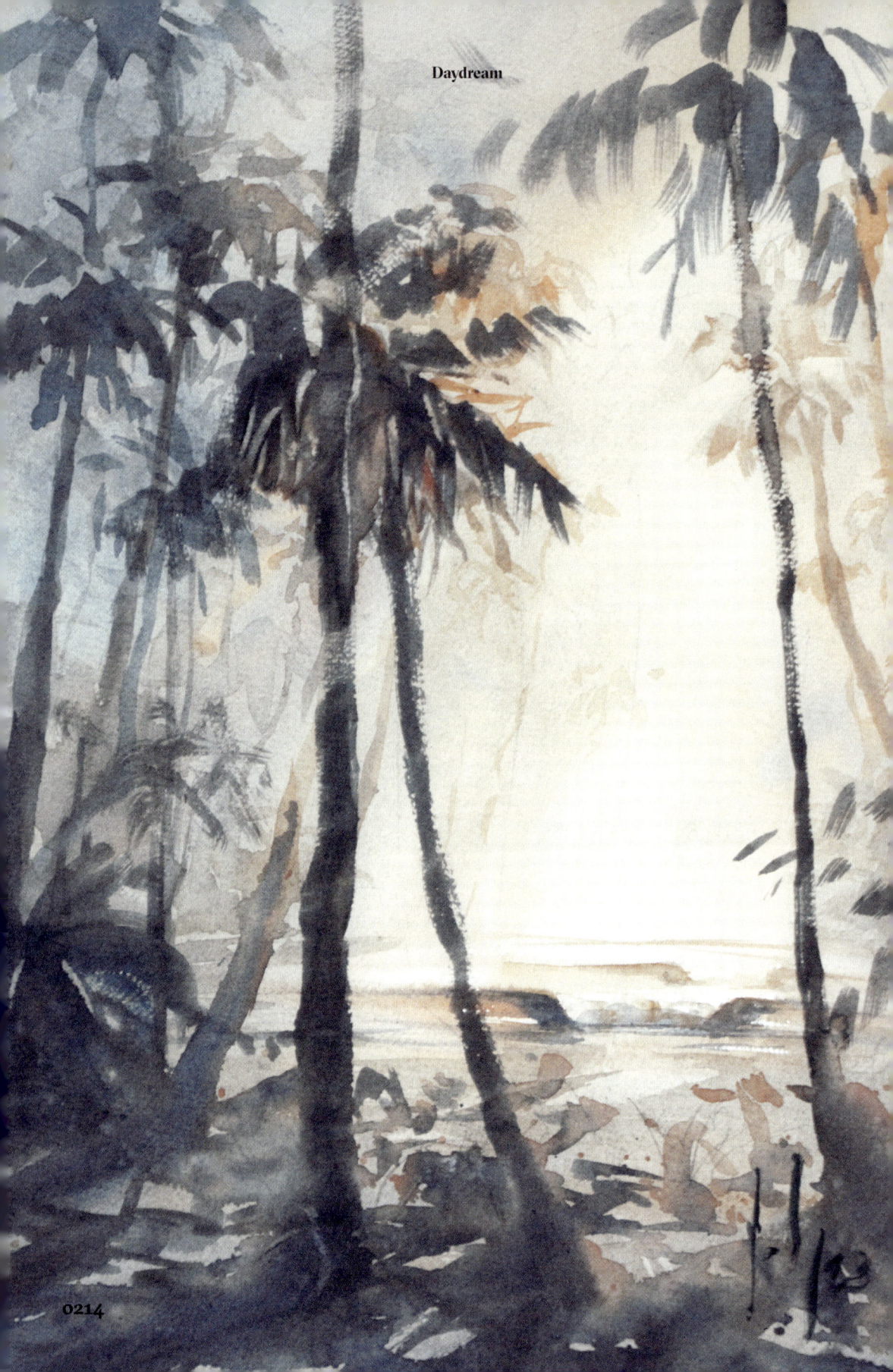

'Daydream' (left) is a place that doesn't exist. 'It's one of many attempts to capture a familiar surf scene that frequently visits my dreams', says Vieira, who mainly paints watercolour art.

'I often find myself in a place where there are no human traces, free from noise and visual clutter. It's a peaceful feeling, a silence that goes through the veins, and makes me feel good.'

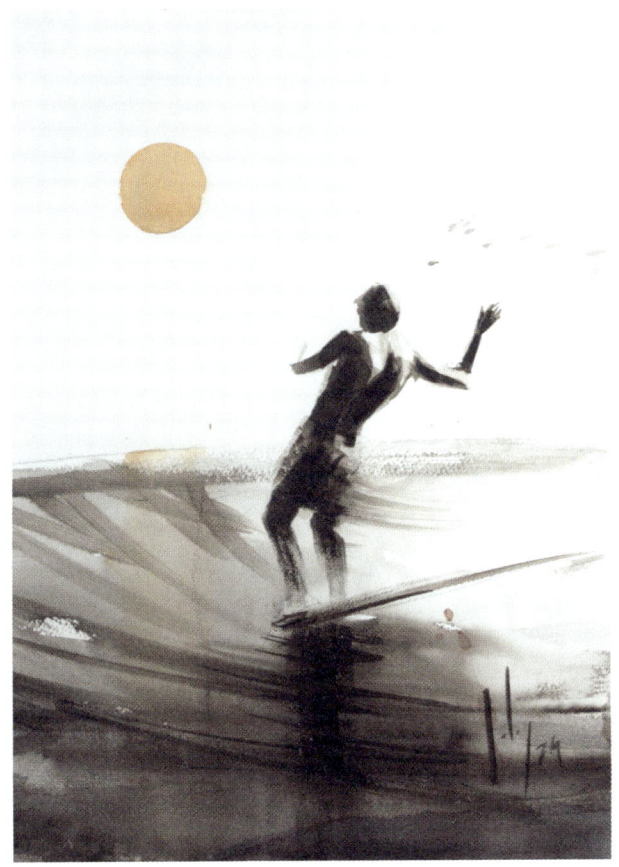

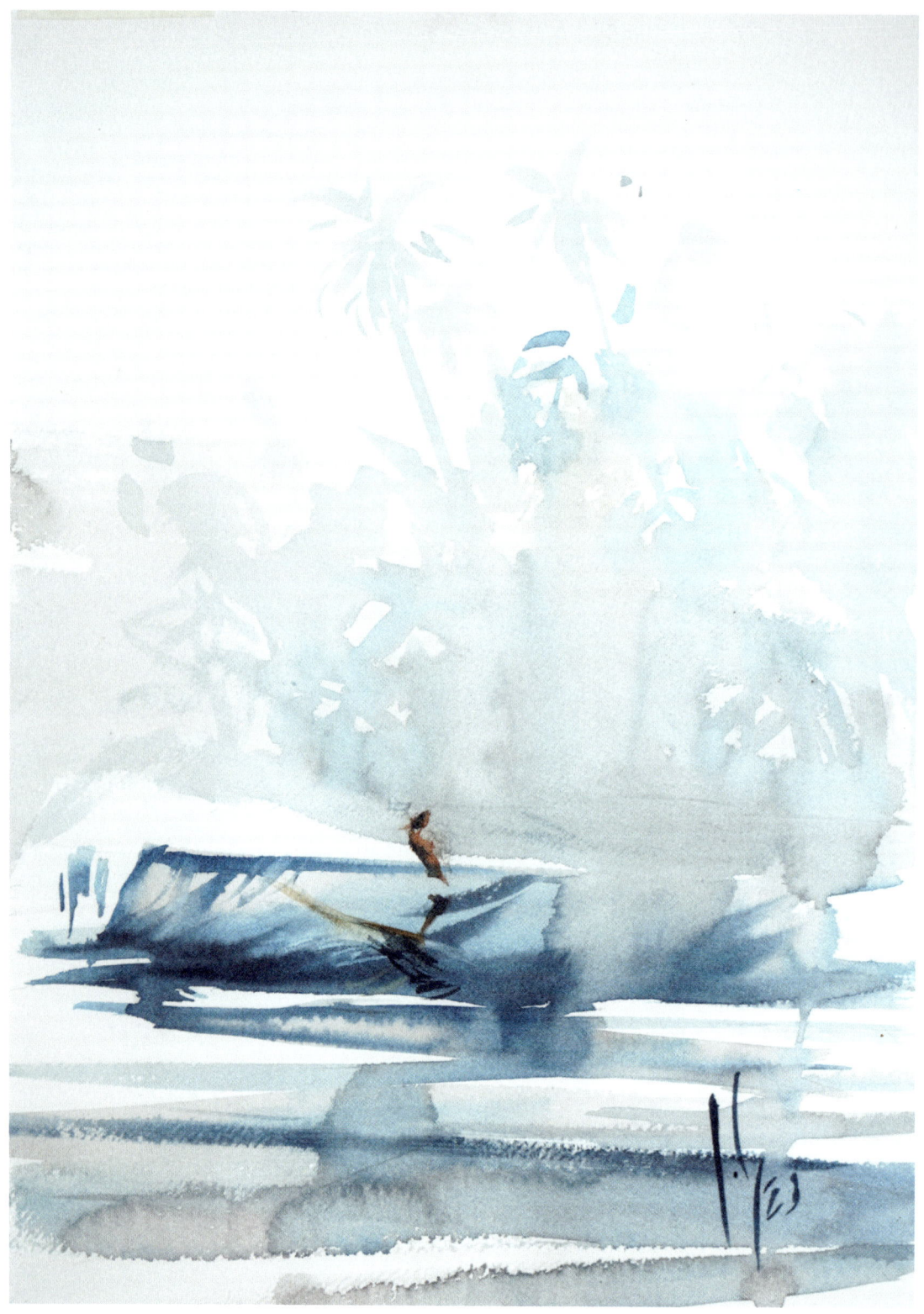

Freedom

Today's surf culture, influenced by industry, tourism and the digital age, has changed from its romantic, raw and pure past

Q & A

Johny Vieira

Who is Johny?
I wonder that too sometimes. But in short, I think I'm a human being who likes to surf and create.

What came first: surfing or painting?
Surfing came first, in 1999. Art came slowly after that. First with sculptures, and then painting, about seven to eight years ago.

If you were to describe your art in a few lines, you'd say...
My art is about the connection between humans and the ocean through surfing. It represents the feelings and balance that surf brings into our lives. All my paintings are watercolour. I use a traditional technique but try to add a loose style to it.

How does the ocean influence your life/work?
In all possible ways. Since my teenage years, most of my jobs have been ocean-related, such as lifeguard, surf coach and surf judge. I've spent a significant part of my life on the beach. When the waves are good, I go surfing. When there are no waves, I turn to painting. The ocean is a source of energy and inspiration for me. Travelling and seeking out empty line-ups with perfectly breaking waves makes me feel alive. These sensations ultimately find expression in my work.

When did you first think: I can do this for a living?
When I was learning how to paint, COVID hit, and I got stuck in the Canary Islands. At that time I was living off sculptures and surf lessons, which suddenly weren't possible anymore. It pushed me to paint daily and try to sell my work, and surprisingly that worked.

When people look at your work, what would you like them to feel?
I want them to feel that we are part of nature, and we don't need much to have a peaceful life. Take a moment to consider the importance of the ocean in our lives.

Do you have an opinion on price setting in the world of surf art?

I have no idea. I just want to be accessible for surfers who feel touched by my art, not for art collectors who wonder if the artist is going to become famous over the next few years. Obviously, I prefer prices that make it possible to pay my bills at the end of the month. To be honest, I'm a terrible salesman.

Do you have a favourite quote that inspires or motivates you?

Normality is a paved road: it's comfortable to walk, but no flowers grow on it,' by Vincent Van Gogh.

What is happening in your life right now?

Over the past two years, I have been feeling a bit down, perhaps not putting in 100% effort into my work. I've been working the minimum, I dedicated more time to myself, and enjoyed life through travel while trying to understand what I want to create next.

Where do you currently live or surf?

I have been living a somewhat nomadic life in my mobile home, travelling around Portugal and Spain over the past year. There are many places to explore and enjoy on this small peninsula.

What is your favourite surfboard at the moment?

I'm loving a 7ft twin fin pin tail from Portuguese master and shaper Cartaxanas (SPO Surfboards), perfect for long wide lines and barrels.

Are there other places in the world where you feel at home?

My home base is Santa Cruz in Portugal, but actually all of Portugal makes me feel at home.

Has surfing given you anything in life?

I guess it has given me a lot more than I can account for: friendships, life lessons from the ocean, job opportunities, and not forgetting my mental and physical wellbeing.

Is there something you are particularly proud of?

I think I'm proud of being me all my life, to have created my own path, living my life the way I think is best for me.

What does surf culture today mean to you?

Surf culture embodies the behaviours, traditions, creations and beliefs of surfers – those from the past and those adopted along the way. Today's surf culture, influenced by industry, tourism and the digital age, has changed from its romantic, raw and pure past. There are more surfers plus more information, but the number of spots remains the same. This means crowds and they have changed our surf experience and the way people behave in and out of the water. It's sad to go surfing when people paddling just a metre away from you don't say 'hi' or 'good morning'. There's a larger group of individuals, but unfortunately with a smaller sense of community. But, on the bright side, more people are making a living from it, and we see more art related to surf. •

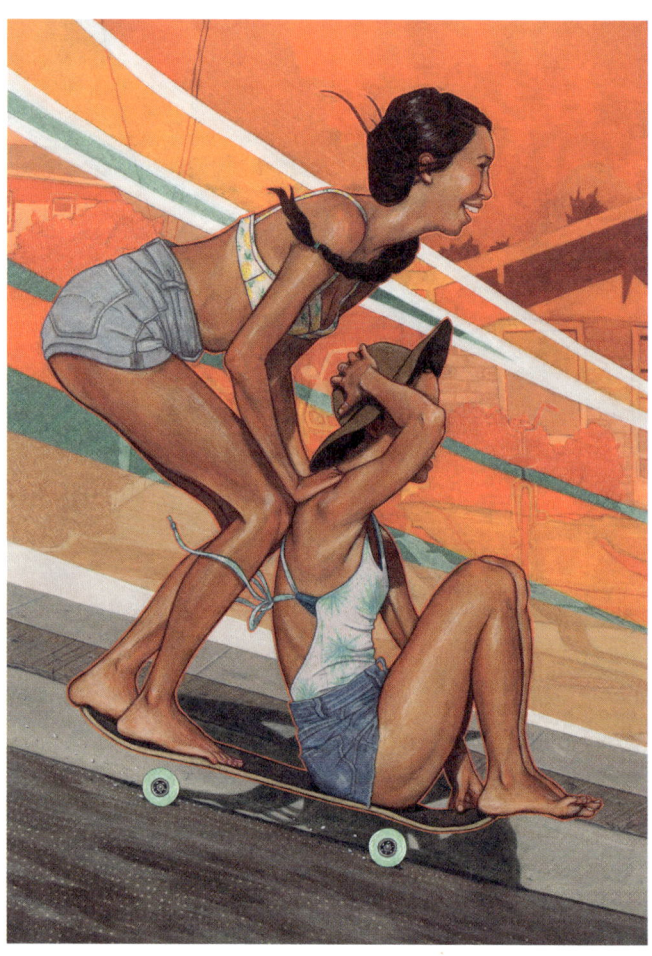

21

Kahili Hill

Surf & skate

Kate Wadsworth

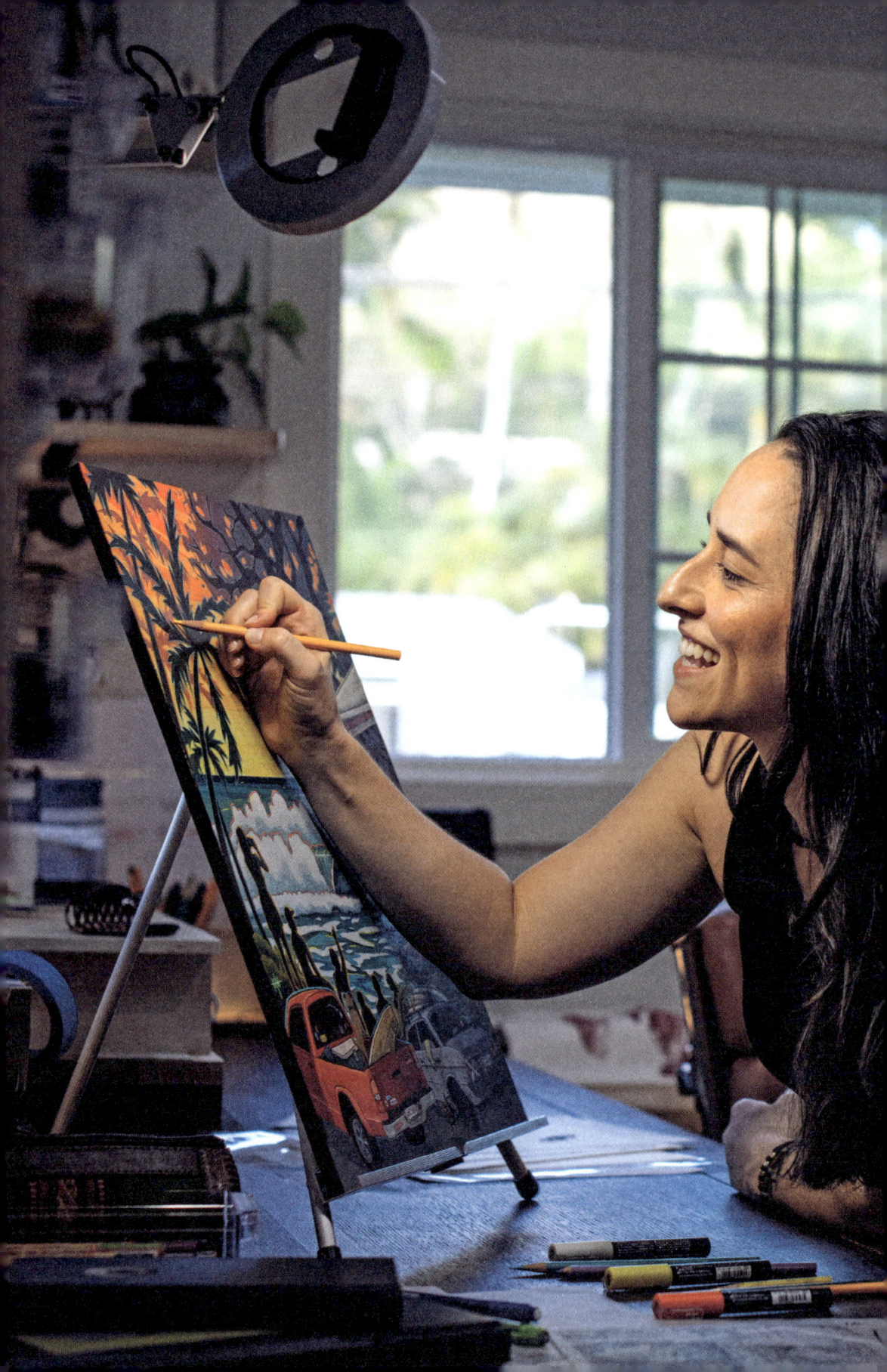

Surf and skate culture are predominant in the figurative works by Hawaii-based Kate Wadsworth. Her art features a sense of summertime nostalgia that makes us wonder about island life.

Moku Manu Surfers

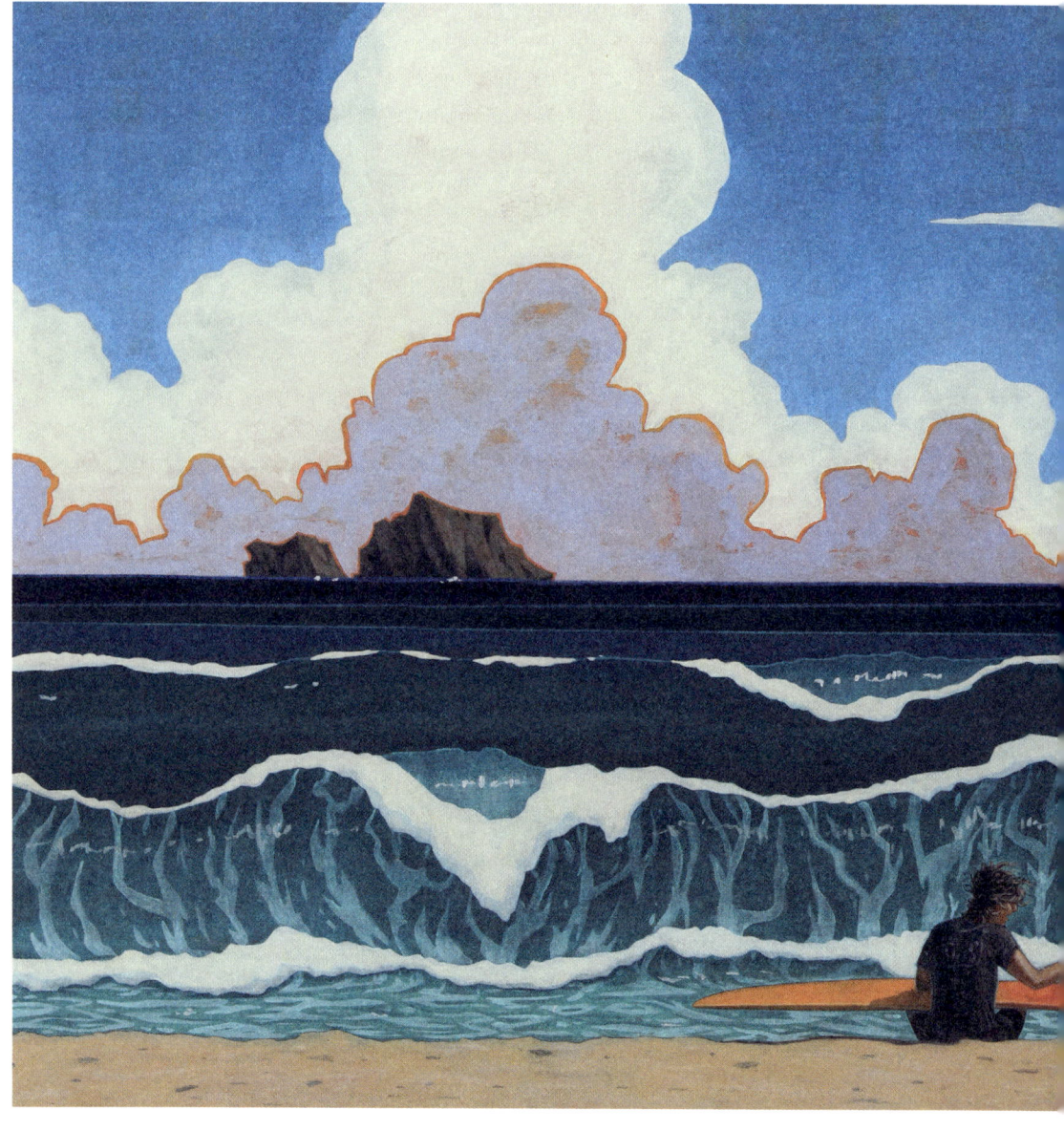

This illustration is based on a specific moment. 'The weather was perfect and the waves crystal clear but crashing hard,' says Wadsworth. 'The foam mirrored the big puffy clouds in the sky. I snapped a photo of a trio of surfers and this was my interpretation of two of them having a friendly pre-surf conversation.'

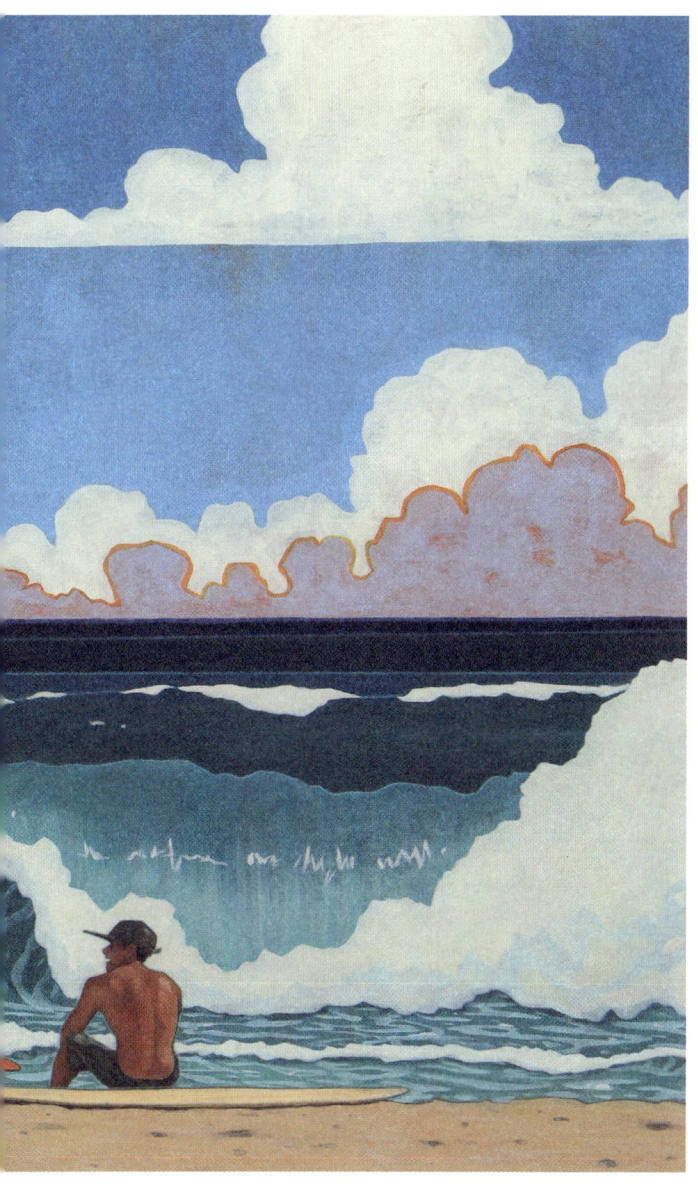

I tend to
illustrate
subjects from
a more light-
hearted side.
In general,
I hope my work
sparks a bit of
joy or silliness

This illustration was created
for a 2020 Vans Pro surf contest,
a qualifying event for the Vans
Triple Crown of Surfing. It's inspired
by the famous winter swell
at Sunset Beach in Hawaii.

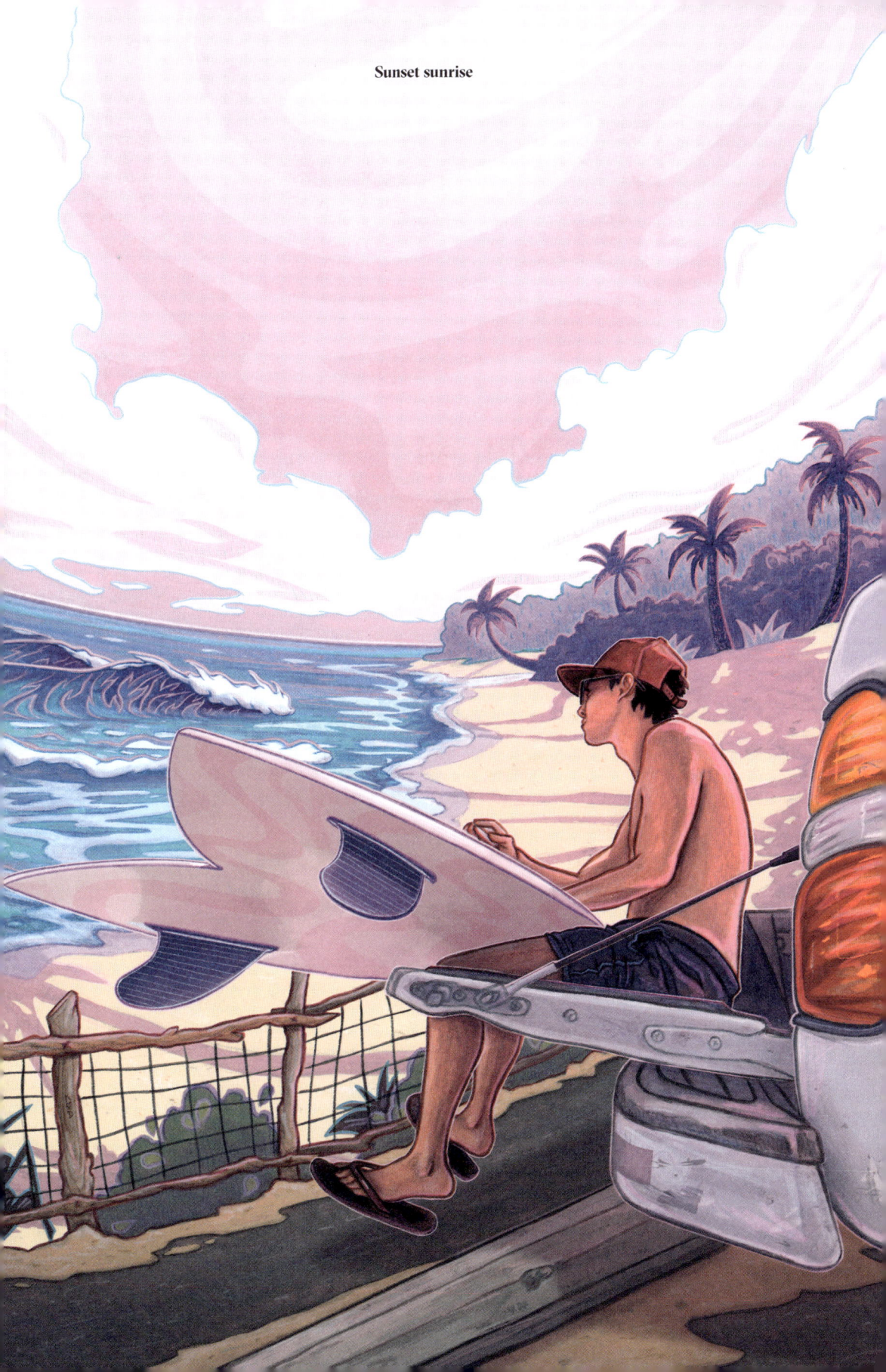

Sunset sunrise

Q & A

Kate Wadsworth

Who is Kate?
I'm an illustrator, graphic designer and muralist from Kailua, Hawaii.

What came first: surfing or drawing?
Definitely drawing. I have been drawing, painting and pursuing artistic things for as long as I can remember. I am also much more of a surf appreciator than an actual surfer. (laughs)

If you were to describe your art in a few lines, you'd say…
I love to experiment with bold colours and exaggerated shapes. You might call it figurative art or urban sketching.

I think the ocean is also present?
The ocean is a place of restoration for me. I spend a lot of time at home behind a desk, so waking up early to catch the sunrise at the beach or going beach camping are some of my favourite things to reset and find balance. Sitting in the sand and watching the waves can be meditative, and I consider swimming in the ocean healing. Surf (and skate) culture was also prevalent in my upbringing and, as an adult, it keeps finding a way into my work. I often illustrate versions of my friends and my favourite places – and living in Hawaii, we're surrounded by the ocean, so it's certainly a big influence and inspiration.

How does your art come to life?
I always start with a pencil in my sketchbook when I'm brainstorming ideas. Once I have a solid concept, I'll bring my sketch onto my iPad and do some colour studies in Procreate or Photoshop. If I want the final artwork to be digital, I'll finish the work in Procreate. If I want it traditional, I'll transfer my final drawing back onto a wood panel (or paper) to be painted with a mix of acrylic paints, coloured pencils and paint markers.

When people look at your work, what would you like them to feel?
I suppose it depends on the illustration and the viewer. I tend to illustrate subjects from a more light-hearted side, and often with a sense of summertime nostalgia. In general, I hope my work sparks a bit of joy or silliness, and creates a feeling of warmth or relatability.

You've had the privilege of working for international clients. Which collabs are special to you?
I've created poster artwork for Vans and Sony; editorial illustrations for *Hawaii Business Magazine*, the *Los Angeles Times* and NBC News; and last year my first picture book was published with Kokila, an imprint of Penguin Books.

What's the story behind the book?
I was asked to illustrate Srividhya Venkat's story *Girls on Wheels*, published by Kokila. It's a wonderful story inspired by the real-life skateboarding revolution happening in India, and follows three friends who learn to skate at their local skatepark.

You were chosen to create an artwork for the Vans Triple Crown of Surfing. Is that a special honour?
Creating the Triple Crown poster was a bucket list item for me. I've been a fan of Vans all my life, and working with them is a dream come true. The event, however, was bittersweet. I created the poster art for the 2020 competition. Because of the COVID pandemic, spectators weren't allowed to gather on the beach and watch like usual. 2020 was a weird year, but it's still one of my favourite projects.

Where do you currently live or surf?
I live in beautiful Hawaii, the birthplace of surfing! So I'm a bit embarrassed to say that I am not a surfer. I tried several times when I was younger, but I ended up taking up paddling instead, with an outrigger canoe club (specific type of canoe, ed.). We'd have practices and races in the ocean, and if the steersman lined us up just right, we'd catch a wave in the canoe.

Do you have a favourite quote that motivates or inspires you?
Maya Angelou said: 'You can't use up creativity. The more you use, the more you have.' •

22

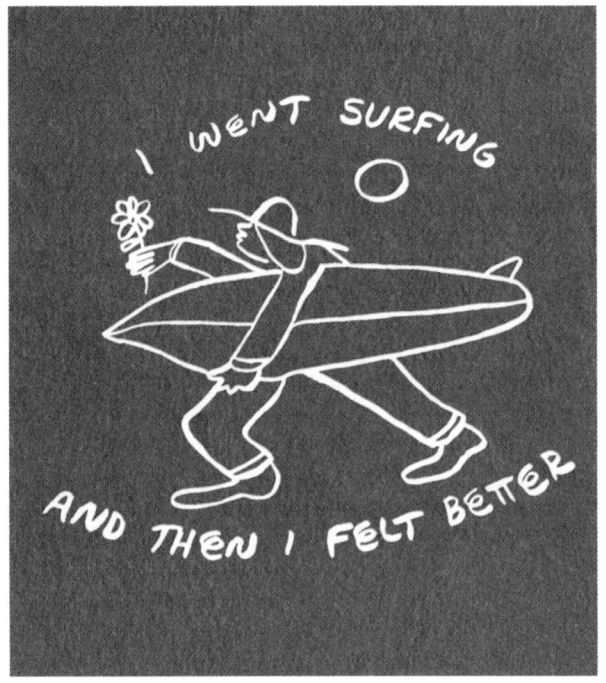

Feel better

Saltwater cures

Ty Williams

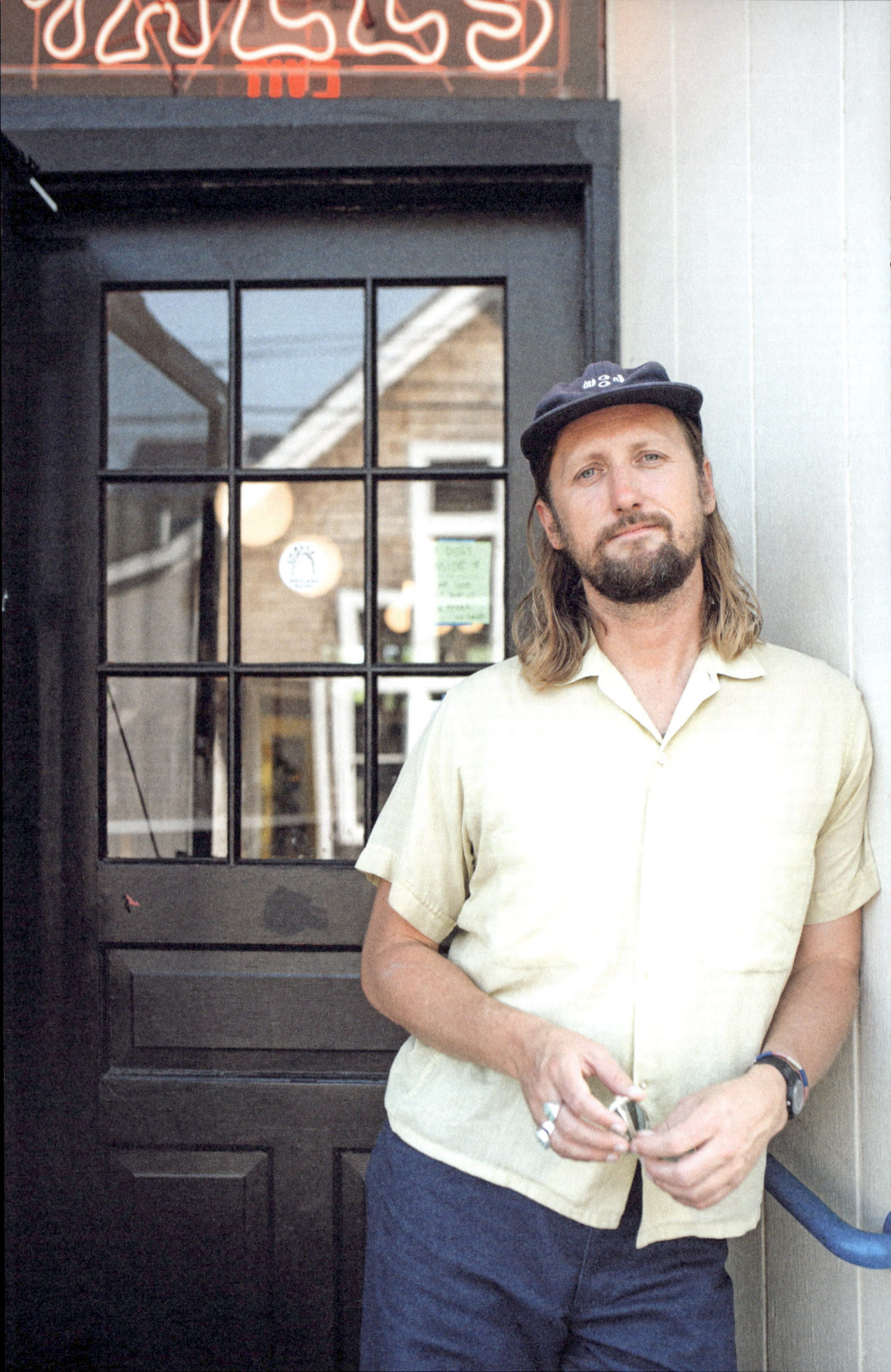

The art of American artist Ty Williams is often described as whimsical and hopeful, always influenced by surfing and the salty New England coastline.

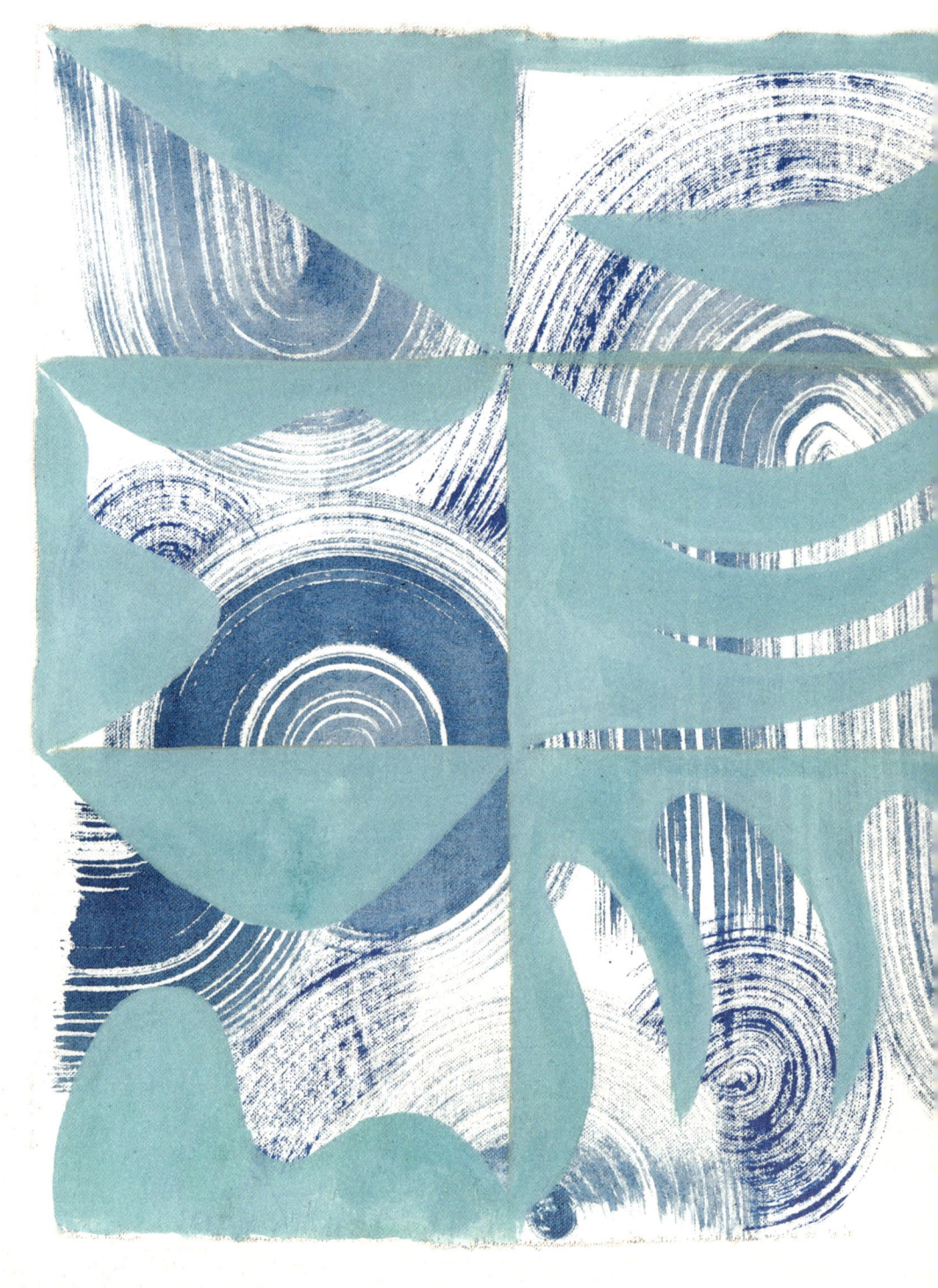

In between tides

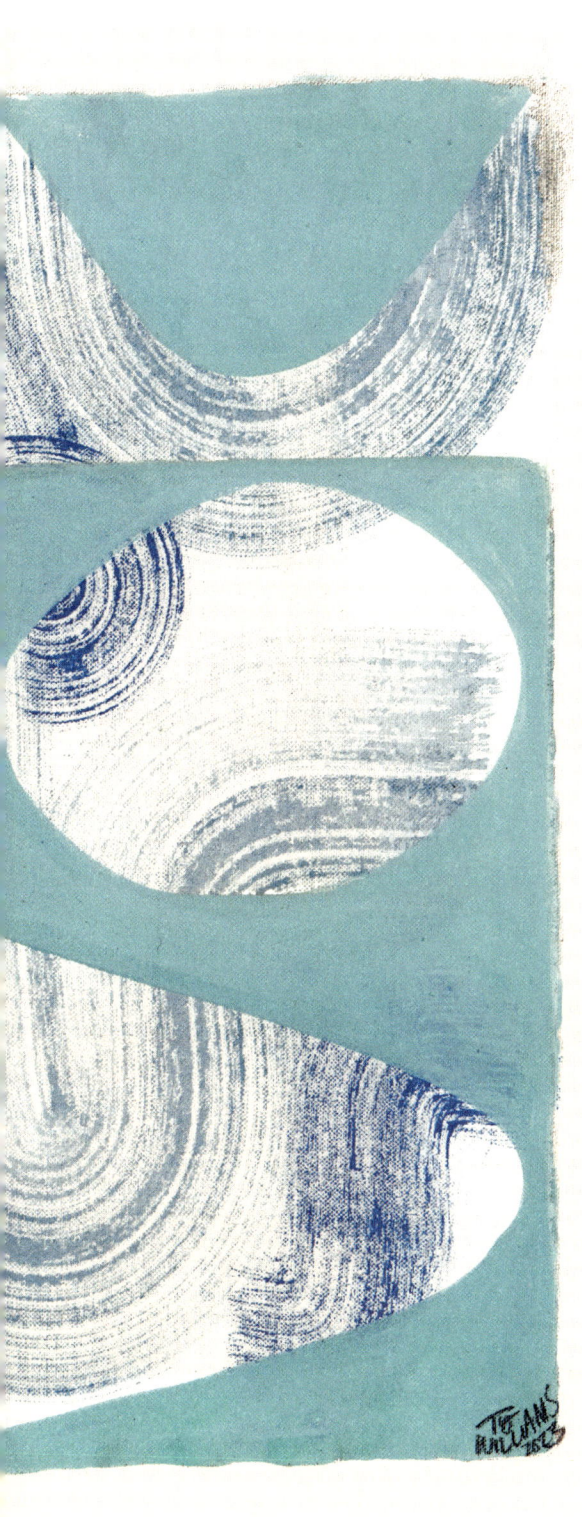

Some of Williams' artworks speak for themselves, such as his cute and rather famous illustration 'salt water can fix that'. However, the American artist also creates paintings open for interpration like this one, 'In between tides'.

Surf culture is
always ebbing
and flowing but
the constant
element that
I appreciate is
the desire to
explore and
ride waves

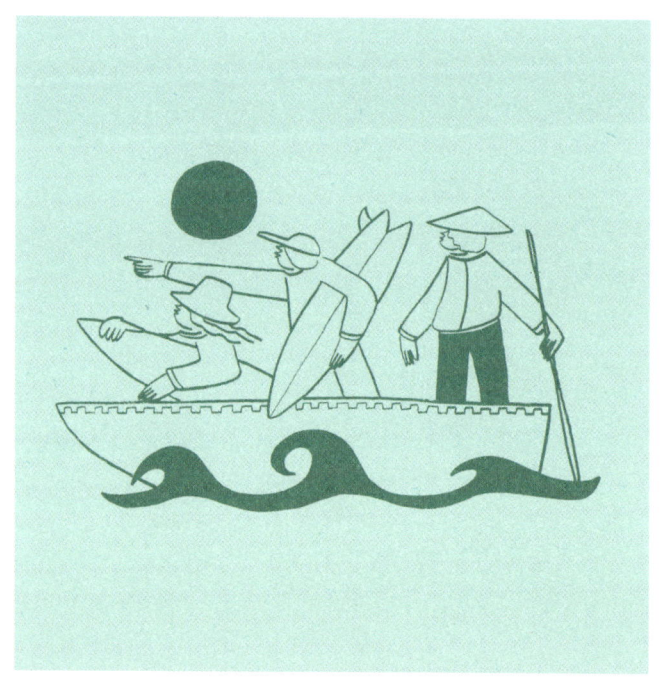

Searching

IT'S EASIER TO FLOW THAN SLAM ON THE BRAKES

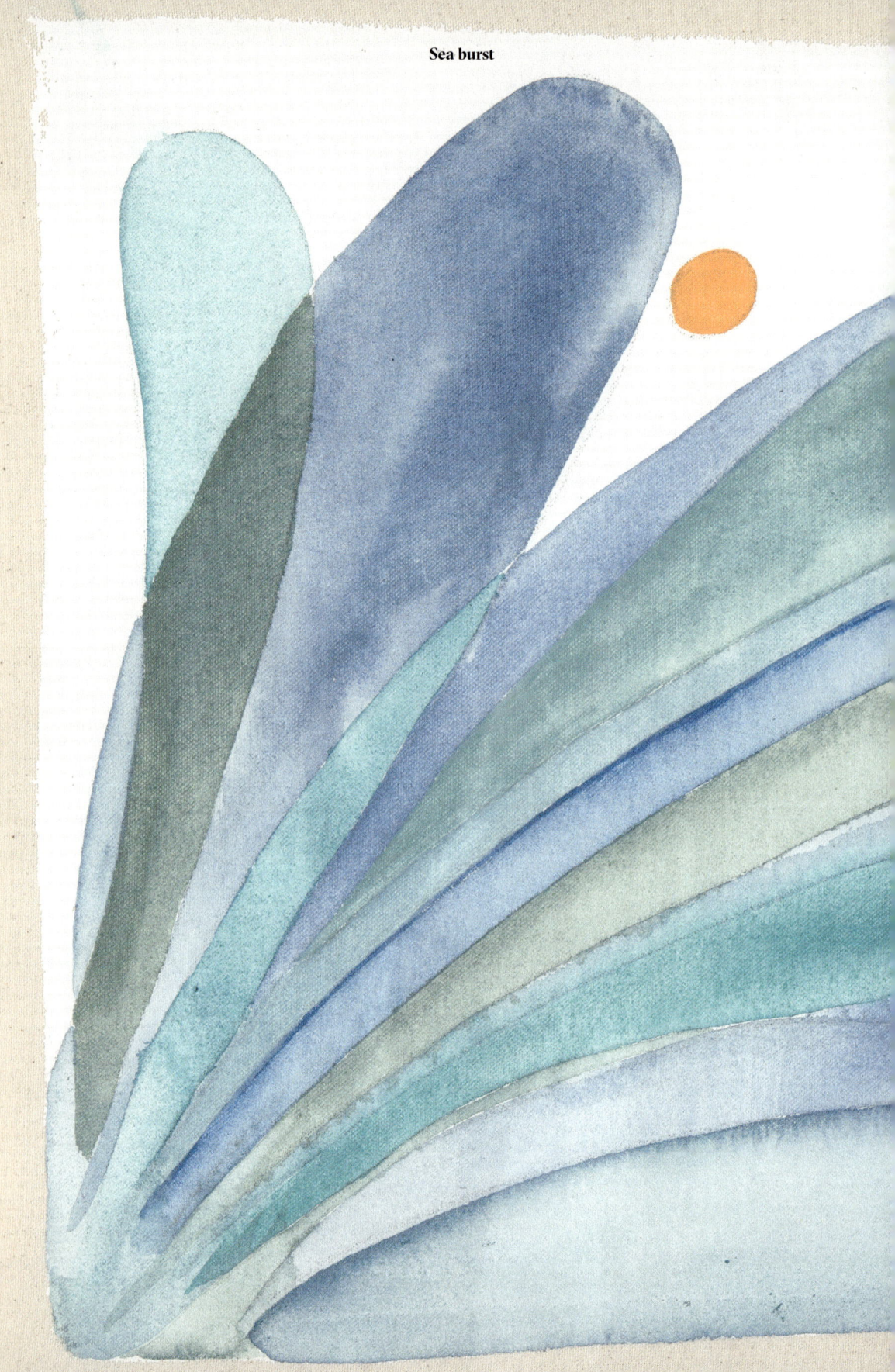

Sea burst

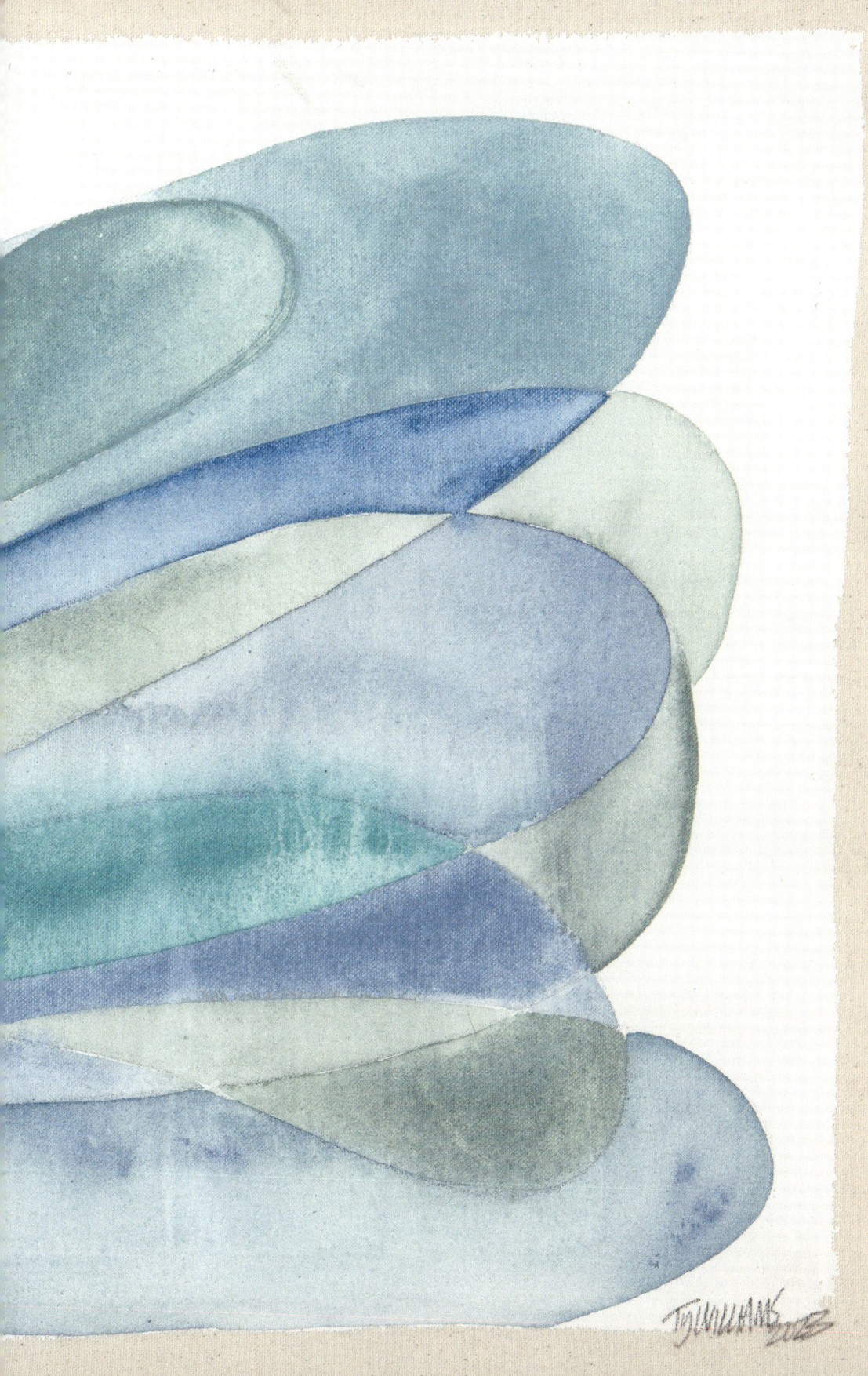

Q & A

Ty Williams

Who is Ty?
I am someone who enjoys being
in the ocean more than on land,
and I may have an addiction to
French fries.

What came first:
surfing or drawing?
My earliest thoughts are of my
mom putting me in front of a
stack of paper and giving me pens
and pencils, encouraging me to
entertain myself while she helped
my dad work on our house. I was
infatuated with the ocean and sea
creatures, but it wasn't until I was
around 11 or 12 years old that
I thought about riding waves.

If you were to describe your art
in a few lines, you'd say…
I've heard people describe
my work as whimsical, and
I'm fine with that.

It seems to have a positive vibe.
Would you agree?
Most of my work is somewhat
hopeful or tender. I like to imagine
it being a relief from the daily
stuff we all experience. I also hide
a little sarcasm in there for
flavour. If people can find enjoy-
ment or some level of lightness
in my work, that's fantastic.

When did you first think:
I can do this for a living?
That's a funny question and
maybe a little hard to answer.
I spent a large portion of my
life working in restaurants, and
drawing and designing on the
side. There was a point in college
when I knew I could potentially
create art for a living, but I needed
the stability of my industry jobs
because it kept the art-making
as a pleasurable endeavour.
I haven't worked in a bar for about
a decade now, but I still find
myself creating art for cafes,
product labels, hotels and bars
because those are the spaces
I know and where I made my living
from the age of 14.

What kind of paper or paint
do you use for your artwork?
I use a variety of papers and
canvases. Usually whatever
is available, I can make work.
I draw everything by hand in
sumi ink. And for paintings lots
of recycled, leftover paint.

240

Do you see a difference between your paintings and illustrations?
My drawings are illustrative, and at my core I think I'm an illustrator. My paintings are more abstract with more patterns. It really depends on what I'm feeling at the time.

Is there something you are particularly proud of?
I'm mostly proud of all the people I have had the opportunity to work with, who have also become friends over time. As I age, I'm finding the best currency is a good community and the one I have feels very special to me.

Do you have a favourite quote that inspires or motivates you?
'Salt water can fix that.'

Where do you currently live or surf?
I live in southern Maine on the northeast coast of the United States. I grew up here and it's where I learnt to surf. Maine has a small, dedicated surf community. Waves are better in winter, so it isn't for the faint of heart, but it's special and rewarding to get a decent day here. I've spent stints living in California, Florida and overseas, but always end up coming back.

What's happening in your life right now?
In addition to painting and designing for different projects, I am currently renovating a little cabin on the southern coast of Maine. It will be a slow process but I'm hoping to get it finished in the next year. I'm learning a lot. --->

Q&A

Ty Williams

Has surfing given you anything in life?

I hope I don't sound like a lunatic when I say this, but I feel that surfing, and time in the ocean, has given me the best parts of my life. My friends, my inspiration, some level of health and even my favourite foods revolve around the ocean and the activities performed in it.

There are some pictures of a cute little van on your Instagram that's almost impossible to not fall in love with it. Can you share its story?

The little van is something I share with my buddy, who imported it from Japan. It's great for a surf check and finding a non-conventional parking spot during a crowded summer.

What would your dream surf trip look like?

My dream surf trip would maybe be a Mexican right-hand point break, or somewhere in remote Japan, with lots of sauna time, amazing meals with friends, and maybe I could convince Bill Murray or Jeff Bridges to join?

What is your favourite surfboard at the moment?

I have a propensity for collecting surfboards (maybe it's a vice?), so picking a favourite is very hard. Recently I've been loving my Deepest Reaches Megafish and I've also been enjoying a little twin fin fish my buddy Trevor Gordon made me. I like having two to three surfboards in my car when I go to surf because I appreciate having options.

Do you think surf culture has changed a lot in recent years?

Surf culture is always ebbing and flowing but the constant element that I appreciate is the desire to explore and ride waves. Surf culture hasn't changed for the individuals that I am inspired by. The people still sleeping in vans and tents, shaping their own boards, growing their own food, sailing on boats, fixing their own clothes etc. will always exist regardless of what mainstream 'culture' is selling. I love that part of surfing. •

Are there other places in the world where you feel at home?

I am a restless person by design and travelling comes easy to me. That being said, I've spent a lot of time in Japan and it certainly feels less foreign to me than most places in the States.

23

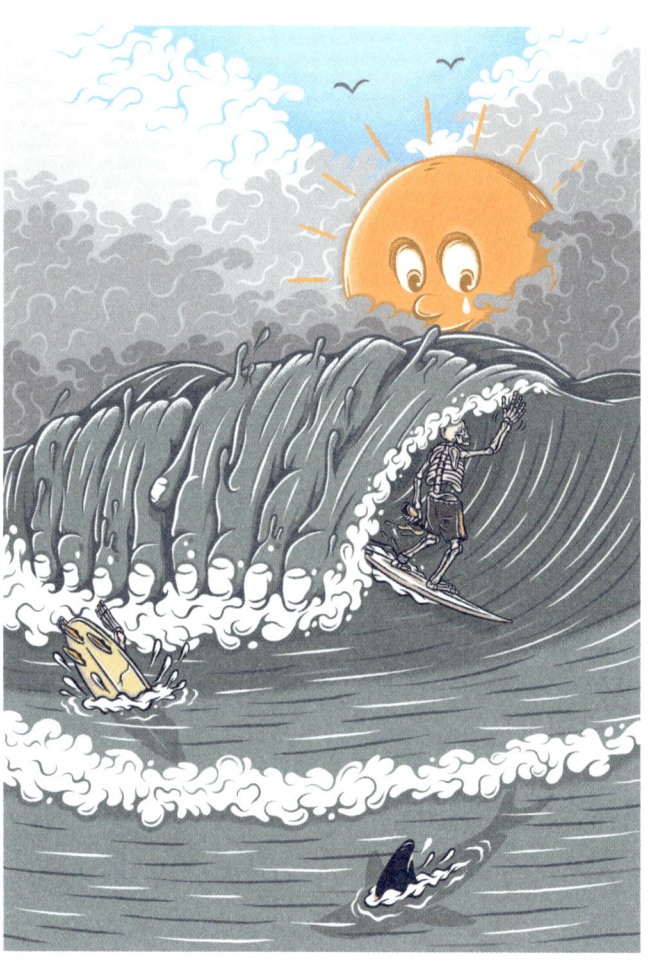

Hello sun

Great waves

Kentaro Yoshida

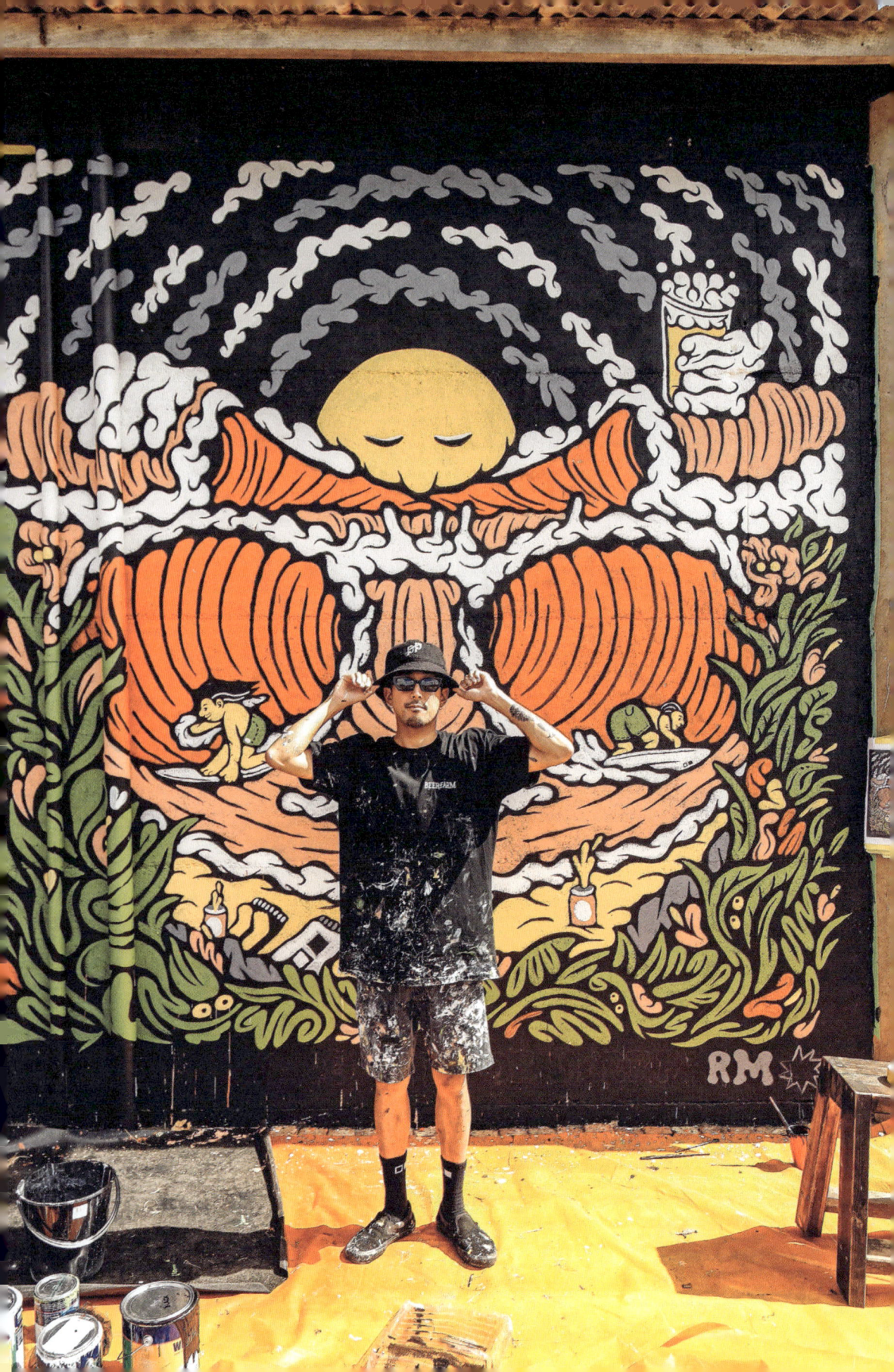

Kentaro Yoshida, originally from Japan, now enjoys life in Australia. His surf art is influenced by Japanese manga culture, where hidden details add an additional layer of depth and complexity to his work.

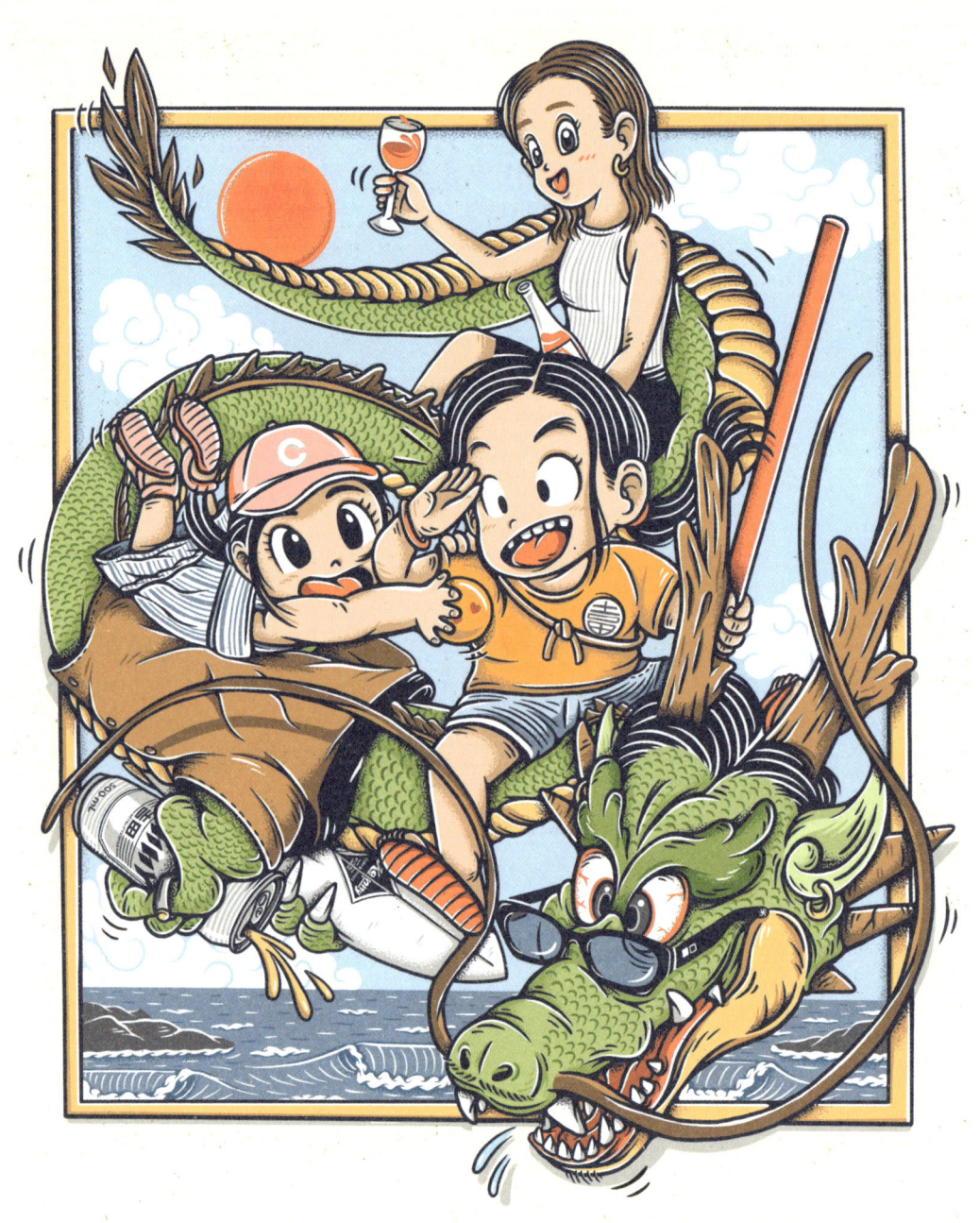

Yoshida portrait

I grew up with
mangas like
Dragon Ball and
Pokémon. They
were my visual
culture as a kid
and my style is
still related

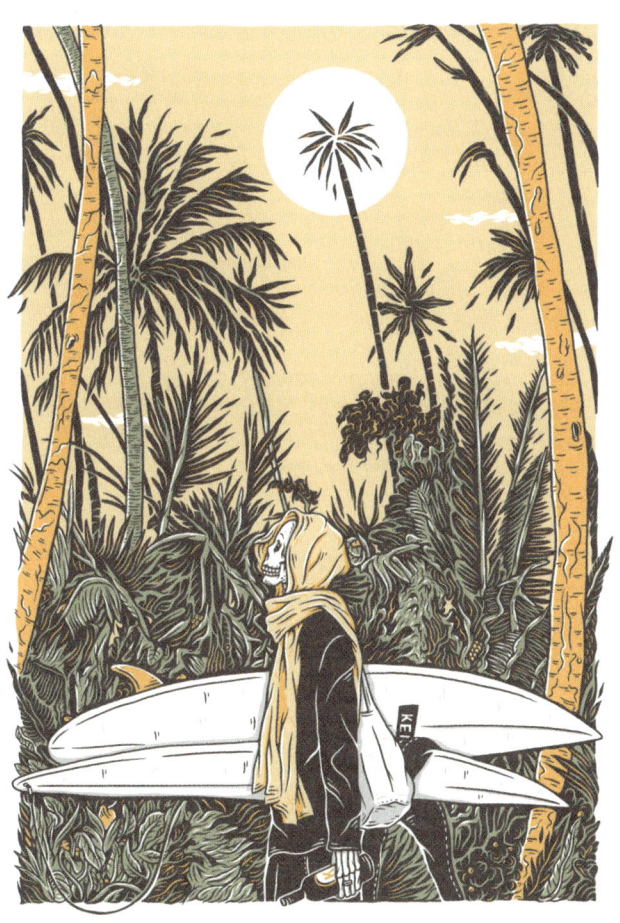

Q & A

Kentaro Yoshida

Who is Kentaro?
An artist originally born near the Toyama coast in Japan. When I was 18, I moved to Australia to pursue English studies. I became hooked on surfing and the community over here, which led me to stay. I consider it my home now and live at the Northern Beaches with my wife and two girls.

Your style is reminiscent of Japanese mangas or graphic novels. Would you agree?
Yes. I grew up with mangas like Dragon Ball and Pokémon. They were my visual culture as a kid. It's the only way I could draw stuff, and my style is still related. You'll also find hidden messages in my work, which is a characteristic often found in manga. Manga artists frequently embed deeper meanings or cultural references. Whenever I work for a brand, for example, I'll dive into their history and add historical references to my paintings. Maybe you won't notice them at first sight, but you do if you look closely. It adds something extra to my artworks, like they are comic stories on their own.

What's the significance of surfers being depicted with skeletal bodies? I'm missing the link: do you see a connection between surfing and mortality?
Haha, no, not at all. The skeletons draw inspiration from the work of Ben Brown, an artist based in Sydney whom I consider my mentor. He's not specifically a surf artist, but I do admire his work. The skeletons don't necessarily convey a dark meaning. On the contrary, I consider my work to be fun.

When did you first think: I can do this for a living?
I earned my bachelor's degree in visual communication and initially worked as a graphic designer and art director. During my time at university, I occasionally painted surfboards for friends or local surf shops. Soon, people began referring to me as an artist, which felt odd and uncomfortable since I hadn't pursued other forms of art. To validate that title or gain more confidence in it, I began doing other work. Surprisingly, people appreciated my art and were even willing to pay for it.

250

You have over 100,000 followers on Instagram. How did that happen?
I joined Instagram back in 2015 when it was primarily known as a photo filter app, with users scrolling through beautiful images. I regularly posted, also sharing glimpses into my personal life. That seemed to work. Nowadays, Instagram has evolved into a platform focused on content creation and business promotion, but that's not how it started for me.

Where do you currently live or surf?
So I live at the Northern Beaches in Australia. I'm goofy and have a particular fondness for left-hand breaks. I surf almost daily, and this played a huge role in my decision to settle here. As a freelancer, I have the flexibility to tailor my schedule around the tides and weather forecasts, which is pretty amazing.

Did you also surf in Japan?
Not till I arrived in Australia and learnt how to surf here. That's where everything came together for me.

Is Japanese surf culture different from Australian surf culture?
For sure! In Australia surfing is almost a national sport, everyone does it and the vibes are very friendly. Japan has a long coastline and lots of spots but localism is deeply rooted. When in the water, you certainly have to respect the older guys and if you're not from the area, I mean, you might as well not enter the water.

Is there something you are particularly proud of?
Moving away from the country where you grew up and settling in a new place is undoubtedly challenging. Over time, I've integrated into the community here and I definitely feel part of it. I adapted and created a life for myself and my family.

Has surfing given you anything in life?
When I arrived in Australia I may have felt a bit lonely, but surfing played a crucial role in helping me find my rooting. Sharing the ocean with like-minded people made my life more fun. Surfing gave me a lifestyle, friends, a community and a positive way of thinking. Whenever I feel stressed, surfing has the remarkable ability to erase those worries. It just glues everything together and guides you on your journey in life. I'm sure many surfers can relate.

What is a perfect surf session in Kentaro's world?
Nothing too extreme, perhaps around 4 feet, super glassy and hitting the water before sunrise to see the sun come up and have her change the colours in the sky. There's really no better way to kickstart your day. •

If you like the artists in this book, go support them.

01_**Erik Abel** Sells prints and more on www.abelarts.com. For originals, go to www.abelarts.com/availableart to see all originals that are available through his galleries.

02_**Ceri Lou Bathgate** Partnered with LAMA in Paris, which is a print-on-demand platform for artists. Head to her website www.tropicoolstudio.com and click 'shop' to be redirected to her shop hosted by LAMA.

03_**Nina Brooke** The best way to buy Nina's work is to sign up to the newsletter on her website www.ninabrooke.co.uk, and get notifications about new collection releases.

04_**Jeanne Beuvin** Prints and postcards via www.lesfillesdusurf.com.

05_**Raül Casado** Originals and prints through www.raulcasado-art.com or by contacting him via his Instagram account @raulcasado_art.

06_**Jonas Claesson** Buy originals, books, prints, clothing, stickers, cards, calendars and much more from www.jonasclaesson.com.

07_**Luís da Silva** On his website www.sickfaces.pt, Luís mainly sells T-shirts and limited edition prints. If you want to buy an original piece, contact him by emailing sickfaces.info@gmail.com.

08_**Pandora Decoster** Contact via Instagram @pandora_decoster.

09_**Jim Drouet** Several galleries represent Jim and the contacts are on his website www.jimdrouet.com.

10_**Jean Jullien** Contact one of the galleries Jean works with, like Alice in Brussels or Nanzuka in Tokyo. Find all the information on his website www.jeanjullien.com.

11_**Taisiia Kordiukova** Through her online shop www.kookumbra.com and on Instagram: @uhuhualoha.

12_**Nick Kuchar** Has his own retail shop in Kailua (Hawaii) and sells originals, prints, limited editions, wearable art and more on his website www.nickkuchar.com.

13_**Fabian Lavater** Check out his website www.lavaterart.com for originals, prints, clothing, phone cases, mugs and more. Fabian ships his art worldwide and it's free on art prints and originals.

14_**Lisa Marques** T-shirts and prints via www.lizzyartworkshop.com.

15_**Lennart Menkhaus** Clothing or art prints on his website www.menkhouse.com.

16_**Quentin Monge** Contact him via his website www.quentinmonge.com or sign up for his newsletter to get updates about new artwork.

17_**Jessica Soparlo** Sells prints on her online shop www.wouldbenudenotto.shop.

18_**Rebekah Steen** Prints, limited editions, originals and merch on her art shop www.goldfishkissgoods.com.

19_**Jonty Storey** Prints and originals via www.cardigan-creative.com. Jonty also takes on (and loves to do) commissions.

20_**Johny Vieira** Visit his website www.wavesbyjohny.com, where you'll find original paintings. Johny also sells prints on his SaatchiArt page www.saatchiart.com/wavesbyjohny.

21_**Kate Wadsworth** Sells stickers, postcards and prints at www.katewadsworth.com.

22_**Ty Williams** His work is sold through his studio website www.imaginefineartprinting.bigcartel.com.

23_**Kentaro Yoshida** Prints for sale on his website www.kentaroyoshida.com.

thank you

Sarah Theerlynck
We are on the same page:
really the only publisher I'd entrust
my paper babies to. She cares,
not only about the details.

Elke Treunen (MAFF)
For bringing Surf & Stay vibes to
an art book! Prettiness on paper,
once again. She's the only art
director who understands me
without words.

**Thijs Demeulemeester,
Iris De Feijter, Sofie Forton,
Katrijn Helsen, Hannelore
Michiels, Sarah Spiessens,
Barbara Uvin, Bellie Vandeburie,
Bruno Van de Meulebroecke,
Klaar Wauters**
For sending support when the
waves were crashing. I wrote this
book during a turbulent chapter in
my life and they gave me a much
appreciated cloak of love.

**The apartment &
waterfront view**
A place where raindrops danced
on water and winds whispered
along the river's edge.I had a seat
by the window, accompanied by
freshly brewed coffee every day.

Lannoo Publishers
First *Surf & Stay*, now *Surf & Art*.
It's our third journey and I feel
fortunate to have a publisher who
believes in my work.

253

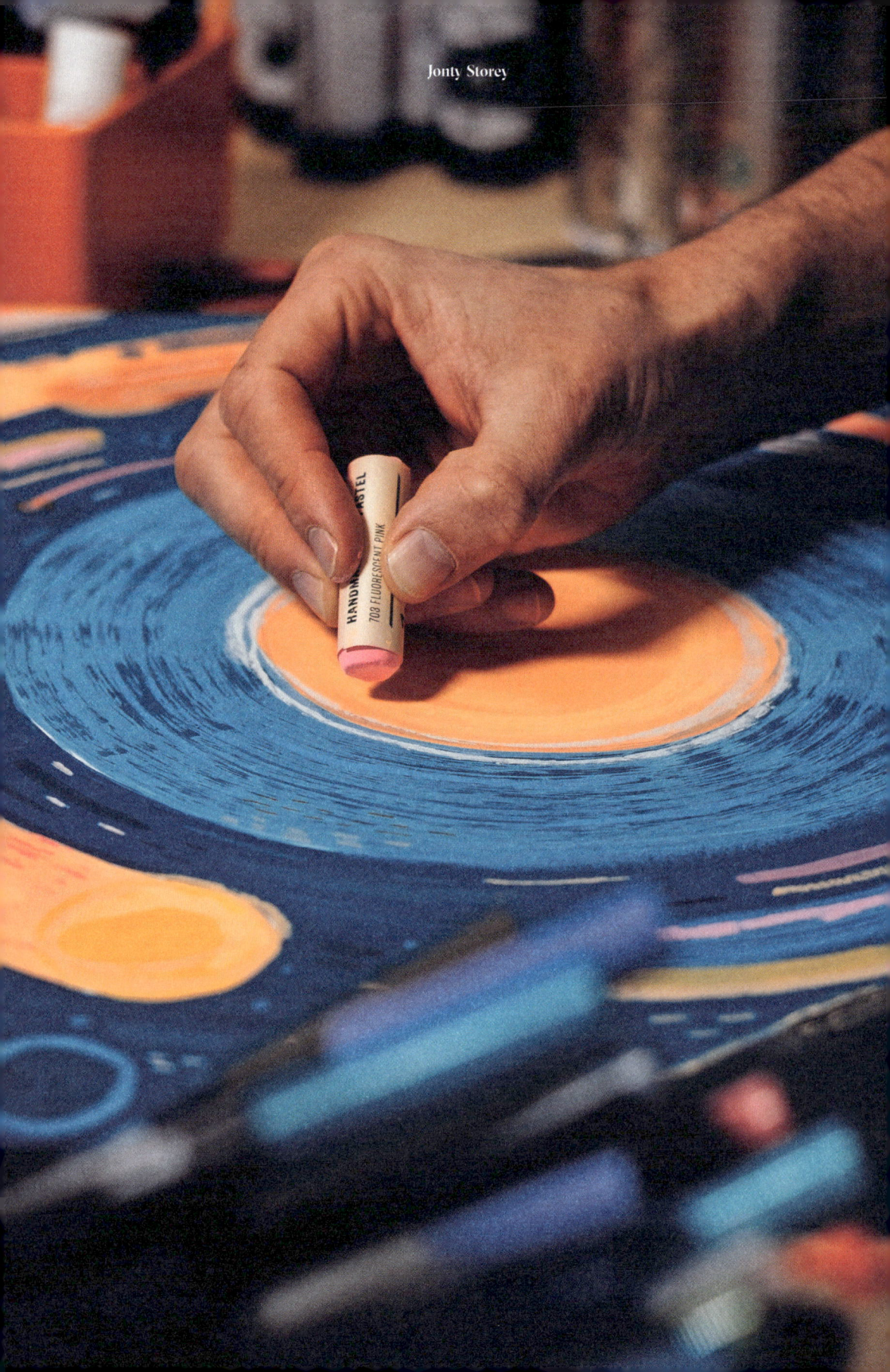

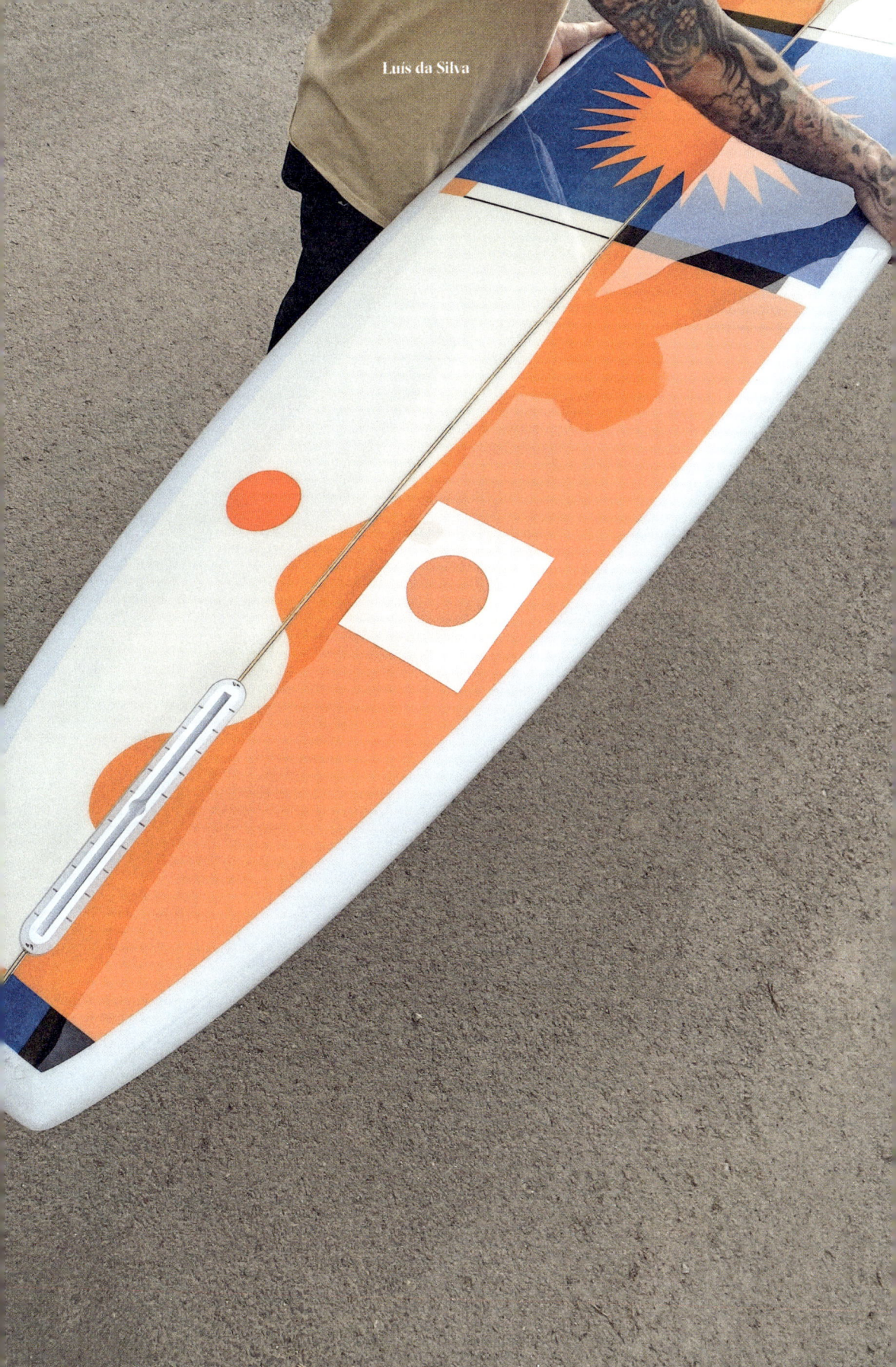
Luís da Silva

Photography portrait pictures

Ceri Lou Bathgate: Greg Hazzard
Nina Brooke: Doon Williams
Raül Casado: Antony Neufcour
Luís da Silva: Simon Fitz
Jonas Claesson: Murray Fraser
Jean Jullien: Antoine Doyen
Nick Kuchar: Andrew Rizer
Lisa Marques: Riemkje Poortinga
Quentin Monge: Marina Germain
Jessica Soparlo: Tianna Grey
Johny Vieira: Daniel Espírito Santo
Kate Wadsworth: Elyse Butler
Ty Williams: Emily Hagen

Concept, texts
and image selection
Veerle Helsen

Book design
Elke Treunen (MAFF)

Copy-editing
Heather Sills

Typesetting
Keppie & Keppie

If you have any questions or comments about the material in this book, please do not hesitate to contact our editorial team: art@lannoo.com

© Lannoo Publishers, Belgium, 2024
D/2024/45/267 –
Thema: AG, SPG, AK –
ISBN: 9789401485098
2nd print run
www.lannoo.com